"*Get There Early* is a completely transformative learning experience . . . an indispensable guide to success in the world of work today and tomorrow."
—ELLEN GALINSKY, President, Families and Work Institute

"Johansen does a great job of showing us how getting there early gives organizations the chance to manage the dilemmas of the future."
—TIM BROWN, President, IDEO

"Johansen is a masterful storyteller. . . . A must-read for the leader facing the dilemma of what to do today to position for the future."
—VERN D. HIGBERG, Vice President, UPS Corporate Strategy Group

"As the CEO of a large faith-based healthcare system, I can tell you that the dilemmas we face and the challenges that present themselves grow more significant by the day. *Get There Early* provides a unique blueprint for leaders in healthcare, non-profits, or literally any other industry to achieve success for their organizations in our VUCA world."
—WAYNE A. SENSOR, Chief Executive Officer, Alegent Health

"Johansen has hit a Grand Slam with *Get There Early*. This stimulating volume helps leaders make sense out of the maze of dilemmas like those we constantly face in Major League Baseball, where we strive to improve the ballpark experience, while also dealing with the growing and ever-changing mix of electronic media delivering our product to our fans."
—CHUCK ARMSTRONG, President, Seattle Mariners

"Anticipating the future and effectively addressing it early is becoming an increasingly critical leadership skill in today's dilemma-filled world. In *Get There Early*, Johansen provides powerful, practical guidance for recognizing and acting on leadership moments at the optimal time."
—M. CARL JOHNSON, III, Senior Vice President &
Chief Strategy Officer, Campbell Soup Company

"Johansen sets out a strategic framework which leaders in any organiza-tion can use to make sense of our volatile, uncertain, complex, and ambiguous (VUCA) world. Most importantly, he explains how foresight can provide the insight that permits confident action in the VUCA World."   —TOM GLOCER, CEO, Reuters Group PLC

"Using foresight to drive strategy helps non-profits to become proactive and innovative. The tools and insights in *Get There Early* are well-honed methods that nonprofits can use to spot entrepreneurial opportunities and enhance their effectiveness."
—CHAD P. WICK, President & CEO, KnowledgeWorks Foundation

"Essential reading for entrepreneurs. Johansen helps us make sense of chaotic inputs in our business lives and provides a helpful framework to think about alternative futures. After reading this book, I am excited about framing the dilemmas my young company is facing today. Entrepreneurs are all about 'getting there early.'"

—CORA TELLEZ, CEO, Sterling HSA

"In our dilemma-laden world, Johansen challenges leaders to be sensemakers, not just problem-solvers. *Get There Early* is must reading for anyone committed to leading and winning in a context of uncertainty."

—JEAN MCCLUNG HALLORAN, Senior Vice President, Human Resources, Agilent Technologies

"Johansen addresses the key leadership challenge of our times—how to create a clear strategic vision for our organizations in an environment of bewildering change and complexity . . . I love his definition of strategic leadership as 'what happens in the space between judging too soon and deciding too late.'"

—WILLIE PIETERSEN, Professor, The Practice of Management, Columbia Business School

"*Get There Early* gives education, business, and government leaders an urgently needed handbook to gain foresight to lead to insights and action to leverage our most important natural resource: our students' minds."

—MILTON CHEN, PHD, Executive Director, The George Lucas Educational Foundation

"It was the poet Rilke who once wrote that 'the future enters into us, in order to transform itself in us, long before it happens.' Johansen teaches us to recognize that future in our businesses and manage towards it long before it happens."

—LISA M. QUIROZ, Senior Vice President, Corporate Responsibility & Inclusion, Time Warner

"The *Get There Early* principles can be applied in nearly every aspect of life. For me, music is a dilemma to be enjoyed, with lots of hidden structure but great freedom to improvise. A great song doesn't need to be a solution to be a success: it's a dilemma that keeps on flowing. In creating this book, Johansen has created a way for leaders to engage with their challenges, much like I compose music."

—CHIP DAVIS, Composer/ President, Mannheim Steamroller, American Gramophone

GET
THERE
EARLY

GET THERE EARLY

Sensing the Future
to Compete in the Present

Bob Johansen

INSTITUTE FOR THE FUTURE

BERRETT-KOEHLER PUBLISHERS, INC.
San Francisco

Berrett-Koehler Publishers, Inc.
235 Montgomery Street, Suite 650
San Francisco, CA 94104-2916
Tel: (415) 288-0260   Fax: (415) 362-2512   www.bkconnection.com

Ordering Information
Quantity sales. Special discounts are available on quantity purchases by corporations, associations, and others. For details, contact the "Special Sales Department" at the Berrett-Koehler address above.
Individual sales. Berrett-Koehler publications are available through most bookstores. They can also be ordered directly from Berrett-Koehler: Tel: (800) 929-2929; Fax: (802) 864-7626; www.bkconnection.com
Orders for college textbook/course adoption use. Please contact Berrett-Koehler: Tel: (800) 929-2929; Fax: (802) 864-7626.
Orders by U.S. trade bookstores and wholesalers. Please contact Ingram Publisher Services, Tel: (800) 509-4887; Fax: (800) 838-1149; E-mail: customer.service@ingram publisherservices.com; or visit www.ingrampublisherservices.com/Ordering for details about electronic ordering.

Berrett-Koehler and the BK logo are registered trademarks of Berrett-Koehler Publishers, Inc.

Printed in the United States of America

Berrett-Koehler books are printed on long-lasting acid-free paper. When it is available, we choose paper that has been manufactured by environmentally responsible processes. These may include using trees grown in sustainable forests, incorporating recycled paper, minimizing chlorine in bleaching, or recycling the energy produced at the paper mill.

Library of Congress Cataloging-in-Publication Data
   Johansen, Bob.
   Get there early : sensing the future to compete in the present / Bob Johansen.
      p.   cm.
   Includes bibliographical references.
   ISBN 978-1-57675-440-5 (hardcover : alk. paper)
   1. Strategic planning.   2. Leadership.   3. Business forecasting.   4. Decision making.   I. Title.
   HD30.28.J645   2007
   658.4'012—dc22   2007014542

First Edition
12 11 10 09 08 07   /   10 9 8 7 6 5 4 3 2 1

Designed and produced by BookMatters; copyedited by Mike Mollett; proofread by Anne Friedman; indexed by Gerry Vanderswaay

To the Institute for the Future community
. . . past, present, and future

Contents

Please look inside the book jacket to find the visual forecast map that summarizes the dilemmas described in this book.

List of Figures   xi

Foreword   *W. Stanton Smith*   xiii

Stan Smith, the senior partner at Deloitte & Touche, frames the book with a practical futures perspective: how can the study of the future lead to better decisions in the present? He has already employed the ideas in this book in a variety of settings.

Preface   xvii

INTRODUCTION   **Foresight to Insight to Action**   1

The Introduction explains what it means to get there early and how doing so can yield advantages — particularly in uncertain times. This book is organized around the Foresight to Insight to Action Cycle.

PART 1

FORESIGHT   **Sensing Provocative Futures**   13

Foresight stimulates leaders to develop their own visions and get there early. Part 1 begins to unfold the Foresight to Insight to Action Cycle with a focus on the foresight zone.

1   Thinking Ten Years Ahead to Benefit Today   15

Getting there early requires foresight and vision. Chapter 1 gives
the context and rationale for ten-year forecasting, as well as
a quick overview of how forecasts are done. If you want to go
straight to the forecast, skip this chapter.

2   Institute for the Future's Ten-Year Forecast   24

Chapter 2 discusses IFTF's forecast for the next decade, which is
visualized in the Forecast Map inside the book jacket. This forecast
is the content base for the remainder if the book. It is a specific
chunk of foresight that leaders can use to stimulate their visions.

3   The VUCA World: Both Danger and Opportunity   45

The Ten-Year Forecast is loaded with Volatility, Uncertainty,
Complexity, and Ambiguity (VUCA). Chapter 3 explores examples
of VUCA dangers and opportunities in military, health, education,
and business settings.

4   What's Different about Dilemmas?   69

The Ten-Year Forecast is laced with dilemmas, many of which
look like problems at first, except that they cannot be solved
and they don't go away. Chapter 4 introduces the key differences
between problems and dilemmas; it lays the groundwork to win
with dilemmas and avoid the temptations of certainty.

PART 2

INSIGHT   Sensemaking to Inspire Strategy   85

How can leaders use foresight—whether or not they agree with
it—to gain insight and inspire it in others? Part 2 shows how
leaders can use the provocation of foresight, with the help of
stories, immersion experiences, and workshops, to create a
clear, compelling, and productive strategy.

5   It Takes a Story to Understand a Dilemma   87

Stories are necessary to make sense of the future. Although
problems can be described with data and solved with analytics,
these methods are not enough to reveal the truths and opportunities
embedded in dilemmas. Chapter 5 discusses how stories help
leaders figure out what's going on and what's possible as well
as giving them a way to communicate their strategies with clarity.

6   Immersion: The Best Way to Learn in the VUCA World   101

The more leaders can immerse themselves in provocative
environments, the more they are likely to understand their
future options for innovation. Chapter 6 introduces a range
of immersion experiences, including simulation and alternate
reality gaming, for first-person low-risk learning that is ideally
suited to a world of great uncertainty.

7   Sensing and Sensemaking   122

To get there early in the emerging future world, leaders need
to tune their own skills in sensing and sensemaking. Chapter
7 shows how small-group workshops can provide powerful
input, building on participants' ideas and using foresight to
provoke strategic insight.

PART 3

ACTION   To Get There Early   141

How can leaders create strategy — drawing from foresight and
insight — and bring it into action? Part 3 helps leaders create action
plans that have both clear direction and flexibility regarding how to
get there.

8   From Insight to Action   143

Chapter 8 gives examples of organizations that have used
foresight to inspire new strategies and new actions — in the
face of dilemmas — and how they made the link between
foresight and insight.

9   Flexing and Flexibility   164

In the world of the near future, winning organizations will
be flexibly firm. Chapter 9 discusses how to create an agile
organization that knows how to sustain a connective web of
shared interests to bridge traditional boundaries.

10   Flexible Firms   184

Chapter 10 gives case examples, as well as a near-future vignette,
that illustrate how organizations can be simultaneously flexible
and firm, to create a culture of readiness and agility.

11 **Foresight from Hindsight**   200

The best leaders and the best organizations are able to learn
from their experiences, especially their failures. Chapter 11
explores ways to derive insight from action, as well as to use
action to suggest future explorations.

CONCLUSION **Making Your Peace with the VUCA World**   215

The Conclusion makes use of stories of personal leadership in
the VUCA world, as well as hints and hows, to help leaders put
the ideas in this book to work.

Notes   229

Bibliography   237

Acknowledgments   241

About the Author   245

About IFTF   246

Index   247

Figures

Decade Map   *inside of book jacket*

I.1   Foresight to Insight to Action Cycle   10

1.1   Institute for the Future Logo: View from a Distance   16

2.1   Determinants of Health Status   43

5.1   Foresight to Insight to Action Cycle: Foresight to Insight   86

7.1   Graphic Recording Captures Insights and Group Memory   130

7.2   Graphic Game Plan by the Grove Consultants International   131

8.1   Foresight to Insight to Action Cycle: Insight to Action   142

9.1   The Fishnet Organization   166

9.2   Options for Communicating in a Networked Organization   174

9.3   Face-to-Face Remains Key for Orientation, Trust Building,
      and Renewal   176

10.1 IFTF's Organization Chart: Organic and Circular   198

Foreword

You may be standing in an airport bookstore or perhaps you see this book sitting on a colleague's desk. You pick it up and thumb through it. You may wonder: "Should I buy this book and read it . . . or not?"

My answer is resoundingly YES, . . . you should!

So why is this book important to read? Because it's a guidebook for what's going to be, for the future that is really not optional—the VUCA world of Volatility, Uncertainty, Complexity, and Ambiguity. Because it will give you an entirely new angle on how to approach your job as a business leader in this VUCA world. Bob Johansen has created a book that is exceptional in its originality and clarity of expression as well as in its effective blending of theory and practical examples.

But you may well ask: "Can I really do the things described in this book and make a difference in my business?" From personal experience, I can again say resoundingly, YES. We all need a better way to engage with the dilemmas that are increasingly apparent all around us. This book provides that better way.

At Deloitte & Touche, we have used the ideas in this book, including the Foresight to Insight to Action Cycle, to stimulate new approaches to reaching young workers just entering the workforce. The outputs of our research, study, and analysis are initiatives within our organization that are designed to (1) leverage the strengths of all the generations in our workplace, (2) raise the quality of communication and understanding among us regardless of generation, and (3) broaden and deepen the pool of talent from which we can successfully recruit externally. Our effort is a research-based practical approach to studying the future; it helps us make better decisions today, decisions that, in turn, will create the conditions for success tomorrow. As a result of applying the concepts in this book, our next-generation initiatives have been able to contribute to Deloitte's considerable commercial success. Bob Johansen, Lyn Jeffery, and their colleagues at Institute for the Future have helped us immeasurably in this task.

The table comparing problem solving and dilemma sensemaking in Chapter 4 is basic training for all of us going forward. In today's marketplace, we have little buffer time between our decisions and their impacts. Mistaking a dilemma for a problem can be costly. It is harder to catch mistakes early when the repercussions of a false step are greater. We must learn to succeed when we are faced with dilemmas, even when we cannot promise or expect clean solutions.

This book (especially Chapter 6) is a great introduction to the value of immersive learning to deal with these uncertainties. Young workers have a lot they can teach us, regardless of generation, about flexibility, collaboration, technology use, and multitasking. The video gaming culture that they grew up in is one that we must learn from in business. Simulations help us learn to be comfortable with ambiguity while still holding to our core values. On this point Bob Johansen does business leaders a service by reminding us that in the VUCA world leaders need to avoid the facile answer or specious clarity that comes at the expense of the truth.

These times are different from the past in degree and intensity of uncertainty. There are risks in being so certain about everything, yet we still must have the strength to make good decisions when decisions need to be made. We all love to have "the answers" at the tip of our tongue, but many of today's "answers" are fundamentally flawed because they don't recognize the complexities all around us. At Deloitte & Touche we use the workshop formats described in Chapter 7 to engage people in the futures context and flesh out issues that we sometimes didn't even know were there.

The ideas in this book have been valuable for me in my private life, as well as in business. About eight years ago I was diagnosed with Parkinson's disease. The world of volatility, uncertainty, complexity, and ambiguity crashed in on me with this diagnosis. I was confronted with dilemmas like the following: How could I continue to work professionally with these new physical challenges? How could I manage the symptoms of this potentially debilitating disease? What new resources might I learn from to come up with my own vision of the kind of life that is possible for me?

I've used the hints and hows from the Conclusion of this book in my own life decisions within my new "normal" that was created by Parkinson's. As I deal with my personal health dilemmas, I've learned to be data based and objective in dealing with my future, yet to remain open to new ways of looking at the data. I've learned to create my own zone of serenity and focus in order to make business contributions at a high level and simultaneously manage this serious medical condition. There is little absolute problem solving for people with Parkinson's; it's mostly about dealing with dilemmas.

In this book, we begin to see inner relationships and make connections that others usually do not see; we learn to "think the unthinkable." On the one hand we may be uncomfortable with the insights that arise from seeing the world differently. However, we need the innovation and creativity that stems from seeing things differently. We understand that we must adapt if we are to survive, much less prosper, in these turbulent times. The right-brain orientation of this book provides a much-needed balance to our overly rational, short-term focus.

So I recommend that you start to manage your own dilemmas by reading and reflecting on the concepts in this book. In this regard Bob Johansen reminds us correctly that we need to understand and analyze the future context as well as the present facts using feelings and reason in equal measure. By acting on the wisdom in this book, you will be getting there early in this emerging world. This very act will help create a new normal.

It has been said that the price of greatness is solitude. So take a bit of time and create some space for solitude (even in the midst of the often frenetic activities around you), to soak up the great ideas in this book and then apply them in your business and in your life. Decide to take a few minutes to see the world in a profoundly better way that will increase your effectiveness in every role you play in life, but especially in your role as a leader.

The external realities described in this book are not optional and they cannot be avoided. Fortunately, thanks to this book, we do have many options for action. However, the time to act is now by learning to get there early.

Join Bob on this journey and enjoy the adventure!

W. Stanton Smith
National Director,
Next Generation Initiatives
Deloitte & Touche USA LLP

Stan Smith was featured in the December 14, 2006, NewsHour with Jim Lehrer *special report on the next-generation workforce by Judy Woodruff.*

Preface

This book started from pain. As I have worked with top-executive teams—especially over the past few years—I have concluded that the most intense pain that leaders experience, the pain that keeps them awake at night, is caused by not being able to solve problems.

For many leaders, the challenges seem to be coming faster and faster. The challenges look like problems at first, but they don't go away. The challenges seem to be getting messier even as solutions become more elusive. For today's leaders, it seems as though solvable problems are morphing into no-win dilemmas before their eyes.

Most of today's leaders, of course, were trained to problem-solve. They see problems everywhere, but they have trouble recognizing dilemmas—even when they see one up close. Dilemmas are problems that cannot be solved, problems that won't go away. Leaders need practical ways to make sense out of complexity when problem solving is not enough.

Twenty or thirty years ago, when today's leaders (including me) were in universities and graduate schools, they (we) were taught the theories and methods of problem solving and organizational control. Most of today's leaders were never taught how to win when faced with dilemmas. In today's world, every profession has become a dangerous profession—every leader is at risk, and the range of risk is growing.

About the time that the Enron scandal broke, I heard a joke about two women in a bar discussing two men who were sitting near them. One woman said to the other: "I love men in dangerous professions . . . like accounting."

This joke is funny because we think of dangerous professions as skydiving or race car driving or stunt doubling in movies, but we aren't used to thinking of everyday jobs as dangerous. Accounting used to be perceived as a conservative career choice, dependable and requiring discipline but certainly not dangerous.

In order to get there early, leaders need to tune their abilities for these dangerous times—to sense the future, to make sense out of threats and opportunities, as well as to decide when and what to decide.

Get There Early is written for leaders, present and future, official and unofficial. If you hold or aspire to a leadership position in business, government, or a nonprofit agency, this book will help you succeed even when faced with a situation you can't solve.

In the age of the Internet, everyone has the opportunity to know what's new, but only the best leaders have the foresight to sense what's important, make sense out of their options, and understand how to get there ahead of the rush.

Get There Early is not just about speed; it's more about timing. The Foresight to Insight to Action Cycle, described in detail in the book, helps leaders make strategic sense out of the mounting dilemmas all around us and pick the right timing for action—as well as the right action.

Get There Early includes a map to the next decade (on the back of the book jacket), drawing from the latest Ten-Year Forecast by Institute for the Future—which has a thirty-nine-year track record and is one of the very few futures think tanks ever to outlive its own forecasts. Our forecasting experience since 1968 gives us perspective and humility. We know firsthand that nobody can predict the future—but we also know that consideration of provocative futures can lead to better decisions in the present. Foresight to insight to action really works.

We struggled with how to present a forecast map within the physical constraints of a book. My colleague Jean Hagan had the creative inspiration to use the inside of the book jacket, which is just the right size for a map. We hope that you will take off the book jacket and leave the map open in front of you as you read—especially when you read Chapter 2, where the map is summarized in text. You don't need the map to understand the content of the book, but we find that mapping is a very important tool for holding complexity in your mind.

Our Forecast Map unpacks a future that requires new forms of leadership beyond the quick-fix problem-solver style so common among today's leaders, who love to solve problems but hate dealing with dilemmas. Leaders must develop the same kinds of complex emergent qualities as the challenges they are facing in the "VUCA world" of Volatility, Uncertainty, Complexity, and Ambiguity.

In creative response to the dangers of the VUCA world, the most successful leaders have a blending of Vision, Understanding, Clarity, and Agility. The Foresight to Insight to Action Cycle helps leaders engage with the dangers and come up with a viable plan of action.

My goal is to help leaders lead—without prescribing exactly what to do. We all need to be leaders in these times of fluid hope; we need to learn to be comfortable leading in this often uncomfortable world. We need leaders who will get there early and take courageous stands—but express those stands and carry them out with humility. We need the skills to move gracefully and interactively from foresight to insight to action.

IFTF has a wide range of experiences with leaders in companies, government agencies, foundations, and nonprofits. I draw from these experiences and spice the book with stories to probe future dilemmas and draw lessons from them.

This book helps leaders resolve the constant tension—a dilemma in itself—between judging too soon and deciding too late.

Bob Johansen
Palo Alto, California, June 2007

Introduction
Foresight to Insight to Action

As the son of a milkman in the small midwestern town of Geneva, Illinois, I was taught to get there early from the start. In the days before refrigeration, my dad got up at midnight to deliver his milk. My first job was getting up with him to help on the milk route, but by that time we had a refrigerated truck and were able to sleep in until 4 a.m. My dad started early, but he got to finish early as well, and he saw things that others did not see. I still remember the freshness of the predawn summer mornings in Illinois when we were up and active before anyone else. Once I was up and out of bed—as long as I was not out late the night before—getting there early had lots of dividends. Getting there early helps you see beyond the problems of the present.

Most organizational cultures today, and most leaders, want to get there just in time, not get there early. Many are willing to settle for getting there "fashionably" late. They focus on quick-fix problems, and they love people who solve those problems rapidly. They hate dealing with the long-term kinds of dilemmas that will characterize the future.

THE VUCA WORLD OF DANGER *AND* OPPORTUNITY

VUCA is an unpleasant acronym, but I have found it surprisingly useful as a way to open conversations about the future. It stands for Volatility, Uncertainty, Complexity, and Ambiguity. It originates from the U.S. Army War College in Carlisle, Pennsylvania—the U.S. Army's graduate

1

school for generals-to-be—which is now informally calling itself "VUCA University."

Sometimes perceived as the most conservative, the most hierarchical, and the slowest moving of the military branches, the army is transforming itself. Assumptions about logical human behavior are being challenged in the face of extremes—like indiscriminate killing of civilians and children, or suicide bombings. In this kind of world, an increasing number of leadership challenges will be embedded in dilemmas—some of which look like problems.

Many people are so fearful and uncomfortable with uncertainty that they have a desperate need for answers. Some will accept only a simple moral equation as an answer, even if there is no simple moral equation. Many people feel an urgent longing for a sense of control.

As an example, consider how often words like *absolutely* are used in your daily conversations. The word *absolutely* gives the speaker a sense of momentary control and comfort in a world where absolutes are hard to find. It is a satisfying word to say, with two opportunities for emphasis: AB-so-LUTE-ly! Listen for this word in your conversations and consider how it is being used and for what purpose. In my experience, the popularity of the word *absolutely* and other strong declarations (words like *exactly*, *precisely*, *of course*, *no doubt*, *undoubtedly*, *clearly*, *utterly*) has increased significantly in recent years. Absolute language is comforting, and demand for certainty will grow in the future.

We all need some comfort and security in life. In order to thrive, beyond just surviving, people must take on dangers and turn around the uncomfortable VUCA acronym by developing the skills and state of mind that I describe as having Vision, Understanding, Clarity, and Agility, all of which will be explored in this book. We need to call attention to the challenges, but we also need provocative ways to generate believable hope.

How can leaders develop their own abilities to get there early, to understand what's going on, and to succeed in a world of dilemmas—without resorting to a false sense of certainty?

GET THERE EARLY

Get there early has a very specific meaning for me, and it is not just about speed. *Get* is an action word, and *there* implies direction and intent: an outcome, a vision, or a goal. *Get there* suggests strategy to me, a direction and a place where you are going, with at least some idea how to proceed and what you might do when you get there. *Early* means at the right time or at least with good timing. Usually, getting there early means getting there before the masses, in time to gain some advantage. If you get there late, you stand in line, and you might not get in at all. If you get there early, you don't have to rush, and you have time to make a good decision.

For corporations, *get there early* means finding new markets, new customers, and new products ahead of your competitors. Toyota got to the hybrid car market with the Prius at a very good time, with a conscious focus on consumers who wanted to change the world with a purchase decision that evolved into a public statement. The iPod was not the first digital music player, but Apple was the first maker to do it right, with great design, ease of use, and functionality. The iPod demonstrates that it is important to get there early but not necessarily to get there first. Success is more about timing than it is about time. Sony got there early with the Walkman for cassette tapes and CDs, but it got there late for digital music players. Success is transient.

For nonprofits, *get there early* means anticipating the needs of your stakeholders and sensing emerging issues before they become overwhelming or before others who don't agree with your issues have taken a commanding position. In the United States, people with great foresight saw that—by getting there early—they could create massive public national parks that never could have been established once commercial land development took over. California's Coastal Commission, established in the early 1970s, was created much later than most national parks, but it still got there early enough to establish public-oriented coastal guidelines that have resisted commercial real estate forces.

Get there early means seeing a possible future before others see it.

Crest toothpaste, for example, was the first toothpaste to be approved by the American Dental Association. Before the ADA endorsement was granted, Procter & Gamble supported large public research efforts on the effects of fluoride, a key ingredient in Crest. *Get there early* also means being able to act before others have figured out what to do. Based on the positive results from the fluoride research, P&G came up with a novel plan for ADA endorsement of Crest. It doesn't do any good to get there early if you don't do anything.

Within UPS, there is an informal cultural understanding that if you get to a meeting fifteen minutes early, you are on time, so that you show respect for others by not having them wait and also increase the productivity of the meeting. UPS is still a get-there-early company, with a culture that requires on-time behavior. Not surprisingly, UPS is one of the most sophisticated corporations in using foresight to draw out insight as input to strategy. Management uses ten-year scenarios to test their strategies on a regular basis, and they have a corporate strategy group that keeps the get-there-early discipline alive. At UPS, getting there early is not an option; it is built into the company's strategy.

I get to airports two hours before flight time, and I bring my work with me. I find that takes a lot of the stress out of travel, and if something does go wrong, I've got time to recover. Some years ago, my wife and I were going to Australia, where I was to give a talk for an Australian government celebration. I dragged my wife to the airport three hours early, only to discover as we checked in that we did not have proper visas for the trip. In those three hours before flight time, we were able to contact the embassy, get special visa photos, rush in a cab to the nearby home of a local Australian official, get an emergency visa, and still make our flight (just barely). My wife has never complained about getting there early since that trip.

When airports are on alert, the time it takes to go through security is unpredictable. Arriving at the airport two hours early has reduced my travel stress—and I get a lot of work done as well. Time at airports and on planes has become a very important opportunity for uninterrupted work for me. In fact, much of this book was drafted in airports and on planes. At least some of the current discomfort of travel is of our own making, when we play a fragile system too closely and stress out when it doesn't work as fast as we want it to work.

When I go to baseball games, I like to arrive right when the ballpark opens, about two hours before the first pitch. That way, we get to see batting practice, and we can relax and watch the scene unfold as the crowd arrives. We become part of a relaxed and expectant gathering that is gradually coming to life. We rarely encounter traffic or lines. Our experience at a ballgame is reflective and pastoral, in spite of the fact that—eventually—we are part of a large crowd at our San Francisco ballpark. Getting there early creates a special experience for us. We get a more personal experience of the game. When we get there early, the staff and even the players pay more attention to us. We wander into places where crowds are not allowed. Almost any experience is changed, usually for the better, by getting there early.

In professional baseball, Billy Beane and the Oakland A's got there early with the "moneyball" approach to talent selection, an innovative approach that uses quantitative measures to forecast player performance—and thereby build winning teams.[1] For years, the A's achieved much better performance results with a small budget than did most other teams that spent much more money on players. Now, however, other teams are applying similar measures, meaning the A's must continue to innovate.

Bill Walsh of the San Francisco 49ers got there early with his West Coast Offense in professional football. The 49ers achieved great success during the Bill Walsh era, but the West Coast Offense is now used by many teams as Walsh's former assistant coaches have moved on to lead other teams. The get-there-early advantage is usually only temporary.

What happens when you have a scheduled meeting but some of the participants don't show up on time? (In a cross-cultural world, with different habits, practices, and preferences with regard to time, coordinating our work—especially our global work—will become increasingly complex.) Those who are on time are left to make awkward conversation, while tardy members essentially waste the time of their increasingly anxious colleagues. What about conference calls in which some participants straggle in late to the call? Remember those awkward exchanges? "Who has just joined?" "When should we start?"

How about starting on time, with an agreed-upon-in-advance protocol for appropriate and inappropriate behavior? How much time is wasted each day by waiting for those who arrive late? I have a friend who joined a get-there-early company, and his first boss was an industrial engineer who was particularly punctual. Using the salary levels of all the people in a given meeting of his staff, this leader always had his algorithm ready so that he could he could greet any latecomer with a calculation of the cost of any delay expressed in dollars. This approach is probably too extreme for most of us, but his staff did learn not to be late for meetings.

Organizations that have a get-there-early culture begin meetings on time, even if everyone is not there. Getting there late is just not acceptable. Once a get-there-early or on-time culture is established, most people show up on time—unless truly extenuating circumstances arise. Getting there early respects the time of others, as long as you don't get there too early.

Getting there early is not about rushing to do as many things as possible, running from one action to another. Doing things in a rush is more of a modern American value than getting there early. To me, *get there early* means getting there ahead of the rush so that you have time to reflect, time to consider alternative paths of action, time to think. I get there early so I don't have to rush.

When I was president of Institute for the Future, I set all of the clocks seven minutes fast. Of course, that works only if you run according to the new time, and some of my colleagues didn't get the concept. Setting your clock ahead doesn't make any difference if you still believe only the original setting. At one point, in friendly rebellion, one of my colleagues brought in an additional clock and hung it in our conference room. Under the matching clock that ran seven minutes fast were the words *His Time*, while the sign under the other clock read *Our Time*. Seven minutes ahead of actual time came to be referred to as *Bob Time*, just as it used to be called *Daddy Time* by my kids when they were little.

Get there early can play out in different ways for different people. You need to decide what get there early might mean for you and how this stance could alter your own leadership. This book will give you lots of options and lots of rationales for why it is good to beat the crowd.

The key is to get out in front—or at least toward the front—of whatever process you are engaged in. In some cases, you'll want to be there ahead of your competition in order to get some kind of edge or advantage. Kleenex, for example, got there early with a good tissue and became the name for an entire category, not just a brand. Most consumers don't say "Do you have a tissue?" Instead, they say "Do you have a Kleenex?"

Getting there early is particularly valuable if you have no idea what's going to happen after you arrive. It allows you to get settled, establish a position, and prepare. If you get there early, you can be centered and ready, while your competitors who arrive late are likely to be disheveled. It helps you think through what might happen, once you are there, and consider alternative strategies with time to think them through. You've got a chance to be ready when others are just rushing in. You can hold the possibilities in your mind while still figuring out what to do and gain a deeper understanding of what was going on before you got there. Getting there early is especially important in times of volatility, uncertainty, complexity, and ambiguity—where figuring out what's going on is not at all easy.

SENSING AND FLEXING

It takes understanding to engage with complexity without becoming mired in it. Leaders must determine when decisions need to be made (sensing) while still allowing for agile course corrections as decisions play out (what I call "flexing"). This determination takes great sensing skills, combined with an ability to make sense out of what is happening and flex your way to success. While judging too soon can be dangerous, deciding too late could be worse.

Part 1 of the book (Chapters 1 through 4) prepares you with a birds-eye view of big-picture driving forces and discontinuities; the map inside the book jacket illustrates a mesh of dilemmas requiring new forms of leadership beyond problem solving. Part 2 (Chapters 5 through 7) helicopters down to make sense out of the present, to draw out strategic insight. Part 3 (Chapters 8 through 11) takes you to the ground level of action, teaching you how to use our approach to win and help others win. The Conclusion offers personal suggestions for applying the ideas in this book to your own leadership challenges.

Get There Early lays out the Institute for the Future's three-step process—foresight to insight to action—that will enable readers to sense, make sense out of, and win when faced with dilemmas. *Get There Early* offers practical methods for sensemaking and flexing, a collection of skills, intuition, content, and style that allow you to:

Develop foresight, to sense and understand the context around the dilemmas that challenge you.   The goal is not to predict what's going to happen but to provoke your creativity and prepare you for your biggest challenges, many of which are likely to come in the form of dilemmas. Foresight is the first step in any good strategy process: the search for external forces and environmental factors creates the context for both strategy and innovation. Leaders are always sensing, as well as coaching others, about what's important and what's not. Foresight is, essentially, the ability to sense what could happen before it happens, the ability to identify innovation opportunities. The result is a strategic vision of where you are and where you want to go, and a pretty good idea how you are going to get there early.

Develop your own insight, and stimulate insight for others.   Leaders are sense makers, and they help others make sense—often by asking penetrating questions. It turns out that foresight is a particularly good way to stimulate insight, to help make sense out of dilemmas and imagine what you might do next. What innovations are possible, given the dilemmas you are facing? Sensemaking is, essentially, a search for an "Aha!" that contributes to your strategy and seeds innovation. Insight is the core element of any good strategy, but insight is scarce, and it doesn't just happen. Insight is most likely to happen as a result of hard work, open-mindedness toward future possibilities, intuition, and a touch of serendipity. Insight must be communicated clearly so that not only you understand it but so also do those whom you need to engage.

Learn when to act and how to learn from your actions.   Decisions still need to be made in the world of dilemmas, but leaders must be tuned to the emergent realities around them in order to decide what to do and when to act. Connection is key, and leaders are always connecting: people to people, ideas to ideas. Many innovations are simply connections that are made for the first time. Leaders need a flexible learn-as-you-go style—since most dilemmas keep changing faccs. Strategy leads to decisions and action—in order to make a difference. Even when the action begins, it must be carried out with agility—in order to respond to the inevitable corrections that will be required. Firm action is needed, with an ability to flex.

The Foresight to Insight to Action Cycle was designed to stimulate winning decisions in a world where leaders must concentrate on dilemmas—while others continue to focus on problem solving.[2] A shift in emphasis is necessary: leaders must be both problem solvers and dilemma managers, but the emphasis must be on the latter.

Even though you can't accurately predict in the world of dilemmas, you can tune yourself in to what is going on around you. You can improve your abilities to sense and make sense. You can learn to be flexibly firm. You can prepare for success in the uncertainty zone created by dilemmas. You can learn how to get there early, at least some of the time.

The Foresight to Insight to Action Cycle provides a simple discipline of readiness. Figure I.1 summarizes the Foresight to Insight to Action Cycle graphically.

I have seen the Foresight to Insight to Action Cycle come together many times with great impact. One example sticks out in my mind as particularly inspirational. In 1999, our forecasts suggested that biotech was becoming increasingly important and that it was mixing in very creative ways with information technologies, as we can see much more clearly today. We presented this forecast to the Global Leadership Council of Procter & Gamble. Our foresight for P&G was that biotech would become increasingly important for many P&G products. The top twelve people at P&G looked around the table and realized that none of

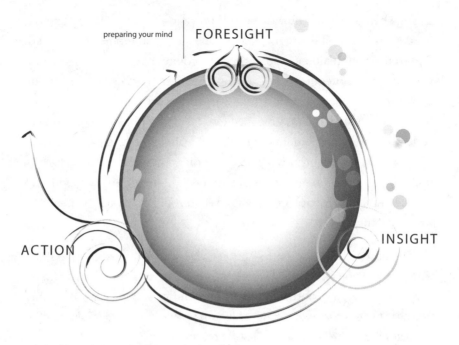

preparing your mind   FORESIGHT

ACTION

INSIGHT

1.1   Foresight to Insight to Action Cycle

them had the expertise needed to make good business decisions with regard to biotech. This was an insight, an "Aha!" moment, for P&G.

The action was to create a Biotech Reverse Mentoring Program for the top twelve people at P&G. We located young PhD biotech scientists, all of them at P&G, who were willing to become reverse mentors for their senior executive colleagues—meeting about once a month for one year. The result was a considerable increase in the biotech expertise of the top executives: they did not become scientists, but they certainly knew a lot more about the business implications of this new area of science. At the end of the year, P&G had a biotech strategy, and you can now see the results of this strategy reflected in many P&G products, especially in detergents and hair care. One of the top executives, A. G. Lafley, continued to use his reverse mentor, Len Sauers, as an informal science adviser even after he became CEO of Procter & Gamble.

This example shows the full cycle: the foresight was that biotech would have major impacts on P&G products; the insight was that the leaders did not have enough background to make good business decisions in this important emerging area of science; and the action was a reverse mentoring program that paired young scientists with the top managers in the company. The follow-up action was a biotech strategy that has now become part of many P&G product strategies.

The Foresight to Insight to Action Cycle can help you get there early, and the greatest value comes from experiencing the whole cycle. Foresight provokes insight, insights spark action, and action reveals lessons that can only be learned in the field, to avoid repeating old mistakes and to suggest new futures to explore. The art of getting there early is achieved through using the cycle again and again.

The dangers of the VUCA world yield to vision, understanding, clarity, and agility, to help leaders resolve the tension between judging too soon and deciding too late.

PART ONE

FORESIGHT

Sensing Provocative Futures

This book recommends that you use ten-year forecasting to improve your foresight and shape your vision for the future in order to get there early and win.

Foresight is derived from listening for, sensing, and characterizing futures that provoke your own creativity. Forecasts—specific chunks of foresight—should be designed to stimulate actions you might take in the present. Foresight can also be derived from experience and observation, when you see something that you believe is a precursor of the future. Vision is your own personal statement, or your organization's statement, of the particular future that you intend to create. Vision is the beginning of strategy.

Even a forecast that never happens is worthwhile if it provokes insight for you. A ten-year horizon provides a futures context for current events and decision options. The best leaders sense the future in order to compete in the present.

Part 1 is focused on foresight as a source of leadership vision. Stimulated by foresight, you can create your own vision—a direction to pursue and an understanding of how to get there early. Part 1 begins to unfold the Foresight to Insight to Action Cycle with more detail on the foresight zone. Foresight is the beginning of the journey.

1 Thinking Ten Years Ahead to Benefit Today

The way you can go
Isn't the real way.
The name you can say
Isn't the real name.
—Lao Tzu, *Tao Te Ching*

Ten-year forecasting provides a unique perspective—a futures context—that helps you create your own vision, for your own organization. Leaders can learn from many different sources of foresight, and this chapter provides a taste of varied approaches. Forecasting helps leaders break out and develop new "ways you can go."

The Institute for the Future's *Ten-Year Forecast* was begun in 1978, when Roy Amara was president of IFTF. The ten-year time horizon was an important choice. Looking ten years ahead, one can see patterns more clearly, even if the details are still unclear.[1] To be most useful, a forecast should be far enough into the future to go beyond an organization's normal planning horizon but not so far ahead that it becomes unbelievable, irrelevant, or too far out. Most of our forecasts focus ten years ahead, but our range for recent forecasts has been from three to fifty years. Our preference is for ten years.

Figure 1.1 shows Institute for the Future's logo, which was created by Jean Hagan. The logo is designed so that when you look at it close up, it is hard to make out the *IFTF*. As you hold it farther away, how-

ever, the IFTF logo becomes clear. Our
goal in creating the logo was to symbolize the fact that a ten-year view is easier
to make out.

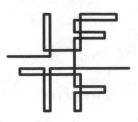

For example, if we look ten years
ahead, it is clear that wireless will be
everywhere—even in many parts of the
underdeveloped world. Cell phone sales

1.1   Institute for the
Future Logo

are booming already in Latin America, Africa, China, and India. Within
ten years, wireless connectivity and sensors will be ubiquitous. It is very
difficult to anticipate, however, what will happen in the world of wireless and sensors when you are thinking just one year ahead.

INSPIRATION, NOT PREDICTION

A forecast is a plausible, internally consistent view of what might happen. It is designed to be provocative. At Institute for the Future, we
don't use the word *prediction*. A prediction is a statement that something *will* happen. A prediction is almost always wrong. Journalists
and others love to highlight predictions that didn't come true, but why
are they surprised? If we have learned anything from forecasting, it is
that nobody can predict the future. Some people who call themselves
futurists are trying to predict the future, but that is more entertainment than research. Fortune-tellers predict the future; forecasters
don't.

The link between thinking about the future and predicting the future,
however, is built into most people's thinking, so it takes some unlearn-
ing for most people to uncouple forecasting from prediction.

A forecast doesn't need to "come true" to be worthwhile. A forecast
should provoke new thought: new insights, new possible actions, or new
ways of thinking about the present. You don't need to agree with a forecast to find it useful.

Herman Kahn, who invented modern scenario planning at the Rand
Corporation and then founded the Hudson Institute, had a unique dis-

claimer in the front of some of his reports that read something like this: "Some of the ideas in this report are deliberately misleading, in order to provoke thought." He didn't tell readers which ideas were deliberately misleading.

By using this disclaimer, Kahn was cleverly opening his readers up, preparing their minds to stay at the perception stage longer. Readers needed time to sense what Kahn's forecast was probing, if only they were patient and open-minded enough to be provoked. He was teaching his readers how to use future scenarios to stimulate their thoughts about possibilities.

One of Kahn's most important books is *Thinking about the Unthinkable*.[2] Forecasting is a way to help us all think in ways we don't normally think. Kahn's unthinkable thinking fueled military strategy. He framed the debate about thermonuclear war in new ways by describing a frightening future in a vivid way that helped policy makers consider the future implications of their action or inaction. The scenarios were designed for the military, but they proved just as useful for war protesters—if they were open-minded enough to read them.

What a wonderful leadership skill: the ability to think the unthinkable and create futures that nobody else can imagine—or to prepare for futures that nobody else thought to protect themselves against.

When I use the Foresight to Insight to Action Cycle with groups, I used to start with a provocative forecast to stretch people so they could think the unthinkable. Foresight is a very interesting place to start, since almost anyone can get excited thinking about the future. It is relatively easy to engage people in a very interesting conversation about the future. It is much harder, however, to link that stimulating conversation to practical things that people can do to make their organization better in the present. You don't want people to look back on a foresight conversation and remember it as stimulating but irrelevant to their present decisions. For this reason, rather than starting with foresight, I now start with preparing the group—before considering what foresight might be most usefully provocative.

PREPARING YOUR MIND

A good leader has a prepared mind—a mind prepared for the always-uncertain future, prepared to think the unthinkable. It means being able to hold multiple realities in your mind simultaneously without jumping to judgment too early.

Preparing your mind is a readiness exercise, to probe where you are as a leader and as an organization, before the Foresight to Insight to Action Cycle begins. Once you know where you are, it is much easier to sense where to start in the vast array of future options that you might consider.

The best sensing is done with an open mind that resists judgment long enough to figure out what is going on—even if what is going on does not fit one's expectations or honor one's values. Often, the most innovative ideas come from engaging with what feels most foreign, from those moments when you have a strange sense in the pit of your stomach that something doesn't fit.

Leaders must resist shutting down or responding instinctively when what is going on does not fit their expectations. The first question to ask when you arrive early in a new situation is, "What's going on here?" If you are having strong reactions, ask yourself, "Why am I reacting this way? Which of my assumptions are being challenged? Do those assumptions deserve to be challenged?"

In business, deep sensing is difficult because we are often rushing for judgment and are rewarded for speed in decision making. Sensing requires a pause, sometimes a long pause. Foresight allows time for a pause. Getting there early implies speed, but you want to get there with enough time to think before you have to act. Sensing requires reflection to get beneath surface reactions and see what is *really* going on, beneath what it *looks like* is going on or what others might like you to believe is going on.

True sensing is hard work because it requires not only watching and listening but also rethinking your own frame for understanding what you are seeing and hearing. Sensing is a discipline of waiting actively—but acting when the timing is right.

Many readers of this book will have taken the Myers-Briggs Type Indicator (MBTI),[3] which is derived from the work of Carl Jung. Jung distinguished between perception and judgment as the basic stages in our ability to engage with the world around us. Jung pointed out that people have differing ways of perceiving and making judgments about life, differing "ways of coming to know." The Myers-Briggs assessment helps us understand our core tendencies: how we tend to perceive and how we tend to make judgments.

Sensing happens first, then judging, but the speed of the shift varies from person to person. The speed with which we move from perception to judgment is especially important when it comes to dealing with dilemmas. Problem solvers cut to the chase right away. Sense makers go slowly at first when dealing with dilemmas so they can go fast later.

Sensing requires the discipline to hold at the perception stage just long enough, before moving to judgment. Foresight encourages you to spend more time sensing, to develop skills in asking questions that matter and resisting answers that don't. The quest is to avoid answers that are premature, answers that reflect only your assumptions—and get to the new insight that might be revealed from more careful consideration.

Roy Amara is the most disciplined futures researcher I have ever met. During his career, Roy emphasized futures research methodology and its importance. But he concluded later in his life that perhaps he had overemphasized methodology. "Futures methodology is less important than I thought," he said at a recent IFTF History Day. This observation came as a surprise to me. He now stresses the importance of thinking through what it is that you want to accomplish in your futures project and then determining what methodology is most appropriate. Preparing your mind may be the most important stage, so that the forecast is most likely to be useful.

APPROACHES TO FORECASTING

Forecasting is a kind of mental fitness practice, comparable to the process of physical fitness. At a gym, for example, you can use tools like weight machines, free weights, a treadmill, a stair-climbing machine, an exercise bicycle, and an elliptical trainer. A cross-training approach is best, using a mix of approaches. And, of course, you need some coaching to put together an exercise program that works for you. Forecasting is a lot like that. Forecasters (like personal trainers) have a range of tools that they use to enhance the development of foresight and sensory skills.

There are many approaches to forecasting that leaders can use to improve their sensory capabilities. These are the core methodologies that we use at Institute for the Future to develop our forecasts:

- **Expert Opinion Aggregation** defines who is most proficient in understanding a possible future and provides a systematic process for articulating and synthesizing expert opinions into a forecast.

- **Expert Workshops** are a specific form of expert opinion aggregation. Expert workshops are typically composed of groups of twelve to twenty-five diverse experts called together as part of a forecasting process.

- **Content Synthesis** draws together the forecasts of others to create a synthesized view.

- **Historical Analogy** draws lessons from the past. Even in times of great change many aspects of life do not change. A historical approach explores what is not likely to change and what lessons have been learned so you don't repeat old mistakes.

- **Scenarios** bring forecasts to life through stories, some of which may include characters and dialogue to help bring people into the daily life of future worlds.

- **Survey Research** uses questionnaires or interviews to elicit attitudes about the future. Although surveys cannot go deep, they have the advantage of providing access to wide ranges of people through stratified samples (across the categories of populations that are important to you) and random samples to draw wide conclusions. Internet survey research has extended this reach even further.

- **Ethnography** is derived from the discipline of anthropology and provides a way to explore underlying culture and values—as well as the patterns of how things work or what's going on in a given setting.

- **Visualization** brings a forecast to life through pictures, human art, digital art, and a variety of other means to help visualize possible futures. The map inside the book jacket is an example of the forecast maps that we do at IFTF.

- **Artifacts from the Future** are hybrids of archaeology and design that use imagined objects to bring a forecast to life. An artifact from the future is a scenario in physical form.

My purpose here is not to do a detailed analysis of futures research methodology, but I do think it is important to give a taste for how forecasting is done before introducing our forecast. At IFTF, we rely heavily on experts. The challenge in expert opinion aggregation is finding the best experts and then reducing uncertainty in their forecasts—while avoiding false consensus.

The Delphi Technique, created by Olaf Helmer and Norman Dalkey at RAND and expanded when Helmer left RAND to become one of the founders of IFTF, is the best known of the opinion aggregation techniques. Delphi is basically an iterative series of anonymous questionnaire rounds among experts, a process designed to explore the uncertainty space and attempt to reduce it. In the early days of Delphi, either a consensus developed around a future forecast or a distinct divide arose that was defended round after round. At IFTF, we still use derivatives of Delphi, although the term *Delphi* is not used as much anymore. Expert opinion aggregation is typically one of several inputs to our forecasts.

The selection of experts is critical. The best experts at exploring the future are rarely the celebrities of today, since celebrity status often reduces one's humility and openness to alternative futures. The best forecasting experts are those who are either not yet celebrities or don't want to be celebrities. We have learned to be very cautious about celebrity experts, although occasionally we find celebrities who still have the ability to forecast beyond the core ideas that brought them fame. In my experience, celebrity and good forecasting rarely mix well.

Typically, we develop data books of relevant facts in advance of any forecast, to get our core team and all the experts at a similar starting point—at least with regard to base data relevant to the forecast. A skilled facilitator runs the expert workshops to ensure that all the experts have a voice and that they "play well" together as they explore all aspects of the forecast. The forecast itself, however, is typically done after the expert input, by people who are expert at content synthesis.

Expert workshops can be a useful input to a forecast. For example, IFTF did a project for the government of the United Kingdom to synthesize views on the future of science and technology looking ahead ten, twenty, and fifty years. We used a variety of published and unpublished sources, with a wiki (an online text-based discussion medium) as a gathering ground for the synthesis and expert panels to review the results of the draft synthesis efforts. In this global expert survey we used in-person workshops, interviews, and an online wiki to gather and synthesize expert inputs. The end product was a forecast map that identified driving forces as well as thematic patterns.[4]

Scenarios, both written and in artifact form, bring a forecast to life. Scenarios can be either more or less quantitative. Some scenarios, in fact, are focused on numbers. Other scenarios are more literary, with characters and dialogue, as in the stories written with the novelist Rob Swigart in Chapters 3, 5, and 10. Scenarios can be used to create and expand a forecast, or they can be used to present the results. Scenarios are also used in some organizations to test or explore strategies after they have been created. The Forecast Map, described in Chapter 2, will provide a rich structure from which scenarios can be generated.

Questionnaire results from large samples lend themselves to quantitative analysis, which can provide a greater sense of confidence in a forecast. Surveys about the future, however, run the risk of not going deep enough with the respondents. Most people just don't think about the future very much or very systematically, and asking them questions about it may not yield valid responses. Surveys allow breadth in sampling, but they do not allow depth—and depth is often important in making a forecast. Surveys are best as one of several inputs to a forecast. In our forecasting practice, we now tend to use surveys later in the research process, to test hypotheses that were developed using more qualitative methods such as ethnography.

Ethnography, the basic methodology of anthropology, is most useful in forecasting when it is applied to deep understanding of individual people or communities. The key is systematic observation. For example, we use ethnography in our forecasting to explore hopes and fears, as well as to understand underlying processes of change.

Ethnography uses much smaller sample sizes than do surveys, but the research goes deeper. Ethnographic interviewing is a kind of hybrid methodology in which interviews are used but with a deep sense of contextual awareness in addition to an interview question guide. Ethnography can provide human and very interesting accounts that are often expressed in stories. Ethnography yields rich input to a forecast. Ethnography begins not with a hypothesis or a theory but with an open mind and sharp listening skills.

DEVELOPING YOUR APPROACH TO THE FUTURE

Although forecasting methodology is important and useful, it is wise not to take any methodology too seriously. Each leader needs to decide what approach he or she will take toward the future. When the Delphi technique was popular, for example, we got many calls at Institute for the Future from people who said they wanted to do a "Delphi study." When we asked questions about what they wanted and why, it became clear that they had little idea what a Delphi study was; it was just the popular phrase of the day with regard to thinking about the future.

In today's marketplace, *scenario planning* is the phrase that many people use to open a conversation about the future. However, it is best not to frame your forecasting interest in terms of any specific methodology.

There are many futures methodologies that can be considered, depending on what you want to accomplish. This chapter was intended to give you a taste of some basic alternatives. The chapters that follow show how these approaches can be used in the Foresight to Insight to Action Cycle that is at the core of this book.

2 Institute for the Future's Ten-Year Forecast

The future is a life seen through the lens of possibility.
—Kathi Vian, IFTF's Ten-Year Forecast Leader

Chapter 2 draws from Institute for the Future's ongoing forecasts of the global business environment, information technology horizons, organizational shifts, and health trends to provide a base forecast for this book, a way to hold the complexity of this decade of dilemmas in your mind.

Our forecast is a plausible and internally consistent view of future forces affecting the global environment, thinking ten years ahead. What are the external forces that will shape the next ten years, with an emphasis on dilemmas that are important for leaders to consider? Our forecast visualizes a future: the global social and technological context within which leaders, workers, and organizations will be living ten years from now.

Any map, of course, is not the territory. A map is a representation of reality, but it is not reality. In fact, nobody really knows the reality of the future; we are all running on approximations, some better than others. The next decade is likely to be characterized by extreme dilemmas and bewildering twists in logic, so forecasting is especially difficult.

The external future forces that will be presented in this chapter invite, and perhaps require, a sense of urgency. In order to respond to the challenges of the future, we need to reflect, tune, and design a flexible approach to leadership—which is what this book is all about.

DIRECTIONS OF CHANGE

Before discussing the Forecast Map, it is important to highlight the underlying directions of change behind the forecast. Think of these directions as historical context for the future that is to follow. The directions of change presage a forecast. In our forecasting at IFTF, we have learned that—even in highly uncertain times—you can still get a pretty good sense of the *direction* of change, even if the particulars are blurred. We are looking here for waves of change. Once the waves are apparent, you may try to ride them or not, but at least you can avoid getting hit by them.

The following statements indicate direction, not destination; we are moving in the direction indicated, but we may never actually get to the end point toward which we are moving.

MOVING TOWARD everyday awareness of vulnerability and risk—in both the developed and developing worlds.   The often competing forces of extreme polarization and new abilities to cooperate characterize this shift. The next ten years will be extremely challenging, and they will feel that way to almost everyone. This kind of world already exists in many parts of the developing world, but the developed world will also experience a dramatic increase in anxiety and sense of risk. The day-to-day personal preparedness disciplines in hot-spot cities like Jerusalem are likely to spread across the developed world as concern over security increases.

MOVING TOWARD an hourglass population distribution where old age is the new frontier, but the kids will be heard.   The developed world will experience its largest elderly populations ever, while the developing world will be driven by youth. The young "digital natives" are those children of the wealthy world who were born into and unconsciously bred for the emerging world of dilemmas and global connectivity.

MOVING TOWARD deep diversity that is "beyond ethnicity,"[1] in the workplace and in society.   Diversity is a dilemma in itself, and it presents major challenges as well as exciting opportunities for innovation. Diversity is essential to creativity.

MOVING TOWARD bottom-up everything, where people interact with the products and services they consume.   New types of loosely connected teams will become the new basic organizational unit for innovation. The grassroots economy, which has deep roots, will be amplified and multiplied by new media networks, games, and hobbies. Hierarchies will be important in some cases, but they will come and go in much more fluid ways.

MOVING TOWARD continuous connectivity where network connections are always on.   Online identities will become increasingly important as people learn to express themselves—and leaders learn to exert leadership—in new ways that are consistent with the new media but are still linked to the old media.

MOVING TOWARD a booming health economy in which health is an important filter for many purchasing decisions—and health risks are on everyone's mind.   Health values will be central as consumers become more health conscious while also pursuing indulgent options in this both/and world.

MOVING TOWARD mainstream business strategy that includes environmental stewardship combined with profitability—doing good while doing well.   Environmental practices and sustainability strategies will become increasingly common and increasingly urgent. Science—particularly the life sciences—will become increasingly important, both as a source of risk and as a way of improving the world around us.

A GUIDE TO THE FORECAST MAP

The Forecast Map inside the book jacket is a matrix-style map, with five driving forces and four impact areas. The map pulls together the core elements of our Ten-Year Forecast, with an emphasis on those future forces that will affect leaders. This map makes it is possible to hold a complex array of interacting future forces in your mind all at once. Please find the Forecast Map on the inside of the book jacket and open it in front of you as you read this chapter.

Expect to be a bit overwhelmed by this map when you first see it. The future is extremely complicated, but this map will help you grasp what's going on.

Each row is a Driving Force that summarizes visually a forecast storyline as you read across. Each column is an Impact Area: People, Practices, Markets, and Places. For each storyline, I suggest below a core dilemma for leaders and organizations. To the far right of the Forecast Map, you'll find what we call an "artifact from the future." Artifacts from the future combine scenario-creation skills with those of design prototyping. This chapter is a text description of the visual map inside the book jacket.

Storyline 1: Personal Empowerment

The word *consumer* is obsolete, but there is no better word to replace it yet. The word *consume* means to destroy. But consumers are not just destroyers or just passive recipients of mass messages, and increasingly people resent being treated as such. Consumers are empowered people whose powers are amplified by the interactive media that they are rapidly learning how to use.

For very large organizations, this personal empowerment creates a dilemma: how can they engage constructively with the increasingly powerful individual people, and networks of people, who buy their products and services?

Beginning about ten years ago, we introduced into IFTF forecasts the concept of the *new consumer* to describe the upscale, educated, innovative people who created new market demand and shaped the mix of products and services. About five years ago we noticed that the new consumer was not just upscale and not just educated in the formal sense: more or less everyone was becoming part of the mix of engaged and empowered people. IFTF's research suggests that engaged consumers are characterized by three bellwether behaviors:

- **Self-agency:** acting with independence, on one's own behalf, but with close networked links to others, so that individual decisions are magnified but influenced by others.

- **Self-customization**: adapting and applying core products or services to their own individual needs, with the expectation that products will be customizable to their needs.

- **Self-organization**: organizing responses and initiatives in ways that are difficult to anticipate.

Engaged consumers are a force to be reckoned with. Engaged consumers can inject a brand with incredible buzz, as did the early iPod users. Apple got there early with a well-designed and compelling product that was promoted mostly by word of mouth, although Apple fueled the fire.

Engaged employees have the same kinds of power, but their power is applied to work. Indeed, many practices of work (for example, time and task management) are being brought home, but influence goes back and forth between home and work as distinctions between work and private life become blurred. An IFTF forecast for a professional services firm, for example, suggested that such work/life crossovers are causing jobs and hobbies to mix, creating "jobbies." Engaged workers looking for self-expression bring their hobbies to work, or their work to their hobbies. Some will seek second or third careers to more fully express their jobby interests.

As I have worked with corporations, I've found it very useful to ask employees about personal hobbies, not just about work. In my experience, some corporate cultures tend to drive people toward exotic hobbies that more fully express their personal identity. If an engaged employee's job does not allow for full expression, the employee will likely be attracted to hobbies that do. The ideal job is one that combines job and hobby, so that the employee will have passionate interest but the results will make useful contributions to the business. Empowered workers seek more flexibility, they want to make a difference, and they have a strong sense of the importance of their own private life.

People are shifting their identities from consumption to creation—including customization and do-it-yourself (DIY). People are adopting tools and organizational practices that foster both self-expression and collaboration. This shift implies a move toward more open economic exchange, with an emphasis on external innovation. A key example is the increase in open-source technology, although different places have different levels of openness. Software in Silicon Valley, for example, is obviously trending toward open source, and in London is also becoming more open source but less so than Silicon Valley.

Personal empowerment will be shaped by the aging baby boomers. First, the aging baby boomer generation has changed every major institution it has come into contact with, and the concept of retirement looks likely to be next on the list. I expect that the word *retirement* will disappear altogether and be replaced by a baby-boomer-type term like *redirection, regeneration,* or *refirement.* Second, we will see increased longevity in this generation, with a possible shift in retirement age, since government retirement benefits promises are becoming harder and harder to keep. Peter Drucker pointed out that the retirement age in the United States was established in the 1930s during a period of employment surplus, when legislators wanted to clear out room in the workforce for young workers. Meanwhile, since the1930s health care has improved greatly, and most jobs involve much less physical strain. Drucker suggested that if all the changes were taken into account, the retirement age in the United States ought to be about seventy-nine, rather than sixty-five. Such a proposal would not be popular with many people, of course, but Drucker was definitely on the right track.[2]

The new retirement will include new forms of empowered work and leisure, new combinations of work and hobbies. The boomers will rethink and reform the notion of careers for fifty-plus in several key ways:

- **Working older:** don't expect the boomers to stop working, unless they get bored.
- **More health expenses and investments in health:** chronic disease meets longer life.
- **Lower levels of government support:** Social Security will not be enough.
- **Expanding, not narrowing, horizons:** the empowered boomers have a big-picture view, so they will continue to reach out and grow.

Meanwhile, labor shortages will create market forces around empowered workers. Most of the labor shortage will be in the knowledge industry, and many companies are exploring ways to connect virtually with educated labor pools in India and other parts of the developing world. Immigrants are likely to fill in any blue-collar shortages, although the politics of immigration will be volatile.

Employers will transition to a more peoplecentric office to promote communication, engagement, and community among its workers. The challenge is to do this for a labor force—from incoming "digital natives" to returning senior alumni—with increasingly diverse needs, expectations, and demands. Think customizable careers, personalized to the special needs of empowered workers.

Increasingly, the old rich and the young poor will bracket the global economy and fuel tensions within it. For those who can afford them, technologies will ease the process of aging.

Workforce diversity will reshape the workplace over the next decade, as the developed world deals with its largest elderly population ever and the developing world offers new pools of young knowledge workers and manufacturing power. The workforce of the future will be shaped by the differing priorities of next-generation workers.

Although most aspects of the future are unpredictable, demographic changes can be foreseen, at least at a general level. Next-generation workers often don't fit the expectations of today's leaders. They are not, however, a "problem" that today's leaders will be able to "solve." Fortunately, this dilemma of next-generation workers is likely to be more of an opportunity than a risk.

Young people have always been different, but the next generation of workers is *really* different. As this unprecedented future takes shape, an unprecedented new generation of workers is entering the workforce with skills and perspective that their elders do not share or—in some cases—even understand.

Although many high-performing baby boom leaders expect to encounter a stream of problems that they can solve—if only they work hard enough—the next generation of workers won't have the same set of illusions. (Yes, they will have other illusions.) Younger workers are likely to be more comfortable improvising their way out of dilemmas. Many of today's kids are already experienced VUCA world players who learned their skills in video gaming worlds that are not as different from business as some may think.

Organizations must prepare for an increasingly heterogeneous workforce in terms of age, nationality, race or ethnicity, and lifestyle. Immigration is changing the ethnic composition of the country, particularly the western and southern regions. Women are having children later in life, and the number of traditional households is declining. Many of the aged will live and work longer, with a strong sense of empowerment.

The first artifact from the future (top at the far right of the Forecast Map) shows how the digital and physical worlds will be blended and used by engaged people. Local information is projected on your eyeglasses as you walk about in a strange city. Jason Tester, who studied human-computer interaction at Stanford and attended the Interaction Design Institute Ivrea in Italy, developed this methodology at IFTF.

Storyline 2: Grassroots Economics

Economies of scale, where bigger is almost always better, are giving way to economies of organization, where you are what you can organize. To get oriented to this still-emerging economic ecology, think of it as eBay on steroids. Everyone can be a seller, and everyone can be a buyer. All organizations—even very large organizations—have the potential to take on a grassroots character. Think personal media, think personalized products and services, and think mass customization or personalization. This economic shift is much larger than eBay per se, but the eBay effect is spreading, setting a tone and breaking new ground. While personalized interfaces are still evolving, the Internet has come a long way already.

A grassroots economics dilemma for very large organizations: how to grow financial performance in an economic environment in which scale is a mixed blessing and you must give the feeling of being both large and small simultaneously?

Scale just isn't what it used to be. It is still important to have scale to reach large audiences, but the scale must be personalized—or at least it must *feel* personalized to the end consumer. And the scale must be localized—even global brands should feel local, or at least not foreign, and their local value should be apparent. Centralized brute-force scale, where growth is driven from a central core, is giving way to decentralized scale, where growth happens organically at the edges. The "grassroots economy" is a group economy organized for cooperation and mutual gain. Groups create new kinds of economic value, some of which is outside the traditional economy. The second artifact from the future (second from the top at the far right of the Forecast Map) shows how computer parts can be recycled and reused by entrepreneurs in the slums of the developing world.

Grassroots economics is a bottom-up engine of innovation, a powerful world for brands, but a world where brands can be extremely fragile. Engaged consumers can threaten the very existence of a brand, as they did with the Kryptonite bicycle lock when a Web video demonstrated how this supposedly secure lock could be opened with a Bic pen.

Business Week calls it "the power of us." Howard Rheingold calls it the "sharing economy."[3] New forms of social organization, enabled by connective technologies and increased mobility, will become new sources of value for organizations that know how to tap into them. Workspaces can be designed to maximize the unique role of working side by side to grow relationships and social networks.

As the traditional culture of consumption gives way to more interactive value creation, we will see increases in the technologies of cooperation and the revival of localism through bottom-up processes. Here the counterculture of the 1960s and 1970s has met the technology culture of the 1980s and 1990s, and these two transformational movements will play out on the economic scene as an intensely social, technologically supported grassroots economy comes into its own.

Personal media are making it possible to personalize content and experiences. For example, camera phones have created a new medium for self-expression, one that is available anytime and anywhere—by anyone. Amateur photographers now have a medium that they never had before. Web sites such as Flickr and YouTube provide sharing venues, as well as bridges to marketplaces for photos and videos. The grass-roots economic driver is moving us toward marketplaces that include both professionals and amateurs, as we are already starting to see in the world of citizen journalism.

Lightweight infrastructure is making it possible to innovate in a more decentralized fashion. In energy, for example, lightweight infrastructure allows power to be decentralized. In telecommunications, cellular te-lephony and Internet access have made it possible to leapfrog the con-struction of landline physical infrastructure. Lightweight infrastructures encourage organizations to rethink the movement of goods and serv-ices. Central infrastructure will still make sense in some areas (in China, for example, both central and lightweight energy infrastructures are be-ing used in varied settings), but lightweight infrastructures are extend-ing dramatically the range of options for innovation.

Grassroots economics will be enhanced by the *geoweb*, which is the linking of the virtual with the physical. Alex Pang at IFTF has referred to this as the "end of cyberspace," since the physical and the virtual will be linked. William Gibson coined the term *cyberspace* in 1984 to de-scribe the place where we go when we are online.[4] In the geoweb, cy-berspace is not a separate place where we go, since our physical places are linked to the virtual. Sensors in the physical world provide location and background data to add to our experience in the physical and vir-tual worlds. During the SARS outbreak in Hong Kong, for example, text messaging services were available to tell subscribers when they were approaching a building where SARS cases had been reported. In the fu-ture you will be able to walk beside a river and check the pollutant lev-els (real-time environmental reporting) or look up the company on the riverbank and check out its credentials—using your choice of filters for the rating—as you walk. Intelligence is becoming increasingly embed-ded in places and things at the same time—with links to social networks.

The distinction between cyberspace and real space is disappearing, but the resulting electronic and physical infrastructure is fueling the growth of grassroots economies. IFTF's 2006–2016 Ten-Year Forecast puts it this way: "This is the decade in which data, sensors, and semantic processing get imbedded in things, people, and places. This world of smart things will look less like the Jetson world, however, and more like an exquisite dance between groups of people and the spaces they occupy."[5]

The Forecast Map summarizes a key historical shift, beginning with the counterculture movement of the 1960s, in which the emphasis was on social transformation. In the 1980s and 1990s the emphasis shifted to technology and network innovation, expressed through the Internet and its many economic impacts. Now the technologies have evolved into media, and the media are becoming the fertile ground for the grassroots economy.

As these economies of connectivity become increasingly visible, innovative businesses will build on that connectivity to create new wealth. The result: commerce will shift by sector and region, with some industries declining while others are injected with new energy.

For example, the grassroots economy allows for the growth of what Chris Anderson calls "long-tail economics."[6] At the end of the current life cycle for many products and services, there are still many people who value the fading product. In fact, the end of the life cycle of a product is sometimes extremely profitable. However, mass-market products cannot focus on niche markets. More customized products and services—and the electronic networks to distribute them—can extract great value from the long tail at the end of a product life cycle.

Networked media, using the geoweb, will make it possible to develop ad hoc infrastructures in areas like security, communications, energy, and waste management. Virtually everything can be "tagged," which means that an item is marked in a way that can be tracked. Many physical things will have RFID (Radio Frequency Identification) tags, which contain much more information about the item than the current generation of bar codes. As things become tagged, search engines will be there to locate the items and use the information. Although manufacturers and retailers have led the development of RFID up to now, the most transformative applications are likely to be those developed by engaged consumers. Expect grassroots economy efforts to create and program tags for everything from photos and children's art to antiques and family treasures. With equal effort, engaged consumers will devise ways to subvert and block tags created by others. The third artifact from the future (third from the top at the far right the Forecast Map) suggests how adhesive home RFID tags might be used by consumers.

Storyline 3: Smart Networking

We are moving toward a global fishnet of connectivity, with regional talent clusters but uneven technological infrastructure and network practices. In a fishnet of connectivity, smart networkers live at the leading edge of market trends, making distinctive and influential choices about entertainment (which are abundant), health, home, policy issues, and elections. The people who make these choices—the people who use products and services, who participate in nonprofit organizations and government groups, who vote—are not just individuals; they are networks of empowered people. Increasingly, brands are selling not just to an individual; they are selling to a social network.

A smart networking dilemma: how to engage in positive ways with these smart networks and networkers that cannot be controlled and only rarely can be influenced in straightforward ways?

Few hierarchies can match up well with a competing network, except in mature industries or stable zones where change is slow. When your customers and competitors are networks, you need to be a network too. There is a definite shift toward networks within and among large companies.

Swarms, or *smart mobs* as Howard Rheingold calls them,[7] are "loosely connected, technology-amplified aggregations of people organizing around fluid topics and incentives" (although many of these aggregations will be *dark mobs*, or smart mobs with bad intentions). Social software, which is focused on amplifying group capabilities, will allow opportunities to create new social capital. Emergent grassroots economies are making it possible to be more responsive and adaptive on a scale that transcends today's institutions. In the world of smart mobs and dark mobs, big companies are big targets; brands are still important, but they are increasingly vulnerable and fragile. Curiously and alarmingly, dark mobs and extreme fundamentalist groups tend to be most adept at new media use.

The testing ground for new bottom-up participation patterns will be the world of gaming, particularly the massive multiplayer online games and immersive environments. This type of entertainment is often self-generated, personal, experiential, and embodied. New skills from the world of immersive gaming, blogging, and peer-to-peer file sharing will filter into the workplace with next-generation workers.

The networked world is becoming a complex mix of virtual and physical, where place is layered with information in a new geoweb (what MIT calls the "Internet of things"). Sensors will be everywhere, acting on people's behalf (on the good days). Connective technologies and mobility have created a host of local and distributed ways of belonging to organizations. Next-generation digital natives to this new networked world have never known life without connectivity. Today's digital diasporas are social networks that have both "roots" and "wings," so they can maintain deep ties and wide reach through a mix of media.

New technologies will give humans the ability to project their identity and presence online. Next-generation workers will be more comfortable in the world of online presence. Entertainment is today's practice ground and proving ground for tomorrow's workforce behaviors.

Networking knowledge will become important to success, for individuals and for organizations. A cohort of people with traditional networking skills and new media practices is defining a new index of networking intelligence—a networking IQ—that sets them apart from others. Networking IQ is basically the combination of traditional networking skills with the application of new media and technologies. IFTF research has identified the following six factors as being most important to networking IQ:

- **Group participation:** how you use networks to engage with others in effective ways.
- **Referral behavior:** how you use networks to link to other resources available through the network.
- **Online lifestyle:** how the network fits in the context of the rest of your life.

- **Personal mobile computing:** how you use the network as you move about.

- **Locative activity:** how you use the network to draw links to specific geographic locations.

- **Computer connectivity:** your skills in linking to computer-based resources.

If leaders are not skilled or at least conversant with blogs, wikis, and other networked media, it will be hard for them to lead. The fourth artifact from the future, the "Reputation Statement" artifact (fourth from the top at the far right of the Forecast Map), suggests how network IQ might be rewarded in the future.

Young people are learning to create and share knowledge in a mixed physical and virtual landscape. Where older workers still struggle with e-mail overload, young digital natives are more able to juggle multiple media, devices, and images. The explosion of social software will challenge traditional notions of focus, workflow, and productivity. Concentration skills will still be important, and perhaps the digital natives will be at a disadvantage with regard to degree of focus. However, the ability to sense context accurately through many channels will be a critical networking IQ ability.

The introduction of more virtual media is likely to *increase* the desire for meaningful face-to-face engagement. Paradoxically, the more time we spend communicating with others by way of machines (such as the phone, computer, or handheld), the more important face-to-face experiences become. In addition, the more time we spend working with globally distributed colleagues, the more important local connections become.

Storyline 4: Polarizing Extremes

Everything, and especially the proliferation of extreme views, is amplified on the Internet. No matter how strange or extreme their views are, people can find others with similar views on the Web and use the Web to organize their collective strangeness. Of course, both positive and negative social change can be organized through the Web, but somehow extreme groups seem more sophisticated at networking than the more moderate ones do. Extreme networks are not problems that can be "solved"; they are dilemmas that need to be managed. While extremist groups have new powers in this world, so do the forces of cooperation.

A dilemma of polarizing extremes: how to engage with extreme groups when you cannot please all of them, especially since they themselves do not agree?

Whether the world is becoming more extreme in its views is debatable, but certainly the extremes are amplified and more volatile. Worldwide, it appears that fundamentalist perspectives (religious, political, and social) are increasing in popularity. Not only do these groups adhere more strictly and literally to their doctrines but they may also reject the separation of sacred and secular life that has characterized much of Western culture over the past century.

Strong opinions, strongly held, will also get more mobile. Although the likelihood of large countries going to war against one another is low, the likelihood of insurgent warfare is high. Dark mobs will increasingly learn the lessons of smart mobs and, probably more so than more moderate groups, will become adept at using mobile technologies and networking mechanisms.

More people will become candidates for extreme fundamentalist views—especially if those people are hungry or hopeless. The gap between rich and poor magnifies this problem of extremes. The gap is difficult to take, especially since these differences are broadcast in everyday media to remind people on both sides of the gap. It is as if the rich rich and the poor poor live on opposite sides of the same street and look out at each other each day. Even if the rich ignore the poor, the poor are increasingly conscious of the excesses of the rich.

The 2006–2016 IFTF Map of the Decade points out the disturbing fact that the number of overweight people in the world is now equal to the number of underfed. Hungry and hopeless people are prime candidates for extreme groups who seek committed followers. If people are hungry and hopeless, their situation is already urgent, and the extreme groups offer at least some source of immediate aid and identity—as well as hope, no matter how unrealistic it may seem to others.

The "connected core" and "nonintegrated gap" regions of the world shown on the Forecast Map highlight the global gap between rich and poor—a gap that shadows the next decade and probably well beyond.[8] For the first time in history, during the course of this decade more than half of the world's population will live in cities. The shift will be greatest in developing countries. Megacities (cities with over 10 million people) will bring growing economic value and urban destitution in developing nations (e.g., China). Megacities will constitute a new kind of wilderness, resembling the most extreme ecologies in nature and eliciting adaptive survival strategies. At the same time, small cities with populations of less than 50,000 will be among the fastest growing in both the developing and developed worlds. There will be a growing distinction between the connected core of economically and technologically linked countries and the unintegrated regions that are less connected. Alongside this global shift in population from primarily rural to primarily urban, the unpredictable impacts of climate change are likely to inflict potentially disastrous effects in heavily populated areas.

These population shifts will strain existing institutions that provide both the infrastructure and social structures necessary for healthy human life. They will also threaten the old wildernesses as people attempt to escape urban congestion.

Dark innovation, innovation by extreme groups for their own advantage, will be important in the next decade, but anyone can learn from these innovations and reapply them in constructive ways. Try viewing again the 1982 movie *Blade Runner*, in which a young Harrison Ford plays the part of a maverick truth finder in a dark urban world of Los Angeles in the future. The most innovative scientists in *Blade Runner* are urban craftspeople working in the burned out core of an infrastructure that no longer functions in the way it was intended. Science continues, but the innovation is on the dark side and the forces of light are difficult to find.

In our world hacking is no longer just a marginal activity practiced by a few malcontents but rather a style of innovation that spawns major economic value not only in gray and black markets but also in legitimate markets. At the 2006 Maker Faire in San Mateo, California, organized by O'Reilly's *Make* magazine, an entire pavilion was dedicated to people hacking Microsoft products in interesting ways. Microsoft sponsored the pavilion in what was a major shift from the company's earlier stance that hacking was forbidden and severely punished whenever possible. Now, at least some forms of hacking are encouraged. There is a fine line between innovation and hacking. In many parts of the world, there is a fine line between innovation and theft.

Storyline 5: Health Insecurity

The baby boomers will fund and fuel what our health researchers at IFTF have come to call the "health economy." The aging baby boomers are determined to change the aging process, just as they have changed everything else as they have matured. Many baby boomers seem to view death as an option that they are not planning to take. They are extremely concerned about their own health, and the wealthy among them are going to be the richest "retirees" in history. Technology drove the last wave of economic growth; health is likely to fuel the next. Health is the bottom line on the Forecast Map because, without health, the future becomes irrelevant. The future is only important to those who are healthy enough to enjoy it.

A health insecurity dilemma: how to grow a culture-of-health marketplace in the shadow of looming global health crises? How many will be able to afford to be healthy?

Many baby boomers will buy anything that will protect their health and well being and help them to stay active longer. Even if they can afford to retire, most baby boomers say they don't want to do it—they just want to work on things they love to do.

As the boomers age, new medical technologies and treatments are making new promises (or perhaps delivering on old promises). In IFTF's ongoing health horizons research we have studied the extremes of life enhancement and life extension in order to begin to sort out emerging patterns. Essentially, the next ten years will see new approaches to extending what the body can do in ways that have been difficult to imagine before. IFTF has identified these styles of creating an extended self:

- **Identity switchers:** those who strive to change their identity through mental and social disciplines.
- **Medical modifiers:** those who use medical or surgical methods to change their bodies in ways that they find positive.
- **Body builders:** those who use exercise and other disciplines to alter their physique.
- **Death defiers:** those who stretch the limits of what is possible and what is safe.
- **Super connectors:** those who use networks to amplify their sense of self and essentially develop a more connective definition of self.[9]

These real-life "X-Men" and "X-Women" are expanding the limits of what is possible, what is healthy, and—in some cases—what is human. They are using various approaches to extend their bodies, their minds, and their social reach. These people at the extremes help to bracket what is possible and motivate what is mainstream.

The language we use to talk about health is also changing; for example, we see the popular introduction of the term *pandemic* (a global or all-encompassing epidemic). The ability to isolate ourselves from global health issues is increasingly difficult because of the fluidity of international travel.

At IFTF, we have done expert panels on climate change since 1977. Until recently, most of the concern was at the fringes of science. Now, the mainstream of science is concerned, and most businesses are seriously considering the possibilities. We expect this concern to grow, along with the variety of responses. The gradual increase in global atmospheric temperature, which has been tracked over the past thirty years and will continue into the future, will have significant—but unpredictable—impacts.

Climate change is likely to have implications for global health. The human herd is not in a healthy state. We may well see declines in health indicators such as longevity and fertility drop and obesity and chronic disease grow.

There are many impediments to health today, in both the developed and developing worlds. Recent IFTF forecasts have highlighted these impediments in particular:

- **Uninsurance:** who will pay?
- **Workforce shortages:** particularly of doctors but also of other health care professionals, with big regional variations.
- **Administrative waste:** health care institutions have never been known for efficiency, but the problems are now highlighted and the solutions are not apparent.
- **Medical error:** even in the developed world, hospitals make mistakes.
- **Lack of incentives for healthy behavior:** threats of lawsuits play a role here, but so do other economic structures that make it hard to provide incentives for healthy behavior.
- **Unhealthy behavior:** even when it is clear what to do to be healthy, many people don't do it.
- **Increasing challenge** of connection between health providers and consumers.

In research that IFTF did with the CDC, we concluded that the determinants of health status break down roughly as shown in Figure 2.1. The surprising and hopeful finding here is that whether you are healthy or not depends largely (50 percent) on your behavior—especially on factors like weight, fitness, smoking, and alcohol consumption. The degree of access to health care is the smallest contributor as a determinant, yet funding for health and health care in the United States is almost the inverse of these proportions. As a society, we continue to invest far more in disease response than we do in behavior change.

Nutrition plays a big role in health, yet nutritious eating is not easy, even in the so-called developed world. As science gets smarter about controlling interactions at the molecular level, engaged people are becoming more aware of their own body chemistry and are intervening in it to achieve health goals. As consumers get savvier about nutrition and food chemistry, they will likely use drugs (or food) to influence their physical health, and also their moods, personalities, and cognitive abilities. Expect engaged consumers to monitor their own body chemistry with increasing precision but varied levels of expertise. The fifth artifact from the future (bottom at the far right of the Forecast Map) suggests a possible "body hacking" movement as such consumers become more adventuresome.

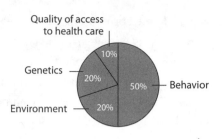

2.1   Determinants of Health Status

Health concerns and environmental concerns are likely to be linked. The first Earth Day was in 1970, almost forty years ago. Now, finally, environmental concerns are coming to be viewed as mandatory for long-term success, not just as something that is nice to do. Global warming, climate change, destruction of resources, biodiversity, disruptions of sustainable food supplies, pandemics, and a host of other factors have driven this gradual shift—which is likely to hit an inflection point of concern within the next few years.

This is one of those forecasts, however, where forecasters have to be careful to distinguish between what they think will happen and what they want to happen. My biggest mistake as a forecaster was failing to anticipate the emergence of sport-utility vehicles (SUVs). Like many others, I experienced the oil crisis of the 1970s, and it seemed obvious to me that smaller cars would dominate the auto scene in the United States. What happened, of course, was something quite different. SUVs were and are a crazed concept from a societal and environmental point of view, but they made perfect sense to individual consumers who wanted a sense of security and control in an uncertain world where gas was still cheap.

Next-generation workers are sensitive to environmental concerns. All generations will be increasingly concerned about their own health, about healthy work environments, and about healthy lifestyles. Health will be defined broadly, to include beauty, nutrition, fitness, lifestyle, and even building supplies, for healthy environments at work and at home. Concern about global pandemics, bioterrorism, and chronic disease is likely to grow. Health and environmental concerns will become increasingly linked in the minds of many people, particularly since the next decade will see dramatic concern about fossil fuels, water, and global warming.

This forecast provides a base for the rest of the book, the foresight that will be used to provoke insight and action. What can we as leaders learn about leading effectively in this kind of future?

Leaders can use foresight of the kind discussed in this chapter to stimulate insights about what individuals and organizations might do. Again, you don't have to agree with a forecast to find it useful.

3 The VUCA World

Both Danger and Opportunity

> The dogmas of the quiet past are inadequate to the
> stormy present. The occasion is piled high with diffi-
> culty, and we must rise with the occasion. As our case
> is new, so we must think anew and act anew.
> —Abraham Lincoln, 1862 Annual Message to Congress

This chapter explores nasty challenges and intriguing opportunities of
the VUCA world. The dangers are characterized by volatility, uncertainty, complexity, and ambiguity. But these same dangers create leadership opportunities that I describe in terms of vision, understanding,
clarity, and agility.[1]

Many people, including some leaders, are already beyond their own
personal capability to cope. The pain can be intense. While nobody can
predict the future, you can prepare. You can't escape all pain, but you
can prepare your mind to engage with painful dilemmas. With a prepared mind, the chances of success are much higher, and the pain is
more manageable, at least partly because you are expecting it. As Louis
Pasteur said, "Chance favors the prepared mind."

The forecast you read in Chapter 2 is the darkest Ten-Year Forecast
we've ever done at Institute for the Future in almost forty years of forecasting, but it is not without hope. Indeed, frightening forecasts can be
motivating; they inspire new action so the dark forecast never happens.
The great storyteller J. R .R. Tolkien made this observation about dark
stories: "Now it is a strange thing, but things that are good to have and
days that are good to spend are soon told about, and not much to lis-

ten to; while things that are uncomfortable, palpitating, and even grue-
some, may make a good tale, and take a good deal of telling anyway."[2]
The same could be said about forecasting: uncomfortable forecasts are
more engaging and perhaps more useful because they are more likely
to inspire action.

The VUCA world is all about change, including both dangerous rup-
tures and positive innovation. Inspiring strategies are hidden in the
volatilities, uncertainties, complexities, and ambiguities that are highlighted on our Forecast Map inside the book jacket. Although the dangers are more apparent, there are many opportunities as well—even if
they are below the surface. Leaders need to flip the VUCA forces, to comprehend the dangers but figure out a way to get there early and win
anyway.

THE ROOTS OF VUCA

My own introduction to the term *VUCA* began the week before September 11, 2001, when I was part of a Deloitte senior leadership retreat at
the U.S. Army War College in Carlisle, Pennsylvania. The Army War College is where rising-star military leaders learn how to be generals, where
successful tactical leaders learn to be strategic. The students learn how
complex government systems work, but they also grow what the army
hopes will become personal social networks for the future—particularly
connections with the growing number of students from other branches
of the U.S. military and the militaries of other countries. The Army War
College is a graduate school for life-and-death dilemmas. "VUCA University" focuses on leadership and strategy.

When I first arrived on the Army War College campus just days before 9/11, it felt like a sleepy liberal arts college that just happened to
be focused on military matters. The campus is in a lovely historic setting. In the quiet dusk, I walked the cinder track where Olympic super-
star Jim Thorpe had run, circling the field where Pop Warner coached
during the time when the campus was home to an American Indian
school. To the side of the grassy campus square, I found a small plaque
commemorating the place where Confederate general and Army War Col-

lege graduate Jeb Stuart burned down most of the Carlisle barracks on his roundabout way to Gettysburg. I saw an old tree that was said to be alive in the days of George Washington, when the campus was used for troop training. All was quiet and calm on the pastoral Army War College campus, without any apparent sense of danger. Security was light.

Now, in the post-9/11 world, the Carlisle campus feels like an armed camp, with security everywhere. The Army War College is focused on the military and societal leadership dilemmas of the VUCA world.

I have been back to Carlisle frequently since 9/11 to lead and participate in seminars with business, nonprofit, and military leaders. Columbia Business School now works with the Army War College to organize these exchanges with a wide range of leaders from business, nonprofits, government, and the military. We focus on lessons for leadership and strategy and what we can learn from one another. The simple answer is, we can learn a lot.

I had very little experience with the military before I began these exchanges, and I had a rather negative view of it: I thought of it as hierarchical and out of touch. Now, having done many of these exchanges, I have come away with great respect for our military—especially for how they are learning how to learn. The army's transformation began after Vietnam, which many think of as a failure in learning.

Unfortunately, it is almost impossible today to separate any discussion of the military from a discussion of the pros and cons of our government's military policy, but that is what I am going to try to do. I'm not here to critique U.S. military policy. Rather, I want to draw lessons about learning that all of us might take away from the intense life-threatening realities of warfare today.

The story that follows introduces the challenges of living, learning, and teaching in the frightening world in which soldiers live. Think of this as a very human story about on-the-spot learning in a life-and-death situation, where no amount of conventional training would have been enough to anticipate what happened.

One afternoon in July 2003, a young army battalion commander from Iowa led a small group of soldiers into the center of a town in northern Iraq. The situation in that part of the country was unpredictable. Roadside bombs, kidnappings, rocket-propelled grenade attacks, and assassinations were commonplace. Antagonism toward the Americans was a certainty. Whether antagonism would lead to violence was less certain but was always possible.

The commander's orders were to begin a relationship with local religious leaders. His mission was peaceful, but his men were understandably nervous.

It was hot as the soldiers marched along a main road, and sweat dripped into their eyes. Small groups of Iraqi men watched them pass, showing neither pleasure nor anger. But as the platoon penetrated farther into the center of town, the groups grew larger. The expressions of the men, at first neutral, grew increasingly hostile. Someone shook his fist. The growing crowd threatened at any moment to become a mob.

A heated discussion began among the Iraqi men, and attention focused on the Americans. The commander raised his arm, and the platoon stopped. Traffic seemed to have vanished from the streets, and a sullen silence fell. By now there were several hundred men advancing toward the platoon. Some were collecting rocks and paving stones, and the mood was clearly threatening.

The young commander looked back and saw more people gathering behind his platoon. He had to make a decision. Standard procedure would be either to retreat with as much dignity as possible or to fire warning shots. Neither option seemed appropriate; the platoon was now surrounded and vastly outnumbered. To threaten violence would work against the commander's intent to make friends with the religious leaders.

He might have thought he had a problem, for which there was some kind of solution. But in fact he had a dilemma with several apparent options, all bad, all leading at best to failure of the mission and at worst to violence.

Instead of reacting by rote (there was actually little to which he could have referred), he took a moment to focus on the desired outcome. His mission was not to fight, to suppress an insurgency, or to attack a stronghold. His mission (his superior's intent) was peaceful, to make contact with local religious leaders and begin an ongoing exchange. Bullets would result in civilian deaths, a public relations disaster, and failure of his mission. Retreat would be a failure even if it were possible, and even no response could result in casualties and possibly death for himself and his men. How could he deal with this dilemma?

In that moment, he improvised an alternate approach, part strategy and part tactic, neither surrender nor aggression. He ordered his men to smile, raise their weapons in the air and turn their barrels down, and to kneel on the ground. They were not showing subservience. After all, they had not laid down their weapons and lowered their heads. They could still respond militarily on short notice if necessary. But they communicated across languages and customs in a clearly understandable way that they meant no harm, that their mission was peaceful.

The crowd stopped in surprise. It seemed to have been spoiling for a fight, hoping perhaps for the bullets if not surrender. Instead they got neither hostility (and a kind of justification for their rage) nor retreat (and so victory). The commander's response defused a potentially dangerous situation, avoided violence, and allowed for the successful completion of his mission on a return visit.

Although the young officer faced a tactical challenge, this story introduces a strategic learning situation. How can organizations teach leaders to deal with dilemmas that cannot be anticipated? The leader in this story was ready in this life-threatening moment, and he reacted instinctively. How can leaders learn to sense what's going on and come up with a successful response?

The VUCA Opportunity

The VUCA world is sparking new ways of thinking and acting—ways to deal with the original dark meaning. The most successful leadership strategy is to flip the danger, like an aikido move in martial arts where you absorb the attack but redirect the energy of the attack in a positive direction. The martial arts teach a relaxed awareness that allows for appropriate and proportionate response, whether that response is an attack, a retreat, or a clever way to manage the dilemma without resort to violence. Aikido practitioners speak of blending with an attack, flowing with its direction and gently spinning it off in a safe direction. The Foresight to Insight to Action Cycle provides a way of engaging with the VUCA dangers in search of opportunities. Such a turnaround is exactly what leaders must do in response to the dangers of today's world.

Consider microeconomics as practiced by Nobel Prize-winner Muhammad Yunus in Bangladesh:

> In 1976, Yunus found himself frustrated at existing attempts to bring credit to the poor of Bangladesh. The economic theory he had learned in the United States simply wasn't working in the VUCA world of rural poverty. Countless numbers were unemployed, unable to make money with their current resources. They needed loans to start small enterprises—loans as small as $20 or even less for investments like buying raw materials for petty trade. Poor people simply couldn't win in the existing finance system. Banking systems excluded the poor, and loan sharks exploited them. Uncertainties and risks for the poor in agrarian societies, including floods, drought, crop failures, health crises, and so much more, were everywhere in their daily lives.
>
> Yunus plunged into this dilemma and saw that he couldn't graft the existing financial system onto the circumstances of the poor of Bangladesh. He needed to change the rules somehow. Gradually, through trial and error, he created microfinance and, eventually, Grameen Bank. He visited the villages and spoke with the people. He saw the world from their eyes, and gradually those factors that had once seemed like insurmountable problems became opportunities for innovation.
>
> Microfinance needed to be local, personal, and part of the community. The personal connections created bridges of trust where once there was fear. He organized borrowers into small homogenous groups, with the members being dependent on one

another to keep their loans. He used social capital instead of financial collateral. In this way, he used the strong sense of community
and social pressure as incentives and sanctions—each person
becomes invested in the others' success, and they all encourage
one another. If one person fails, the entire group fails, unless they
assist one another. Loans didn't require collateral, but repayment
schedules were strict and extremely regular on a weekly basis—
in very small increments.

Grameen also looked at the social conditions—such as shelter,
water, sanitation, family planning, education, and other basic
needs for survival—that had frustrated past attempts to develop
economic self-sufficiency.

Unlike traditional banks, Grameen focused almost exclusively
on women, who generally looked out for the health of the entire
family and so, family by family, increased the health of the village.
Women have much higher repayment rates than men.

Using the new principles of microfinance, Yunus reversed the
age-old vicious cycle of low income, low saving, and low investment into a virtuous cycle of low income, injection of credit,
investment, more income, more savings, more investment, and
more income.

The VUCA world of poverty in Bangladesh is now being turned
around with a combination of vision, understanding, clarity, and agility.
The challenge is finding a way to engage honestly and create a winning
strategy within the chaos that you encounter. Here are some emerging
principles:

Volatility yields to Vision.   *Vision* means having a clear intent, a clear direction for your actions. Vision is much more important than foresight,
since vision seeks to create a future—not just study the future. With
clear vision, creative space opens for innovation within the parameters
that you specify. A bold vision sees beyond volatility, with a kind of calm
perspective that is not trapped by the assumptions of the present. For
example, Muhammad Yunus said in 1996, "One day our grandchildren
will go to the museums to see what poverty was."[3] In a 2006 interview

he declared, "58% of the poor who borrowed from Grameen Bank have now risen out of poverty. There are over 100 million people now involved with micro credit schemes. At that rate, we'll halve poverty by 2015. We'll create a poverty museum in 2030."[4] That's vision, and it is important to note that he didn't begin with this vision: it emerged as he learned in the field. Now, while most people assume a continuing gap between the rich and the poor, Yunus is engaging with that gap and working on practical ways to overcome it. In doing so, he motivates not only his own organization but also many others. That motivation will be amplified by his winning of the Nobel Peace Prize.

Uncertainty yields to Understanding.   In the face of uncertainty, listening and understanding can help leaders discover new ways of thinking and acting. Listening leads to understanding, which is the basis for trust. In order to understand, you must learn to listen carefully without judging too soon. The VUCA world creates an urgency to act quickly, but sometimes it is a false sense of urgency. The best leaders have the presence and calm to listen before talking, to open an opportunity for deep understanding. Understanding is a prerequisite to trust, and trust is vital to building community. The Grameen Bank is based on trust, with a reliance on local social networks. Traditional approaches to banking often begin with an assumption of mistrust and create systems of financial collateral to protect themselves against risk. Authentic gestures of trust can be extremely constructive, as Yunus has shown. His response was one of understanding: he went into the villages and listened to poor people—and he asked many questions. He began by loaning $27 to a group of forty-two people. He gained their trust, and in turn they trusted the new system. His understanding and consequent credit strategy became the groundwork for the Grameen Bank and what has now become a worldwide network of microfinance innovation.

Complexity yields to Clarity.   Leaders must help others make sense out of complexity. The VUCA world rewards clarity because people are so confused that they grasp at anything that helps them make sense out of the chaos. At times, clarity will be rewarded, even when it turns out to be wrong. Clarity is good, and we should strive for it, but not at the expense of truth. The thoughtful leader's quest is to be both clear and accurate, simple but not simplistic. Clarity is usually possible, even when there is no control. Muhammad Yunus realized that traditional banking methods didn't work amid the immense complexity of poverty. Simplistic solutions did not work. Yunus sorted through the complexity and came up with a clear strategy: peer pressure that encouraged them to repay the loans and grow their own communities, and a focus on loans to women, because they tend to benefit the whole family more than do loans to men. The benefits of microfinance are personal, practical, and clear.

Ambiguity yields to Agility.   In an ambiguous world, leaders must be ready for surprises. Leaders can't surrender to ambiguity—that would lead to paralysis and confusion. Rather, leaders must learn how to be agile and responsive to attack. The VUCA world rewards networks because they are agile, while it punishes the rigidity and brittleness of hierarchies. Yunus learned that the hierarchical structures of traditional banking would not work in the developing world. His approach to microfinance is networked and flexible, lightweight, and replicable. Microfinance models have now multiplied across countries, cultures, and circumstances with remarkable agility.

We all have our personal VUCA moments, when our own life becomes volatile, uncertain, complex, and ambiguous. Personal crises hit everyone at some point. In these moments, we are challenged to respond. Absorbing a crisis like losing a child is jarring for anyone, but the most positive response is to engage with the crisis and figure out something—anything—you can *do* to rechannel that negative energy. The most dramatic example of this rechanneling that I ever saw was provided by the Biehl family from my hometown of Geneva, Illinois. Amy Biehl was a Stanford student who went to South Africa to work with poor people but was killed by an angry mob of the same people she was there to help. Her parents, while still grief stricken, envisioned and worked personally to create the Amy Biehl Foundation to carry on the work of their fallen daughter. In an amazing act of forgiveness, they actually met and worked with her killers to create this amazing turnaround.

The VUCA world is all around us, with more or less intensity. Those of us in the less intense environments can learn from those in the more extreme ones. Here are some examples that show how vision, understanding, clarity, and agility are proving successful for leaders in a variety of different organizations.

Examples of Positive Response to the VUCA World

Strategic Intent. The military response to the VUCA world relies heavily on "commander's intent," sometimes called "strategic intent" (which I prefer), as a way of managing the dilemmas. Strategic intent is a clear, compelling, and concise statement that includes the following:

- **Purpose:** What do you want to accomplish? How is this purpose related to the larger mission or enterprise?
- **Method or task:** What needs to be done?
- **End state:** What ends are we pursuing?

Strategic intent, with decentralized authority to execute and innovate within the boundaries of that intent, provides a practical way to engage with chaotic situations. A strategic intent should cascade across levels in the hierarchy (at least two levels down) and across organizational boundaries to provide a consistent direction and message. A strategic intent statement can be a bridge from the most senior officer to the on-the-ground leader who engages personally with those who must bring the intention to life in a practical way.

At its best, the military's strategic intent provides consistency without dogma. A strategic intent makes it more likely that a mission can be accomplished—even if the leader is killed or even in the absence of communications. At its best, strategic intent facilitates agile response to unanticipated events through a consistent take-charge mentality within the framework of the intent. In the military, there is little room to question strategic intent but great flexibility with regard to how that intent is carried out.

Of course, it is not just the army that is experiencing this shift toward asymmetrical warfare on the physical and virtual battlefield. John Arquilla, who is professor of defense analysis at the Naval Postgraduate School in Monterey, has become the leading voice exploring the emergent realities of "net warfare," in which the great wars are between "nations and networks."[5] The world of asymmetrical warfare is obviously different from the worlds of business and nongovernmental organizations (NGOs), but there are important similarities. Competition in business is becoming more asymmetrical. For most companies, their competitors are also collaborators in some arenas. The competitors of today are not likely to be the most important competitors tomorrow.

In this world, nobody is really in control. For people who are experiencing more chaos than they can absorb, who are outside their comfort zone, clarity looks like relief, and the need for relief feels urgent. But clarity is hard to find in this world, and control is often impossible. Clarity is good, but not if it is simplistic, not if the clarity is obscured when it comes to important aspects of the truth. The young commander in the story above understood his commander's intent, which was to make friends with the local religious leaders. He improvised his way out of a very difficult situation while still holding to that intent.

The Army War College teaches leaders that strategy is hard work and that it demands critical thinking—a mix of clarity and complexity. With strategic intent, the vision is clear. The challenge is to develop the agility to respond to the chaotic world within which the intent must be pursued.

Health in a VUCA world.   The threats to health are everywhere, from global pandemics to the products we use in our homes. Health has become a filter for purchase of a wide range of products and services, beyond just response to disease. Now, health criteria are important for food products, beauty products, cleaning products, and even products to ensure healthy housing, air, and water.

The Centers for Disease Control and Prevention (CDC), based in Atlanta, is focusing its strategy on global health and safety—but health is what everyone is most concerned about. The CDC has also recognized that, even though it is a U.S. government agency, health is a global challenge. Pandemics are a concern because the world is interconnected in many ways, including the spread of infectious diseases. The dilemma for the CDC, and for us all as a global society, is how to be responsive to treating and preventing disease while creating more effective approaches to long-term health. The vision for the CDC is long-term health. The CDC is attempting to raise the health aspirations of Americans, encouraging us to focus on healthy living within the context of radical uncertainty.

Meanwhile, the CDC is also the center for emergency health response. Its new Emergency Command Center in Atlanta has sixty-six workstations, sixteen large-screen displays, and fourteen team rooms circling the Command Center. The CDC is better prepared than ever for global health emergencies, even though it is placing its emphasis on heading off the crises before they occur. The new Command Center was developed with corporate support through the CDC Foundation, a creative organizational structure that allows the CDC to mount new initiatives with business without going through the normal governmental procedures that are just too slow be able to respond to global health emergencies.

On 9/11, the CDC had only crude emergency response facilities that it set up in a temporary conference room. In the six years since 9/11, the CDC has responded to twenty-five health emergencies with "command center" activities, which led them to create the more permanent— and much more advanced—Emergency Command Center. Using simulation gaming, it now practices to develop its agility in responding to the next health crises, which are uncertain in nature but certain to come.

The following are the CDC's strategic imperatives, all of which address various facets of the chaotic world around us:

- **Health Impact Focus:** Align CDC's people, strategies, goals, investments, and performance to maximize impact on people's health and safety. (Alignment in this case is a kind of strategic intent about overall direction and purpose.)
- **Customercentricity:** Market what people want and need to choose health. (The CDC is increasingly market sensitive and market savvy.)

- **Public Health Research:** Create and disseminate the knowledge and innovations people need to protect their health now and in the future. (Networks are used heavily within the CDC to spread news about innovations and prepare for rapid responses to emergencies.)
- **Leadership:** Leverage CDC's unique expertise, partnerships, and networks to improve the health system. (This imperative links back to clarity and intent, as well as to the CDC's increasingly wide circle of network connections beyond government.)
- **Global Health Impact:** Extend CDC's knowledge and tools to promote health protection around the world. (Health concerns, no matter how locally defined, are increasingly global. Health issues bleed across national boundaries.)
- **Accountability:** Sustain people's trust and confidence by making the most efficient and effective use of their investment in CDC. (The CDC has an incredible public relations challenge, to engage with diverse people and organizations all around the world.)

Notice how these imperatives bridge the goals of both creating a sustainable health culture and responding to global health crises.

Whereas health care (that is, disease response) used to dominate, the CDC is now making a major strategic push around healthy choice making. Although it is still very interested in the health care system, it is taking a growing interest in health behaviors that are more basic and more likely to have lasting impacts.

In order to hone its own readiness, the CDC executive leadership team uses a set of global scenarios against which each of these strategies has been tested. How might each strategy do in a range of possible future worlds? Readiness exercises like these prepare the leaders of the CDC for the dilemmas that they face, but they also allow them to periodically reevaluate their strategies and the tactics they are using to bring them to life.

Public Education for a VUCA World. Although every other major institution has gone through radical changes in the past few generations, public schools are changing more slowly—except for the core of amazing teachers who bring life and hope to the classrooms. It is almost as though the public school administrators were hoping the VUCA world was not really there, even though any teacher or student could tell you it *feels* chaotic already inside many schools.

The KnowledgeWorks Foundation (KWF) is an operational foundation based in Cincinnati that has a focus on improving education for disadvantaged kids. IFTF does an annual forecast for KWF on external future forces likely to affect education and learning, thinking ten years ahead. Our goal is to identify high-impact zones in which investments by KWF are likely to have major impacts on improving education for disadvantaged kids.

One of the dilemmas we identified is the tension between the marketplace for increasingly personalized learning and the social mandate of the public schools to provide foundational education to everyone—regardless of background or income. New media, especially interactive media, are introducing new ways to engage with students and new opportunities for learning—but access varies depending mostly on ability to pay. Public education is funded mostly from public sources, but new media learning resources tend to be marketplace driven. What is the role of public education in a marketplace-driven learning environment?

Other directions of change in the world of education, each of which introduces dilemmas that challenge educational policy makers, are highlighted below:

- **VUCA Community Schools.**   Increasingly, schools need to be safe zones, centers for hope and positive expectations. Tension is greatest in urban communities, with extreme conditions of wealth and poverty, uncharted social challenges with increasing diversity, and few shared norms to guide constructive change. A school can be a healthy life advocate, playing a core role in communities in dealing with problems such as youth obesity. Community schools can provide a vision for dealing with the volatility of most communities. To be successful, this vision must be understood and shared widely.

- **The Learning Economy.**   The trend is from reliance on a dominant system of public schools toward a diverse marketplace for learning and from one-way classroom-style learning to multiple ways that are personalized to the needs of the learner. Think of this as a grassroots economy for learning, a direction that is likely to be a challenge to the centralized methods of the public schools.

- **Realignment of the Learning Professions.**   The learning professions, such as teaching, are moving toward becoming agents for formal and informal learning, from "sage on the stage" to "guide by your side." Teachers unions are major players as the incumbent learning agents and can be a source for innovation or an impediment to constructive change.

- **Pervasive Learning Ecologies.**   The trend is toward anytime, anyplace learning, with a blending of the virtual and the physical. Schools need to help frame conversations about learning within a community, with an emphasis on providing opportunities for disadvantaged kids. Youth, even poor youth, are growing up with media all around them. These digital natives have the media savvy to learn in new ways if teachers can learn to use the media that the kids already know how to use.

- **Deep Personalization.**   The trend is toward customization for everyone, with experiential lifelong learning. Empowered learners with smart networking skills are developing new ways to learn. Listening, understanding, and trust are required to deliver authentic personalization.

The VUCA world is creating dilemmas of learning for disadvantaged kids that can't be solved with either-or thinking. New strategies are required that go beyond problem solving. The education and learning hot zones summarized above present new challenges, but they also highlight new opportunities for change in how kids learn and how teachers teach. Public schools could be an important part of the learning economy, but the challenges for them are extreme.

Science in a VUCA World.   Science issues fuel confusion, but science can also help us understand the volatility, uncertainty, complexity, and ambiguity around us. The changes underway in science and technology are vivid and evident to anyone who is paying attention. From stem cells to biotech to global warming, it seems that there is a science and technology story in the newspapers every day, and most of the stories concern both hopes and fears.

IFTF did a study for the government of the United Kingdom that synthesized forecasts of science and technology, thinking out ten, twenty, and fifty years ahead. This was an independent outside look, to provide input to science policy makers in the United Kingdom. In this project, we did a series of expert panels and drew together forecasts from around the world. We created an online exchange among experts as a way of synthesizing the forecasts as the project unfolded.

The workshops we did with scientists, policy makers, and thought leaders made apparent a core dilemma: science and technology developments always happen in some social context. Science and technology don't create the future, but they do enable and amplify it. Technology forecasters must take stock of the social climate within which the technology is developing. In effect, every technology forecast must be a social forecast, or at least it must contain social assumptions. Here are the six core science and technology drivers identified by the IFTF study, with a note regarding the societal issues each will raise:

- Small world, with sensors everywhere, meaning that the geoweb discussed in Chapter 2 will become practical on a very large scale. Anytime, anyplace sensing will play out in a world that is worried about both safety (from terrorism and many other threats) and the privacy of individuals.

- Intentional biology, with new possibilities to guide human life at the molecular level. Such abilities raise great possibilities for use and misuse, with very different views of what may constitute misuse. The world of intentional biology is loaded with the possibilities for unintended consequences.

- Extended self, with new possibilities to extend the human body, the mind, and the senses. Again, social norms and values will shape what is accepted as part of the range of human diversity and what is out of bounds.

- Mathematical world, with new capabilities to visualize very complex patterns in comprehensible ways. Big-picture patterns become more visible in this world, but these patterns may not match the assumptions or beliefs of some groups within society.

- Sensory transformation, with new abilities to sense and process what is sensed. Simulation will become more practical as a learning medium in this world, which will introduce new ways to develop disciplines of readiness.

- Light infrastructure, with a move from centralized grids to flexible smaller-scale infrastructure. Energy conservation and sustainability could improve in profound ways using light infrastructure. Societal attitudes toward sustainability could reach a tipping point over the next decade, with more practical and affordable ways to be environmentally sound.

Technology and science have major impacts on society, but society shapes the kinds of technology applications that actually come to the marketplace. Society can slow down or speed up a core technology evolutionary path, not to mention bending that path in significant ways. In California, for example, a public initiative was passed to support stem cell research. A coalition of conservative groups, however, brought a lawsuit against stem cell research that kept the initiative from being implemented for several years. Eventually, the public initiative was translated into active programs, but these NGOs delayed the start and shaped what actually happened.

Both science and technology present many problems that can be solved, but they also present many dilemmas that are much more profound, and it is the dilemmas that become clear when you look ten, twenty, and fifty years ahead. The future world is a high-tech world, with deep roots in science but also a with long roots to the past, and many of these roots are resistant to change from both science and technology.

Leisure in a VUCA World.   Ocean cruises and theme parks are examples of what Joe Pine and Jim Gilmore call the "experience economy," in which the experience *is* the product and service. Pine and Gilmore talk about the overall economic shift from products to services to experiences to transformations.[6] Leisure is still important, but it will play out in a world that is increasingly concerned about safety.

Cruise ships can provide authentic experiences that lead to personal transformations. For example, a cruise offers a family quality time alone for the parents, amazing activities for the kids, and family time for meals and other group activities—in the comfortable world of a cruise ship—which nowadays is very comfortable indeed. Cruse ships go to interesting places while traveling in a contained, comfortable, and safe environment.

In recent years, however, the VUCA world has broken into the comfortable world of cruising. Higher fuel prices are an obvious pressure for the cruise lines. More questions are being raised about the environmental effects of these giant ships, even though the newest ships have greatly reduced their negative environmental impacts. In fact, the water treatment and recycling capabilities on modern ships are impressive indeed, and the fuel used by a cruise ship is far less than that if all the guests took individual automobile trips. Still, cruise ships *look* environmentally suspect.

The cruise lines are sailing conspicuously between the developed and the developing worlds, moving back and forth across the gap between rich and poor in giant-size vessels that embody and advertise wealth. Imagine a luxury cruise liner pulling into a harbor in the developing world. (I have never seen a humble-looking cruise ship.) People (most of them poor) on shore rush out to see the fantastic ship towering over the sea. The first glance from shore is a vision of incredible extravagance, embodying a luxury experience that the local folks could never afford or possibly even imagine. When they go ashore, the advantaged passengers come face-to-face with the disadvantaged residents. Many types of encounters are possible.

Cruise companies are working to be perceived by guests and by local ports as both international and supportive of local development. Their international side calls for them to offer travel opportunities to attractive spots around the world. In addition, cruise companies want to draw passengers who might be based in very different parts of the world. Their local challenge is to figure out how to engage in positive ways with each port of call so that cruise ships are seen as welcome guests at each stop. Some cruise companies arrange for local contributions of food, money, or time by their guests when the ships visit foreign ports. By working with local NGOs or government groups, cruise ships have the opportunity to design positive experiences for their guests while also contributing to the local communities that they visit. Cruise companies want respect and support from both sides of the rich-poor gap.

The cruise companies' dilemma is figuring out how to facilitate positive guest experiences while maintaining good relations with the areas where the ships visit. Cruise companies must balance competing needs, wants, and perceptions in order to create both positive business models and a positive brand reputation with regard to environmental and social impacts. They offer safe adventures with many options on board that range from rock climbing to surfing to personal growth experiences, but they also face new challenges as they cruise the VUCA world.

Theme parks are similar in some ways to cruise ships, but they exist in a more self-contained world. In an anxiety-laden world, safety is a priority—particularly for parents. For kids, however, adrenalin rushes are highly valued, and they want the rush at an earlier age than ever before—probably because of the vivid media experiences with which they now grow up. Can kids be scared safely?

Walt Disney World in Orlando, for example, is one of the safest places in the world. It feels very safe to parents, but it also provides exciting experiences for their kids. The dilemma is to provide both experiences authentically: safety that reassures the parents and thrilling experiences for the kids. It is getting harder and harder for theme parks to win in the throes of this dilemma.

Theme parks provide the potential for transformative experiences. Within the context of a theme park, transformative entertainment can go beyond traditional products and services. Disneyland and Walt Disney World, for example, provide rides and attractions that are an amazing mix of theater and thrill. Where other theme parks emphasize brute force thrill and adrenalin rush by shock, Disney does it with artistic and theatrical flair. The parents and grandparents are likely to understand and appreciate this difference, but it is a challenge to reach the kids— who are coming to theme parks with much richer experiences and expectations than the kids of the past (who are now the young parents). Parents will continue to have safety concerns, however, and the fears are likely to get worse, not better. The safely scared dilemma will be increasingly difficult to manage.

The Outrage Industry. Out of all the companies with which I have worked, Target is the only one for which a community relations person has been present at every workshop I have done—across the company. Target's relationships with its local communities are a visible part of its corporate strategy. Target stores are in local communities, and the corporation makes a noble attempt to be active local contributors. Five percent of Target's profits are dedicated to the local communities they serve.

Just as it is difficult for large corporations to develop intimate relationships with individual customers, it is difficult for a large corporation to engage with many different local communities. Even within a single community where a single Target store is located, there are many different kinds of people and many different views on most issues. Target is very community minded, but the communities it serves are extremely diverse. It is difficult if not impossible to please all community members. Target's community commitment gets played out in the real world of communities in which people do not always agree on what is appropriate.

For example, Target team members (Target employees) are trained to be inclusive and situational in dealing with their local communities, to honor whatever cultural values and traditions are appropriate for a particular guest. Team members offer greetings in the stores appropriate to "the holidays," not just Christmas, although they are also taught to be situational. If a guest says that she is buying a Christmas present for her mother, for example, Target advises its team members that it is appropriate to say "Merry Christmas" to the guest when she is leaving.

Target's flexible and situational holiday language, however, was perceived by a portion of the Christian community as an affront to their beliefs. During the 2005 holiday season, Fox News reported that Target had instituted a policy against "Merry Christmas" greetings at their stores. From what I could gather by talking with Target people, Target had no new policy. Rather, Target was making an ongoing effort to be inclusive of the diverse people in the local communities where their stores are located. The Fox News challenge, however, was polarizing, and it implied that a new policy was in effect: Target was accused of killing "Merry Christmas" and telling its employees to replace it with "Happy Holidays." For Fox News, it was an engaging story of the controversial sort that it seems to love—even though the story was not true, as best as I could tell.

Target was forced to engage with a range of diverse community groups on an issue on which it was impossible for everyone to agree. There was no single greeting that would please everyone in all of Target's local communities. Not surprisingly, some community voices were louder than others. I spoke with Target employees who fielded some of the calls in response to this story. Some impassioned Christian callers were outraged and did not want to hear Target's side of this story. The Target representatives listened and tried to put the Fox story in context.

Target's organizational dilemma is about how to keep its strategic commitment to communities while *also* engaging positively with the very different parts of each community where Target has a store—some parts of which will never agree with one another.

This story is an example of what is starting to be called the "outrage industry," referring to news or entertainment personalities who focus on stimulating outrage—with no particular purpose in mind other than stirring things up. In other words, the outrage industry practitioners are not advocates of a better way; they just want to stimulate outrage. Indeed, Fox News has made a very successful business out of stimulating outrage. People love a colorful story, even if it is not true. Outrage can come from the right or from the left, but the result is increased amplification of stories and anecdotes that contain both information and misinformation, to which retailers and others must respond.

Chapter 2 and the Forecast Map talked about the driving force of extreme polarization. The outrage industry is an artifact of the VUCA world, which fuels polarization. Many of the people with strong opinions are sincerely interested in a particular kind of change, but their voices become mixed easily with those from the outrage industry who are churning stories. Being on the receiving end in this world of dilemma by innuendo is usually a no-win game, yet many corporations have to play the game. As one executive said to me, "We often have a choice, when confronted with accusations like this, of looking stupid or looking evil. When I'm faced with this choice, I always choose looking stupid. It is easier to recover from looking stupid than it is from looking evil."

Insuring against loss in a VUCA World. What is *insurance* in a VUCA world? It seems like an overpromise to sell insurance in a world that has fewer and fewer guarantees. Insurance has traditionally meant indemnification of loss if something bad happens. Indemnification is still possible, but nothing can be truly insured. Readiness is a much more believable and more useful promise, a stance that prepares people for possible loss without overpromising with assurances that nobody can really provide with any degree of certainty.

One example of this readiness is the geoweb and the world of sensors, described on the Forecast Map inside the book jacket and in Chapter 2, that provides, for example, new resources for home monitoring of water leaks, fires, or other risks that homeowners take. These kinds of ambient intelligence are becoming possible, where what used to be static objects can be transformed into aware surroundings as digital technology becomes embedded in physical objects that are part of our daily lives. Using sensors, pattern recognition, and user profiles, new services can monitor and respond as needed. Today's household alarm systems only hint at what will be possible as geoweb technology advances and as services are introduced to take advantage of these new readiness technologies.

State Farm Insurance, for example, is moving toward readiness in its services, while still providing indemnification along the way. The company helps homeowners assess their risk and develop their own readiness strategies. There is a basic shift underway in the insurance industry as consumers realize and accept that nobody can really "insure" that bad things won't happen. This was always true, but it is even truer now. Rather than assurances that may be unrealistic anyway, we must all prepare for and take risks that we choose to take—with a good understanding of the tradeoffs and the readiness procedures that are appropriate. Indeed, the insurance industry is gradually evolving toward a focus on risk, risk transfer, risk advice, and readiness services. Although most businesses hate risk, the VUCA world is fueling a crop of companies that thrive on it.

I did a series of workshops in London, and beforehand the meeting organizer presented an evacuation plan in the event of an emergency. I did a meeting in Geneva, Switzerland, after that, and an executive from London kicked off the meeting. He asked if an emergency briefing was required in Geneva and, before getting an answer, said, "I'm going to do an emergency briefing anyway, since it's the right thing to do." In Jerusalem, such routine readiness preparation is even more evident than it is in London. In the United States, however, most people still pretend that we will solve the "terrorist problem" and someday return to normal. The VUCA world is here to stay; it is the new normal.

This world is riddled with safety and personal risk dilemmas. People want to be better prepared, more ready for the uncertainties we are all facing. We are all becoming more conscious of these risks and more open to services that help us prepare. We all want assurances, and we'd love to have our safety insured, but nobody can do that. The dilemma for insurance companies is to figure out how they can continue to offer indemnification as appropriate while also beginning to offer new services that encourage people to be more prepared for and able to deal with a world where nothing can *really* be insured.

Networks of empowered people will want to be better prepared, more ready for the uncertainty that we are all facing. Smart networking will make it much easier to share these practices, some of which will be shared in an open-source way and some of which will be provided as services by insurance companies and other risk advisers. Interest and advocacy groups, including those with extreme views, are likely to have major impacts on the emerging field of readiness technology and services. Insurance companies do not have a great reputation in many parts of the world, so they will have reputation management challenges. If traditional insurance companies cannot respond to this emerging market demand, new players and new services will arise in their place.

The VUCA world is affecting all aspects of life, as the cases above suggest, and the responses are becoming increasingly interesting. Each response illustrates an open-ended learn-as-you-go style of learning that moves beyond traditional problem-solving styles of leadership.

4 What's Different about Dilemmas?

Obedience to the law is the dry husk
of loyalty and faith.
Opinion is the barren flower of the Way
the beginning of ignorance.
—Lao Tzu, *Tao Te Ching*

When you come to a fork in the road, take it.
—Yogi Berra

This chapter helps you engage with the dilemmas in your world so you can get there early and compete in the present. The Foresight to Insight to Action Cycle is a framework for sensing and making sense out of dilemmas—even if you cannot fully understand or control what's going on.

The biggest challenge for leaders is to learn to live with—even embrace—the tensions inherent in dilemmas. How can you prepare your mind to win when you are faced with dilemmas, to win what appear to be no-win games? Dilemmas disguised as problems are particularly dangerous. If you engage with a dilemma as if it were a problem, you may get there early, but you are not likely to win.

Most leaders understand the methods of problem solving very well; these methods have worked in the past, and they still work in some situations. For leaders, however, dilemmas have become more important than problems. This chapter will help you make the shift from problem solving to dealing with dilemmas. You need to figure out ways to succeed even when you cannot solve.

Many of today's senior executives are simply not prepared for the dilemma-laden environment of today, let alone tomorrow. It is debatable whether we have more dilemmas now than we used to (each generation seems to feel that it has the most complex and challenging of times), but there is no debate that there are many dilemmas now. As I work with senior executives, I find that they immediately recognize the notion of a dilemma and the challenges that dilemmas present. Few leaders would claim that their organizations are facing today's dilemmas optimally, while even fewer would claim to be prepared for tomorrow's dilemmas.

Most of today's leaders were taught—many of them very well—to solve problems. Of course, there are still many problems to solve. The solve-and-run approach, however, is dangerous when applied to dilemmas. An expectation of solution can lead to frustration and false urgency when a solution doesn't appear. The twisting lack of clarity implicit in dilemmas does not yield to the analytics of problem solving. The mysterious aspects of dilemmas remain puzzling, even after the analytics have been exhausted. Many of today's senior leaders must step back and learn another approach—if they have the discipline and humility to do so. Getting there early buys you the time to look around, to sense what's going on.

Another title I considered for this chapter was "Knowing Too Soon," which comes from Ursula Le Guin's interpretation notes from the *Tao Te Ching*, where she says, in reference to the quotation that introduces this chapter: "The word I render as 'opinion' can be read as 'knowing too soon': the mind obeying orders, judging before the evidence is in, closed to fruitful perception and learning."[1]

As I was working on the first draft of this chapter, I mentioned Ursula Le Guin's commentary on the limitations of opinion to my wife, who is a constitutional lawyer. She immediately saw the similarity between Le Guin's insight and the classic views of Justice Oliver Wendell Holmes about the limitations of words: "A word is not a crystal, transparent and unchanging, it is the skin of a living thought and may vary greatly in color and content according to the circumstances and the time in which it is used."[2] Words take on a life of their own, with built-in assumptions and baggage. We hear words, but we don't necessarily understand them—at least not right away.

The language of problem solving inhibits problem solvers, who tend to assume either/or. The world of dilemmas requires us to shift our words and our thinking to embrace both/and. When we're dealing with dilemmas, we need words that can be used with flexibility. We need the ability to avoid taking our words too seriously. The words of problem solving are holding us back as we struggle to engage with dilemmas. It is so tempting to "know too soon," to assume that the comforting words and methodologies of problem solving will get us through. They won't.

Problem solvers have been taught to move fast. Shooting from the hip feels good to them. Winning when you are faced with dilemmas, however, requires an ability to hold complexity in your mind without knowing too soon and without taking words or data too seriously. If you get there early, you've got time to sort out a situation. Some leaders shoot from the hip because they get there late and don't have the time to do anything else.

With dilemmas, you need to listen for what's behind the words, what's beneath the data. We need the discipline and the restraint to avoid forcing a premature decision or trying to solve a problem that has a dilemma lurking inside. If you get there early, you've got more time to decide if you're dealing with a solvable problem or a dilemma. You need time to live with a new situation without become mired in it. Decisions still must be made in the world of dilemmas.

High-performing successful baby boomers are often exquisite problem solvers. Indeed, it was a baby boom leader who came up with the slogan "You're either part of the solution or you're part of the problem." But what if there are no solutions? What if the "problems" don't go away?

I was personally introduced to the world of dilemmas when I went to divinity school in 1967. One of my motivations for studying religion was the uncomfortable feeling I got when approached by campus evangelists when I was in college. I was a college basketball player at the University of Illinois, and these evangelists loved to recruit athletes. I was often met after practice or on campus and walked home by one of their recruiters, who were always very nice, very sincere people with an eye to conversion. Something just didn't seem right about their logic to me, but I wasn't sure what. Divinity school allowed me to understand that life is not a problem that can be solved by one simple religious answer or one conversion experience; it is a dilemma with which we have to be engaged. I believe that religion can play a constructive role, but life is complicated, and our dilemmas vary from person to person.

In divinity school, I was part of a fellowship program designed to attract students who did not have a commitment to the ministry but who did have a curiosity about religion. I was lucky enough to attend the same divinity school as Martin Luther King Jr.; the school was Crozer Theological Seminary, which is now part of the Rochester Theological Union.

When Dr. King was killed in 1968, the school introduced a course that re-created the intellectual influences on Martin Luther King while he was in seminary. My professor in this program, Kenneth W. Smith, had taught Dr. King, who had started to develop his strategy for dealing with the race dilemma while he was at Crozer, an American Baptist seminary in the social gospel tradition. Dr. King was influenced deeply by social ethics leaders like Walter Rauschenbusch, process-oriented theologians like Pierre Teilhard de Chardin, and of course spiritual and social activists like Mahatma Gandhi, who introduced the notion of *satyagraha*, or "force of truth," that underlies nonviolent direct action.

When Martin Luther King was at Crozer, race relations in the United States were deeply polarized. Dr. King learned how to engage with the dilemmas of race relations without getting stuck in the polarities. He learned how to live in the necessary tension between judging too soon and deciding too late. Premature judgment in his world could lead to more polarization and sometimes to violence. Deciding too late would mean missing opportunities for change.

Looking back at the civil rights movement that Dr. King inspired, we can see that polarization was everywhere (on all sides), and there were milestone moments where a single act or event—like the refusal of Rosa Parks to move to the back of the bus—that could change the course of events. Dr. King held strongly to his vision of a promised land, where all races would live together, but he had great strategic and tactical flexibility regarding how to get there. Dr. King listened, reflected, and prayed in order to gain a deep understanding of the situation. Racial relations was not just a problem to be solved for Dr. King, it was a complex series of dilemmas that required great discipline, a clear vision, and a strategy for moving forward. He had to avoid knowing too soon, but he still had incredible courage to act at critical moments.

For me, going to Crozer was a changing point in my life. Divinity school allowed me to explore world religions and to begin to understand the dilemmas of life that religions address. Religions have always wrestled with the basic dilemmas of life. The varieties of religions, however, have varied needs for clarity. The uncertainties and alternative approaches to life are apparent when you look across religious and mythic traditions, if you can avoid getting stuck in one point of view.

The "problem solvers" of the religious world are those who believe that theirs is the *only* way. These groups have solved the dilemmas of life, or so they believe. Rule-based ethics, however, can go only so far. Empathy-based ethics is required in a world that is so diverse, with so many different views of life. The evangelists who tried to convert me in college were religious problem solvers, probably with the best of intentions but with little understanding of the complexities of the world.

This chapter probes the nature of dilemmas—as compared to problems that have clear solutions—and the potential for engaging with dilemmas as a source of inspiration.

CAN YOU TELL A DILEMMA FROM A PROBLEM?

Modern dilemmas have evolved beyond the traditional definition of *dilemma*, which focused on an either/or choice between two bad options. Webster's defines a dilemma as "State of uncertainty or perplexity especially as requiring a choice between equally unfavorable options."[3] In today's complex world, choices are many (we face not just *di*lemmas with two choices, but *tri*lemmas and *multi*lemmas)—even as the context within which dilemmas are arising is becoming more intractable. The Wikipedia definition of *dilemma* questions the traditional definition with its focus on two equally bad choices: "Many modern dictionaries consider this restriction needless and allow the word to be used colloquially to refer to a difficult situation with any number of choices."[4]

Based on our experience with leaders in corporations, government, and nonprofits, I suggest the following characteristics for modern strategic dilemmas.

- Unsolvable
- Recurrent
- Complex and often messy
- Threatening
- Enigmatic and confusing
- Puzzling, with two or more choices—and decisions are still required
- Possibly positive (dilemmas with attractive but competing options are possible)

In our problem-solving culture, we are quick to write off as oxymorons things that don't *seem* to go together. I have a vivid memory of my first morning in China, reading a local newspaper that referred to the Chinese "socialist market economy." The words jumped off the page at me. In the United States, we tend to think of *either* socialist *or* market economies. The Chinese, however, say "socialist market economy," and they really mean both, not either/or. The Chinese socialist market economy is becoming much more relevant to companies from the United States and other parts of the world as they become engaged in China. In the West, we think either/or, but in China it is perfectly normal to think with ambiguity about the socialist and market forces. Sometimes one must be satisfied with partial or ambiguous answers.

We get stuck, especially if we are constrained by time, on what we perceive as contradictions in terms without exploring deeply enough how apparent misfits or opposites might align together to create new opportunities. The socialist market economy is certainly no oxymoron in China, nor is it a problem the Chinese are trying to solve. The socialist market economy is a way of life for them.

The relentless search for an absolute answer can paralyze a leader, delay a decision, or even lead an organization in entirely the wrong direction.

The difference between problems and dilemmas is not just a language thing, although language certainly plays a role and language does embody assumptions. Problems and dilemmas require different kinds of engagement processes. Table 1 summarizes the key shifts in leadership emphasis from problem solving to winning when faced with dilemmas. Getting there early requires an ability to make this shift toward dealing with dilemmas while still honoring the problem solvers of the world.

A problem is "a question or a puzzle that needs to be solved."[5]. Typically, at least in current thinking, a problem has a binary (either/or) solution, or at least a clear solution. Problems are there to be solved. It is fun to solve problems, and you get a sense of accomplishment. As we're taught by dictionaries and our modern culture, problems feel like they "need to be solved."

In a world of dilemmas, we still have many options for response, but usually the options aren't simple, and usually they don't come in pairs. Yes/no will not be enough. What's beyond the yes/no? What might be a third way, or a fourth, or a fifth? Expecting a binary solution can get you in big trouble in the world of dilemmas.

Most of today's leaders, and most of today's organizations, are designed to problem-solve—not to win with dilemmas that have no single solution. Many methods of management have emphasized the quest for control. They have tended to be linear, sequential, and driven by time. "Organization man" was an ideal: the human who learned to live and problem-solve within clear linear organizational structures.

The ideal manager today, in many corporate cultures, is tough and fast: "I'm a better manager because I make tough decisions, and I can solve tough problems faster." As a result of this very understandable and solid training (which used to work in most organizations and still works in the more operational or mature parts of some), many of today's leaders expect to solve problems, and they are frustrated when solutions don't happen—no matter how well they organize, how well they problem-solve, how hard they try, and how fast they run.

TABLE 1. PROBLEMS AND DILEMMAS: KEY SHIFTS IN LEADERSHIP EMPHASIS

	Problem Solving	Dilemma Sensemaking
Frame	Operational, with an emphasis on analytics in search of certainty	Strategic, with an emphasis on foresight and stories in a context of uncertainty
Initial Goal	Respond Consider options, but quickly reduce them to the two best possibilities	Reframe Consider options, but reframe to explore and hold complexity in your mind
Decision Orientation	Decide—the faster the better—on the best possible solution Reverence for speed	Decide with cognizance that there is no solution, but figure out how you can win anyway Reverence for reflection, but you still need the courage to act
Time Orientation	Oriented toward short-term relief Go fast	Oriented toward long-term success Go slow initially, so you can go fast later

Process	Run to execute the chosen solution and avoid failure at all costs Fix the broken parts quickly	Prototype rapidly—"fail in interesting ways"—and learn from failures Try out many scenarios
Belief Orientation	Faith that certainty is possible, with a trust in reason and analytics to get you there	Acceptance of uncertainty, with intuition accepted as a valid contributor to decision making in the face of uncertainty
Best Organization Structure	Chain of command with consistent problem-solving methodologies	Decentralized network for flexibility within a structure of strategic intent
Best Way to Learn	Learn by way of rule-based training in problem-solving methodologies	Learn by way of immersive experiences and principles-based simulation gaming
Academic Roots	Engineering and psychology	Life sciences, anthropology, and comparative religions
Downside Risk	Judging too soon	Deciding too late

THE PSYCHOLOGICAL BENEFITS OF HAVING ANSWERS

Almost everyone likes an answer. Answers feel a lot more secure than questions. In the face of uncertainty or complexity, however, a set mind-set can close too soon and too rigidly. A fixed mind-set will see only the familiar pieces of a puzzle—not the things that don't fit.

Leaders must learn how to thrive in uncertain spaces—while listening to and perceiving what is going on—without jumping to judgment too soon. Rapid judgment is great when it is appropriate to the situation, but premature judgment can be downright dangerous. When so many people are hungry for a simple moral equation, the times are ripe for premature judgments.

Fundamentalism is kindled and fueled by uncertainty. A voice inside says, "This is too much for me to handle" or "I need an answer, right now." In today's world, *fundamentalism* has become a politically loaded word as more and more people move beyond the threshold of uncertainty where they can live comfortably. Naturally, they strive to relieve their own pain. Predictably, fundamentalism is growing.

How do you live comfortably in an uncomfortable world? From a psychological point of view fundamentalist thinking can give comfort, even in times of great discomfort. Fundamentalism gives the comfort of certainty—even if that certainty happens to be wrong.

Fundamentalists (whether religious, political, managerial, social) embody determination and a strident sense of mission, and they proffer clear—usually simple—answers to even the most complex questions. The psychological essence of a fundamentalist message goes something like this: "Things aren't as complex, confusing, and uncertain as they are trying to make you think." (There is often a clear "they" who is the enemy.) "Just believe in us, and all the things that are confusing you will make sense."

Most important, a fundamentalist group gives its members a sense of identity and belonging, even in the midst of extreme uncertainty and confusion. Answers are comforting in themselves, but the greatest psychological value of fundamentalism is a clear identity and a compelling sense of belonging. Of course, people who are hungry and hopeless are most in need of identity and belonging. Choosing a fundamentalist filter for your life can make things easier for you, at least psychologically.

But fundamentalism runs the risk of becoming dysfunctional at an organizational or societal level. It can drive its adherents to maintain an inappropriate course into greater and greater danger. If fundamentalism is wrong in dangerous times, it can be dead wrong.

Fundamentalism focuses the light in one place and ignores the darkness elsewhere, much like the Nasrudin Sufi story about the man searching for his house keys under the streetlight—even though he lost them somewhere else—"because the light is better there."

A fixed mind-set can lead to confrontation, and when fixed mind-sets confront one another, the result is usually polarized conflict and sometimes violence. Minds are fixed on both sides and are not easy to soften. Fundamentalism is characterized by listening narrowly but generalizing broadly.

Because he believes so deeply that he is right, a severely self-righteous person doesn't realize that he is behaving in a self-righteous manner.

From inside a protective bubble of self-righteousness, the world feels like a better place: volatility is calmed by an image of order, uncertainty disappears, complexity becomes simple, and ambiguity appears to be resolved. Dilemmas look like solvable problems.

In the IFTF 2005–2015 Ten-Year Forecast, we included a driving force that we called "strong opinions, strongly held." Consider a threshold of self-righteousness: it is one thing to believe that you are right but quite another to believe that not only are you right but that others are wrong. Unfortunately, large numbers of people globally are going to the dark side of the righteousness blade. These people have concluded that they have the answer, and they don't want to discuss questions or alternatives. In extreme situations, they want to convert, get rid of, or ignore those who don't believe as they believe.

Of course, the world has always been complex and has always offered up dilemmas of life that people have experienced. One of my favorite books when I was in divinity school was *The Wisdom of Insecurity: A Message for an Age of Anxiety*, by Alan Watts. As you read his description of the "age of anxiety," keep in mind that he wrote this book in 1951:

> There is, then, the feeling that we live in a time of unusual insecurity. In the past hundred years so many long-established traditions have broken down—traditions of family and social life, of government, of the economic order, and of religious belief. As the years go by, there seem to be fewer and fewer rocks to which we can hold, fewer things which we can regard as absolutely right and true, and fixed for all time. . . . As a matter of fact, our age is no more insecure than any other. Poverty, disease, war, change, and death are nothing new. In the best of times, 'security' has never been more than temporary and apparent.[6]

Closed mind-sets are not new (there were quite a few in 1951 when Watts was writing the words above), but are the number of people and groups with "strong opinions strongly held" increasing in number or in importance? This question is impossible to answer, but certainly fundamentalist views are amplified by the hyperconnectivity of today. Within our staff at Institute for the Future there are differing views. Some of my colleagues believe that there are more extreme groups now; others feel that the number of extreme groups is about the same but that the Internet and other media now amplify their identities and impacts. My opinion is that there are more extreme groups today. Certainly, life's dilemmas are more amplified today and spread more rapidly around the world. There are now many people, in both the developed and developing worlds, who cannot cope with the uncertainties all around them.

What is clearly new is that almost everyone sees the extremes now, often in vivid color. A splendid array of media spread messages across the rich-poor gap—often inaccurately but almost always vividly. The puzzling and gnawing uncertainties are all around us every day, with few places to hide. If the world is too overwhelming, more people will adopt the comfort of certainty, the relief of righteousness.

But there are also many well-fed people in the rich world who are beyond their own ability to engage with the uncertainty all around them. We all must learn to live with uncertainty in large doses, but we also must learn to live with the much more extreme and self-righteous behavior around us.

How do reasonable people whose minds are filled with questions engage with those who have only answers, or those who are just trying to stir things up? How do organizations engage with extreme groups, extreme individuals, and extreme points of view? In a world where nobody knows—nobody *can* know—the answers, how can leaders at least be ready to engage with everyone?

DILEMMAS AS A SOURCE OF INSPIRATION

Winning when you are faced with dilemmas requires a prepared mind. The first discipline is to resist jumping to premature conclusions. Unless you are in an extreme situation where you absolutely have to respond immediately, reflection is usually more useful than reaction. Leaders need to learn to live with, and even embrace dilemmas. Dilemmas can be a source of insight and inspiration if you can figure out how to engage with and learn from them. Leaders need an ability to hold, listen, and learn—while resisting the temptation to know too soon. In addition, leaders need the courage to decide when the time is right.

There are still many problems that have binary solutions and it is very important that someone solve them. Looking ahead, however, most problems with binary solutions will tend to be tactical, important for successful execution but more appropriate for the operational people within a firm. Strategic thinking will be dominated by dilemmas. The senior leaders in the firm who create and implement strategy will be dealing with dilemmas most of their time. If you're not able to engage creatively with dilemmas that have no solution, you are stuck in the wrong frame with the wrong tools.

Dilemma-management skills and arts are quite different from problem solving skills, as you can see in a glance if you look back at Table 1. Expectations, methods, and outcomes are all different. Wrestling with complexity and ambiguity is really hard work. It is tempting to go for an easy answer. It takes time to think things through.

The ideal leadership state in emergency situations is somewhere be-

tween decisive and righteous, but the immediate challenge is to listen—
to figure out what's really going on. Once a leader is over the righteousness threshold, it is hard to go back. Once a dilemma has been sold
as a problem, it is hard to recast it as having no solution (that is, re-
casting it as a dilemma) without being perceived as having failed. Casting a dilemma as a problem is leading oneself into a corner with no easy
exit on the good side of failure.

When trying to decide if a new challenge is a problem or a dilemma,
you will do better to expect a dilemma most of the time. Mistaking a
problem for a dilemma usually means only a mistake in time—because
problem solving (when it works) is faster than dilemma management.
Mistaking a dilemma for a problem can be far more costly.

The events we most want to know about are those that have not yet
happened: we would like to be able to predict the future, and we would
like it to be a world of problems with foreseeable solutions. But prediction is not possible. Because the world is uncertain and chaotic, it
is best to be prepared to respond to abrupt changes—even to expect
them and practice for them through effective use of simulation gaming
and immersion experiences. Nonlinear events are not only disruptive,
they are often both surprising and out of context. Preparation is in itself a salve, but it has the additional practical benefit of providing readiness when change occurs.

Baby boom leaders are now beginning to experience a gap in expectations created by what used to work for them—as compared to the
challenges of today, and especially of tomorrow.

While many baby boom leaders expect to encounter a stream of
problems that they can solve—if only they work hard enough—the next
generation of workers won't have the same set of illusions. Younger
workers are more likely to be comfortable improvising their way through
dilemmas—rather than trying to solve problems that cannot be solved.

The mixed-generation firm is likely to have better development resources to deal with this future if we learn how to tap those resources.
For now, however, it is important to understand the differences between
problem solving and dilemma management and to develop people who
are comfortable dealing with dilemmas.

In the world of problem solving, there is usually one winning solution and one winner for each problem. One winner, one loser: a zero-sum game. But there is a special hope implicit in dilemmas: it is often possible to come up with win-win strategies—where there is more than one winner. Win-win solutions require cooperative approaches to resolution, and open-source strategies are becoming increasingly sophisticated and increasingly available. Cooperative models can work even when competition continues.

IBM, for example, used to sell primarily hardware and software in a competitive climate. In the current marketplace, IBM rarely sells hardware and tends to give away software. While it cooperates in the increasingly open source and cooperative world of software, the company competes aggressively in the world of high-margin services. Often, cooperative strategies work best in the world of dilemmas. Since it is a very important model for what is to come, we will talk more about the IBM strategy in Chapter 10.

Andrea Saveri, Howard Rheingold, and Kathi Vian are doing ongoing research on social dilemmas and the cooperative strategies that are emerging to deal with them—in both social and business contexts. This work helps to sort out those complex dilemmas where rational competitive behavior can lead to irrational social results. Fortunately, cooperative networking tools have been under development for more than thirty years now, and they are beginning to have practical impacts:

> Connective and pervasive technologies are enabling new forms of human and machine interactions and relationships; they will present business institutions with a host of new possibilities for organizing people, processes, relationships and knowledge. These forces will accelerate a shift in business strategy *from solving concrete business problems to managing complex business dilemmas*, which in turn will require a broader set of strategic tools and concepts than are provided by competitive models.[7] (italics added)

This ongoing stream of research has identified a series of tools and frameworks for dealing with dilemmas, tools that include seven "tuning levers" for organizations and leaders:

- Structure (for organization and for cooperative exchange)
- Rules (and principles that guide interaction)
- Resources (available to fuel the organization)
- Thresholds (that are important to any of the players)
- Feedback (that might be provided to lubricate the process)
- Memory (of previous organizational learning, as well as decisions made)
- Identity (both in person and in online worlds)

These tuning levers are basic to leadership in a world of dilemmas. In Chapter 9, we will use these levers to consider how flexible firms can be structured so that they are better able to engage with dilemmas. Leaders need to understand how each lever can be used to tune specific aspects of their own organization.

Dilemmas are messy and frustrating, but they are also fertile ground for new insights and new inspiration, to create strategy that succeeds—even when you cannot solve. Dilemmas must be held in one's mind and *exercised.* Dilemmas cannot be exorcised by quick judgment or eliminated with analytics. As Voltaire said, "Doubt is not a pleasant condition, but certainty is absurd."

Dilemmas must be understood through stories and experiences. The story lines that follow the forecast in Chapter 2, for example, provides context for the Forecast Map inside the book jacket. The story in Chapter 3 about the young leader in Iraq provides a real-life context for discussing the VUCA world and commander's intent. Stories, an ancient medium, will become even more important in the future world of dilemmas.

PART TWO

INSIGHT

Sensemaking to Inspire Strategy

Part 1 made the case for foresight, forecasting, and leadership vision. Part 2 is an exploration of how leaders can extract insight from foresight, as input to strategy. Foresight is everywhere, but insight is rare.

Stories help leaders make sense out of the VUCA world. Immersion experiences provide practice grounds for learning to live with dilemmas. Workshops are an important way to make the link between foresight and insight, to use group creativity to coax out insight that is robust and practical. Insight is a necessary prerequisite for a winning strategy, and that insight must also be expressed with clarity if it is to have the greatest impact.

Foresight is inherently provocative, but leaders must draw lessons from the provocation if they are to create a clear, compelling, and productive way forward. How do leaders gain insight and inspire it in others? Part 2 explores the foresight to insight zone of the Foresight to Insight to Action Cycle. (See Figure 5.1.)

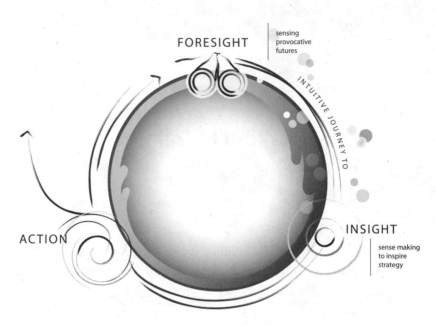

FORESIGHT

sensing
provocative
futures

INTUITIVE JOURNEY TO

ACTION

INSIGHT

sense making
to inspire
strategy

5.1   Foresight to Insight to Action Cycle: Foresight to Insight

5 It Takes a Story to Understand a Dilemma

Study the hard while it's easy.
Do big things while they're small.
The hardest jobs in the world start out easy,
the great affairs of the world start small.
So the wise soul,
by never dealing with great things,
gets great things done.
—Lao Tzu, *Tao Te Ching*

You need stories and storytelling to peel back the wicked complexity that was introduced in Part 1, to help you make sense out of dilemmas.

Whereas problems can be solved with data and analytics, dilemmas need stories. Throughout this book I use stories, including personal stories, case studies, and vignettes, to bring dilemmas to life.

Stories about dilemmas are not just stories; they are mystery stories. As the *Tao Te Ching* teaches, stories communicate "the hard while it's easy" and "big things while they're small," even when the dilemmas involved are complex. The "wise soul" is the leader who is adept at listening for the unfolding tale.

A problem is a mystery that can be solved. Dilemmas, on the other hand, are mysteries that keep their mystery. Problem solvers strive to take the mystery away, but those who understand the truth of dilemmas engage in—even delight in—the mysteries and the continuous learning opportunities that they present. Data and analytics can be useful to help make sense of the world, but data and analytics are not enough.

Story*telling* is only part of the leader's challenge. *Listening* for stories is just as important, to untangle dilemmas, reach some kind of "Aha!" and develop winning strategies. Sometimes the best stories about a dilemma will arise where you least expect them.

The most useful stories about dilemmas are simple but profound. Sometimes stories about dilemmas can motivate organizations, if only you can bring them out from the everyday noise and confusion. An "elevator speech," for example, is a concise summary of an organization's strategy. If you got on an elevator with someone important to you, how could you tell the story of your organization from the time the elevator door closes to the time that it opens again? What's the essence of what you do? Most great elevator speeches are simple but compelling stories.

Deep organizational change happens when good data, good analytics, and good stories come together in a compelling harmony of action. Leaders have to tease out the stories that give clues about what's going on and what insights and possible actions are suggested by the dilemmas they are facing.

Our understanding of modern dilemmas can benefit greatly from the ancient art of storytelling. Stories are narratives of life events with a point of view. Data and analytics address the what; stories probe the why. Data reflects rationality; stories reflect emotion. Data reveals answers; stories reveal questions. Questions, it turns out, are more useful than answers when it comes to dilemmas.

A story is a moving account of a series of events in a form that captures emotion and provides a sense of meaning for the reader or listener. Involving people in a story means getting both their hearts and their minds engaged. Stories are dynamic and flowing.

Joe Lambert and Nina Mullen, who work in the domain of digital storytelling (the next step beyond bulleted PowerPoint presentations, we can all hope), have a simple but compelling definition of a story (drawing from E. M. Forster):

> If you say "The queen died, and the king died," that is a chronicle.
> If you say "The queen died, and the king died, from grief," that is a story.[1]

I would add: if you say, "The queen died, and the king is missing," that is a mystery.

A Story about Silicon Valley

Let me tell you a story of a positive dilemma that I think fuels creativity in the San Francisco Bay Area where I live.

I have been working in Silicon Valley since before it was called that. My story of why Silicon Valley works as a hotbed of innovation is based on what I see as a dilemma between the "culture of ideas" and the "culture of money" in the valley.

The culture-of-ideas people love ideas and love to exchange them, to see ideas mix and grow.[2] They are willing to give away ideas, trusting that they will get back even better ideas in return. Subgroups of the culture-of-ideas people are intent on changing the world, and they are convinced that their ideas can have an impact.

Meanwhile, the culture-of-money people in Silicon Valley are intently focused on making as much money as possible, through the commercialization of technology and ideas. Subsets of the culture-of-money people (who knows how many?) are driven by greed, an irrational quest for wealth at almost any price.

Both of these Silicon Valley social networks need each other, however. The culture-of-ideas people need money to bring their ideas to life. The culture-of-money people need ideas and innovation to inspire new businesses and attract investors. There are a few people in Silicon Valley who are part of both cultures (ideas and money), but only a very few. Some culture-of-money people, however, have moved toward the culture of ideas after they have made a lot of money. Neither of these two dominant cultures particularly likes the other—even though both recognize that they need each other.

The tension between the poles of this dilemma, the tension between ideas and money, is what provides the energy for Silicon Valley innovation. This dilemma fuels innovation. If this dilemma were "solved," I believe the creative energy of the Valley would dwindle.

Telling a story like this can open interesting conversations. The story introduces key players and introduces tension. The story invites engagement and debate: who are these culture-of-money people? Who are the culture-of-ideas people? How do they engage with each other? Is this story the most accurate way to describe the creative energy of Silicon Valley?

There are many different kinds of stories. Below are several stories that reveal important aspects of dilemmas we see all around us.

Fitness Dilemma Stories

In order to engage with dilemmas and consider how to prepare your mind to win, let's start with a dilemma that almost everyone can relate to personally: weight management. Anyone with a weight "problem," knows that weight management is really a dilemma that must be managed in an ongoing way—not a problem that can be solved once and for all. You cannot consider all the options for controlling your weight, reduce the options to two, choose the best one, and you're done. One-time weight *loss* can be considered as a problem, and certainly many are successful at taking weight off for a time. The real challenge in weight management is not taking it off but keeping it off.

Weight Watchers International has become very successful by realizing that although most people know what they must do to reduce their weight, they need help and support to keep it off consistently over time. As with any dilemma, clarity is key, and Weight Watchers offers *"Weight Watchers Family Power: 5 Simple Rules for a Healthy Weight Home."*[3] You can read the book, which is very clear, but you'll probably need the programs—or at least Weight Watchers' business model assumes that many people will need its programs to follow through. Paying for the Weight Watchers program at each event in cash is part of the personal discipline that the organization tries to create.

Solving the problem of weight loss is only one step in the ongoing dilemma of weight management. Because expectations are so important in any behavioral change, it is important to realize that weight management looks like a problem—and indeed problems are inherent in any weight-management process—but weight management is a problem you cannot "solve." People—especially Americans—long for a pill or an operation or some other form of magic that will solve their weight *problem*, but weight management is a dilemma that cannot be solved. Until you prepare your mind with that expectation, your efforts to sustain a healthy weight will be futile.

Weight management is a good example of a personal dilemma, since most of us can understand the challenges on a personal level, but weight management is now becoming an organizational and societal dilemma as well. Private behavior (resulting in obesity and associated rising costs of health care) is now becoming a public policy dilemma of great concern. Health care costs, and employer concerns about those costs, may be the issue that mobilizes action around obesity as a social policy issue. Somehow, we all need to learn how to live with this dilemma—both individually and as a society.

To some extent, obesity is in the eye of the beholder. How is *obese* defined? Is obesity a personal responsibility, a social responsibility, or both? And who has authority to answer these questions? Health care costs, and employers' concerns about those costs, were what finally provoked action around obesity as a social or an organizational issue.

Leaders of large corporations have begun to advocate fitness programs that are bringing the dilemmas of weight management to work. Programs like Corporate Athlete,[4] for example, offer individual and team-based experiences to help leaders manage the dilemma of their own fitness. The Corporate Athlete program includes interviews with family members to test the accuracy of a leader's self-reporting of his or her own behavior about sleep time, nutrition, time with family, stress at home, and other important aspects of healthy living. A growing number of corporations have realized that the pressures of top-executive leadership are lifestyle pressures that include both work and private life. Here's the compelling business logic for change: if corporations can help their leaders navigate the intersections of work and private life—including weight management—performance will be higher, and health care costs will be lower.

Consider these words from A. G. Lafley, the CEO of Procter & Gamble, in a *Fortune* magazine article describing his lifestyle changes after doing a Corporate Athlete program that has now been adopted widely at P&G:

> I've learned how to manage my energy. I used to just focus on managing my time. I'd be up in the morning between 5 and 5:30. I'd work out and be at my desk by 6:30 or 7, drive hard until about 7 p.m., then go home, take a break with my wife, Margaret, and be back at it later that evening. I was just grinding through the day.
>
> During my first year in this job, I worked every Saturday and every Sunday morning. Now I work really hard for an hour or an hour and a half. Then I take a break. I walk around and chitchat with people. It can take five or fifteen minutes to recharge. It's kind of like the interval training that an athlete does.
>
> I learned this in a program called the Corporate Athlete that we put on for P&G managers. I did the two-day program, where I also learned to change the way I eat. I used to eat virtually nothing for breakfast. Now I have a V-8 juice, half a bagel, and a cup of yogurt. And I eat five or six times a day. It's about managing your glycemic level. You don't want to boom and bust.
>
> The other piece of the Corporate Athlete program is spiritual—things you can do to calm the mind. I've tried to teach myself to meditate. When I travel, which is 60 percent of the time, I find that meditating for five, ten, or fifteen minutes in a hotel room at night can be as good as a workout. Generally, I think I know myself so much better than I used to. And that has helped me stay calm and cool under fire.
>
> A key to staying calm is minimizing the information onslaught. I can't remember the last time I wrote a memo. I write little handwritten notes on my AGL paper, and I send notes, a paragraph or less, on my BlackBerry. I prefer conversations. That's one reason my office and our entire executive floor is open. The CEO office is not typically a warm and welcoming place, but people feel they can come in and talk in mine. We have goofy-looking pink and chartreuse chairs with chrome frames and upholstered backs and seats.
>
> I still work weekends, though not the killer hours I used to. On Sunday nights, [HR chief] Dick Antoine and I get together at his house or my house or on the phone and go through some part of our leadership development program. We started doing this shortly after I

became CEO, because I know that the single biggest contribution I will make to this company is helping the next generation of leaders become the best that they can be.[5]

These are not the kinds of personal lifestyle topics that successful CEOs usually discuss with anyone, perhaps even themselves—let alone discuss in national magazines like *Fortune*. In a world of increasing dilemmas, however, concerns like this will be magnified, and approaches to dealing with these concerns will be key to leadership success. A.G. Lafley is a leader who loves to engage with dilemmas, but he still has the courage to decide.

Of course, there will be organizational challenges such as the question of how deeply involved a corporation becomes in a leader's lifestyle choices. For example, is it appropriate to use physical fitness as a criterion for advancement to top-executive levels? If so, how would physical fitness be measured? Would it be appropriate, for example, to reject a person for a top leadership position because he or she was visibly overweight? Although this subject is not culturally appropriate for discussion in most organizations at this time, the answer in the near future is probably going to be a "yes." A few years from now, I expect the answer will be "of course."

A Parenting Dilemma Story

If you are lucky enough not to have a weight-management problem but still want an example of a dilemma that is close to home, consider the "problem" of parenthood. Having a child means having a host of problems, some of which can actually be solved. But the overall challenge of raising a child is much more a dilemma than a problem. Consider this story:

I have a friend, a woman with a Stanford MBA, who vividly recalls her experience of standing in front of her clothes dryer while her baby with colic lay crying violently in a baby chair on top of the warm vibrating machine. She had been told that setting the baby on a dryer was a method for solving the problem of a crying baby, but this "solution" was not working with her baby. She remembers thinking, based on her experience and training as an MBA and as her baby cried on: "This project should be over." She learned through her own personal experience of having children that the "project" of parenthood would never really be over, it would just evolve into different stages.

Although she had a wonderful education, earned at great universities, she never had any training to be a mom—except what she observed within her own family and her network of friends. Nobody ever told her that this problem was really a dilemma she should not expect to solve. Perhaps some parents pass on this wisdom to their own children before the kids become parents. More typically, however, young parents are stuck with their instincts and their educational preparation—which for most of us has concentrated on problem solving.

With kids, you can sometimes solve problems and breathe a sigh of relief (the baby does actually stop crying sometimes), but only until the next life stage or, for some children, the next day—when you are confronted with a very different dilemma. There is very interesting parental space between judging too soon (each kid is different) and deciding too late (discipline is important). Parenthood is a gift, but it comes with many challenges that cannot be solved, although they can be managed if you have appropriate expectations, unconditional love, great dedication, and a little luck.

A Story of Future Collaboration to Address a Dilemma

The stories in this chapter so far have been real-world stories describing experiences in Silicon Valley, with weight control and fitness, and with parenting. Now, we turn to a narrative vignette that is based in the future, with characters, dialogue, and a situation causing tension.

The ten-year forecast in Chapter 2 and on the Forecast Map suggests that global warming is coming faster than most experts expected. Yet global warming is one of those challenges that is difficult to address within our current framework of decision making. David King, the chief science adviser for Tony Blair, has said that global warming is a bigger global crisis than global terrorism. Yet public consciousness is much more focused on terrorism. Global warming, if it does turn out to be a crisis, is not likely to hit with vigor until we are beyond the terms of current politicians and business leaders. The forecast implied in the story below (a plausible, internally consistent view of what might happen) is that global warming is coming faster than expected. The insight is that, to adapt to or forestall global warming, the world needs global social and behavior change. The actions needed to seed such changes are far from clear, but they would certainly involve global NGOs, government agencies, and corporations. Applied science will play a major role to deliver sustainable energy as well as safe, nutritious, and affordable food globally. The following vignette provides a taste of how this could play out.

Circa 2016
TIME: 9:30 a.m. Shanghai
       7:30 p.m. Denver
       9:30 p.m. New York
      11:30 a.m. Melbourne

Benny Cheng entered the public work-play space in Melbourne at 11:00 a.m. precisely and saw Lucius Tran, who was already drinking his usual Perrier and cranberry juice. He had unrolled his flap-top computer and was working his way through the International Times English Crossword Download.

"Hi, Benny," Lucius said with a grin, waving at the seat beside him.

"You order yet?" Benny asked, sitting down. Under the level of the sound baffles, the space was surprisingly private.

"No." Lucius brushed his dark hair out of his eyes. "I thought we had the meeting first and lunch after. It's still a little early for lunch."

"Right." Benny checked the on screen clock. "Let's see. Xin is two hours behind us, but she'll be in the Shanghai lab at 9:30 her time. The Advisory Group will be in the UN conference center in New York. They're twelve hours ahead of Shanghai. And it's early evening in Denver, where Aycha will join us. I think everything's set, and we still have a little time to spare."

"OK." Lucius turned the computer so the screen camera could cover them both. "Whenever you're ready. But since we have a little time, maybe we could check in with Aycha first? I'd like to be clear about the Kenya Protocols."

The top of Aycha's head appeared in an onscreen window. She brushed her dark curls aside as she looked up. "Hi, Benny, Lucius. How are you guys?" Beside her they could see a small child, a precarious tower of blocks, and the rest of her living room.

"We're fine," Benny said. "Melbourne has lovely weather, even if it is winter. Warm and mild, which of course is completely abnormal. How about Denver?"

"Torrential summer rains, severe thunderstorms, and a sleepy child, so give me a minute or two." Aycha turned to her child and cooed, "Come on, Poppins, time for sleepies."

Aycha sighed. "I'll be back," she called, carrying the child out of view. She was back in minutes. "Time?"

Soon they had Brian Dougherty and his GWBAG (for Global Warming Business Advisory Group) team at the UN in New York and Xin Li-Pint in Shanghai in their own windows on the screen. Since this was a public place, the two wore headsets and sat in a subtle cone of privacy.

"Everyone connected?" Benny asked. "Xin, can you see Aycha, our East Africa and South Asia adviser?"

"Certainly," she replied in perfect English. "Pleased to meet you."

"As you know," Benny began, "since the UN Millennium Ecosystem Assessment, there has been a growing consensus that climate change is coming. At that time the forecast suggested a fifty-year time frame. Now, eight years later, the time frame has shortened considerably, and pretty much everyone agrees that we—and as you know, by 'we,' I mean the members of the Global Warming Network, which is everyone from national governments and the UN down through global business and NGOs to local farmers—must coordinate our actions immediately.

"This insight, and it is not a small one, means exercising

sensitivity to local cultures and customs, particularly around agriculture, while still making some big behavioral changes—"

"And don't forget health," Aycha put it.

"We know this," Dougherty said. "And we know the actions we have to take are complex. The Global Business Summit fully agrees with the goals of GWC. Everyone now agrees that our economic activities must become sustainable and affordable globally, and soon. That means major changes in business models, packaging, energy consumption, and health and food development and distribution. Without a healthy world, there will be no business opportunity." He spoke dramatically, but in a matter-of-fact way, without irony.

"Yes," Xin said. "But the food supply is changing, mostly shrinking. Under current conditions we cannot sustain our lifestyle and perhaps not even our population. We cannot increase arable lands. In fact, they will decrease as the climate changes. World food supplies are in jeopardy."

She paused. "Technology can help—Shaolin, Ltd.'s technology, but there are no magical answers. Still, we've got to move ahead with what we've got. I heard that there are still legislative problems in the United States with our organo-ferrite research?" She was always the most direct of the group.

Brian nodded. "There have been problems, but most of the religious and ethical opposition has melted away since the fires in Appalachia. Everyone seems to understand that the world has changed for real, and that to adapt we too must change culturally, and perhaps even physically. This will be a massive and complex effort, but without it the disruptions could be truly apocalyptic."

"All right," Benny said. "Lucius, you had something to say?"

Lucius brushed his hair back with a nod. "As a reminder, there are three stages to this process," he said. "We've completed the first two: we have a solid forecast on warming and good data on the time frame. That knowledge has put the pressure on and forced us to recognize that the faint, partial reactions of the world to date—Kyoto, carbon trading, clean fuels, bioengineered foods, and so on—were going to be inadequate in the face of the immensity of the crisis.

"That insight led to the formation of this group, the Global Warming Network, which is expanding daily. We already have educational and training programs on every continent, including Antarctica. We have teams doing surveys of local farming practices, local health concerns, and local responses to climate change. We are forming plans in every region to influence those customs and practices, aided by national governments, nonprofit foundations and consortia of pharmaceuticals, food, energy, and transportation companies.

Consensus is growing on the actions we need to take, and everything looks promising. But the future, as we all know, is uncertain. That's why I asked Dr. Xin to join this meeting. Her company's organo-ferrite research could help significantly by providing a truly economical way to integrate energy, food, and health. Dr. Xin?"

"Thank you." Xin looked steadily into the camera as she spoke. It seemed she was talking directly to each of those present. "As you no doubt know, our research examines the total planetary energy budget, not food or energy in isolation. Although we began as a Chinese pharmaceutical company, we now partner with a major food company and an energy company to make our products planet—and human—friendly.

"Organo-ferrites in conjunction with biotech in agriculture might help counter past mistakes. They can help fix carbon while allowing us to grow more nutritious food on less land, using far less energy. Shaolin, Ltd., expects to gain something, of course, but we are essentially donating most of our profits to this collective effort. Of course, we have the added benefit of knowing this can help make a positive contribution. Our only real question, now," she added, "is whether Mr. Tran's company can handle distribution."

Lucius jumped. "Of course. We're an Indonesian company, but we have offices all over the world. We're a major partner in the consortium and are fully behind the effort. Our questions for Shaolin revolve around three things: safety, efficacy, and price. And speed. OK, four things."

"Our prototypes are in the fields," Xin answered, "Preliminary results are in. China can ramp up production, but your company will have to handle distribution, and the educational NGOs are going to have to be on the ground ready with education, training, logistics, volunteers, and a host of other matters."

"Well," Lucius said, "that's where Mr. Dougherty's group comes in. They're experts in global organizational processes. Businesses like Wal-Mart have been working on this problem for a few years already and are willing to take the lead. Isn't that right, Mr. Dougherty?"

"Of course. Businesses may be late to the party, but they know where their interests lie. The GWBAG board has approved the action plan Benny has sent us, all 900 pages of it, I might add."

"Excellent. We all agree, then?" Benny said. "Tomorrow is launch day. We hope to have the social science research finished within ten years. The agricultural reform project might take less time if organo-ferrites turn out to be the energy saver and nutrition enhancer we hope. Volunteer education teams are ready to begin work in over 180 nations. Are we ready to bring in the regional directors to give them the go-ahead?"

Dougherty and the others in New York nodded. Aycha said, "Yes." Xin smiled for the first time.

Benny nodded at Lucius, who forwarded the invitations to the seven regional directors. He was well into the introductions when the desolate wail of Aycha's child calling from her crib interrupted them.

"You all go ahead and get acquainted," Aycha said. "I've got another short meeting to attend to."

The vignette reveals a process that is futuristic but still messy because of the wide mix of people, perspectives, organizations, and priorities that are involved. The foresight about global warming is, by the time of this meeting, widely shared as important. Although the participants in the meeting still argue about details and response options, they are agreed that they have to do something and that they have to work together on a global scale. They face global warming that is much more urgent than most of them had expected, but they have considerable resources to collaborate on a global scale. This is a story of global collaboration in the face of the global warming dilemma. There are no magic solutions in this story, but there is the potential for progress.

You don't have to fully agree with a forecast in order to have it provoke insight about strategy. Global warming is looming as an increasing challenge for almost everyone—including most informed experts. Given this forecast, what strategies are possible, for whom? Businesses and NGOs seem most likely to act, with politicians going to work on it only if they sense a shift in popular opinion around this issue. The story brings out the dynamics of engaging with and beginning to respond to the immense dilemma of global warming. The risks of mistaking this dilemma for a solvable problem are extremely high.

Leaders must learn to hold uncertainty in mind without rushing to premature judgment. Getting there early is great, but not if you are both early and wrong. Leaders must learn how to prepare their minds to engage with complexity, beyond the ways of problem solving. Stories are an important part of this preparation.

Stories are used throughout this book to help unpack dilemmas and begin to deal with them. Stories animate complexity and make it real for people. Both listening for and telling stories are useful leadership skills that too many leaders undervalue. Stories are closely related to immersion experiences, which will be described in Chapter 6. Immersion experiences are stories brought to life. Simulation games allow players to step inside a story and take a role in that world. It takes a story to understand a dilemma, and it takes an immersion experience to provide first-person learning within that story.

6 Immersion

The Best Way to Learn in the VUCA World

Simulation builds calluses.
—Doug Campbell, U.S. Army War College

Immersion experiences allow leaders to learn rapidly and viscerally. Immersion helps at every stage of the Foresight to Insight to Action Cycle. It provides a way to get there early before committing to go there at all.

Immersion can help leaders experience a possible world of the future to get a feeling for what it might be like. Immersion helps you see things from different points of view to provoke insight. Immersion helps you try out different ways of being so you can develop your own agility.

Immersion experiences can help leaders extract strategic insight from their experiences. Immersion is a deeper way to learn than is reading, listening, or even seeing. Leaders get to dive in and learn in a first-person way without playing for keeps until they are ready.

I use a wide definition of immersion that includes simulations of reality, alternate reality games, 3-D immersive environments, role-play simulations, reverse mentoring or shadowing, theater, ad hoc immersion experiences, and case studies. My interest is in low-risk learning environments that help improve agility and readiness.

The VUCA world is constantly shifting. It takes a very flexible approach to learn how to lead in this world. Can you learn to hold multiple realities in your mind simultaneously without jumping to judgment too early or deciding too late?

Ambiguity can be satisfying and productive if you are prepared for it. We need ways of learning that help us learn first to accept the realities of a situation and then to practice enough that we can thrive in VUCA environments.

I first learned about immersion experiences when I was in graduate school, at a time when it seemed as though simulation gaming for learning in business, government, and schools would take off and grow rapidly. In 1969, John Raser wrote an amazing book called *Simulation and Society,* in which he said:

> Simulation is "In." Simulation is likely to become a standard research technique due to the following developments in the social sciences: dramatic advances in machine computational and analogizing capabilities; greater emphasis on rationalized decision-making procedures; increased recognition that understanding social phenomena requires examining complex systems of interaction rather than isolated entities; a growing tendency to approach problems from the perspectives of several different disciplines simultaneously; and the increased popularity of a philosophy of the social sciences that insists on multi-variate analysis, rigorous specification of assumptions and relationships, and theories that are temporally dynamic rather than static.[1]

While he was overly optimistic regarding the popularity of simulation gaming, Raser was correct in his assessment of its value. In 1969, simulation gaming was not really in vogue, except with a small but enthusiastic group, including some of my professors in graduate school. All the points that Raser made in 1969, however, are true to an even greater extent today. Simulation gaming is a powerful learning medium.

Simulation gaming for business learning, however, has a big problem. Many people (particularly older people in business) just don't want to "play games," particularly when they are at work. Those who reject simulation games and other immersive experiences for business learning, however, are the ones who are out of step. They have to change if they are to be ready for the world of the near future—or even the world of today.

A "serious games" movement has developed, but it has had limited impact to date. Simulation of reality is a tall order and is easy to criticize as lacking in its ability to replicate from the real world. As a learning medium, simulation and all types of immersion experiences are gaining in popularity. In the military, emergency-preparedness, police, and firefighting communities, simulation gaming is already well accepted and is widely used. In most business, government, and nonprofit organizations, however, simulation gaming is still unusual and is perceived as at least a little weird. Immersion experiences, however, are finally starting to take off.

Simulation gaming allows you to practice in a realistic but low-risk setting. If your world is fast, simulation allows you to slow it down and then speed it up again as your skills improve. If your world is complex, simulation allows you to simplify it so you can grasp what's going on, then gradually bring the complexity back up to real-world levels or beyond. If your challenge seems too big, simulation allows you to bring it back down to size so you can learn to live in it.

Consider the story I told in Chapter 3 about the young leader in Iraq. How might others learn the abilities he demonstrated before they encounter the kind of life-threatening situation that he endured? Certainly routine training approaches are not enough, and may even be more harmful than helpful. In situations like the one in the story, there are no rules to follow, no fixed body of knowledge to transfer. The most appropriate pedagogy for this type of learning is simulation, alternate reality gaming, or some form of first-person immersive learning experience.

I don't mean just simulations of reality; I mean immersion experiences in the widest sense, with many variations. The key element of immersion is first-person learning. I'll use the term *immersion* to designate this broad definition. Fortunately, many of the same benefits of full-scale simulation can be derived from immersion experiences, which are easier to design and more attractive for participants.

Consider a spectrum of immersion experiences, in order from most to least involving for the learners:

- Simulations of reality, where some aspect of the real world is being modeled so that it can be experienced. Simulation gaming can be an attempt to simulate a real-life situation, in order to create a low-risk learning environment within which new skills can be developed and practiced. Simulations, of course, can mislead participants or backfire if they simulate the real world inaccurately—which could give the learners a false sense of confidence. Direct simulation of the real world is very difficult in most situations, but sometimes it is possible and often even the attempt to simulate is worthwhile—even if the result does not replicate reality.

- Alternate-reality games, where individuals, small groups, or massive numbers of players engage in hypothetical worlds, sometimes in digital environments and sometimes in real-world settings. Alternate-reality gaming is not necessarily a simulation of anything real, but it is a compelling immersive environment with challenges—again, a low-risk world where people can learn in a first-person way. In alternative reality games, people "play" themselves in a different setting.

- 3-D immersive environments, where people role-play an alternative identity in an online setting. There is no story and no "game" in these worlds other than what the players themselves create. For example, some young people with autism use 3-D immersive environments like Second Life to practice social skills.

- Role-play simulation games, where learners play a role in an interactive simulation that draws from real-world experiences. The learner plays a role and is given a taste of new situations and practice with possible responses.

- Scenarios, where a story is brought to life. A text scenario may be more like a hypothetical case study, while a physical scenario (such as a movie ticket or some other hypothetical product from the future) is more like an artifact. The point of scenarios is to animate a forecast and engage with the users. For example, digital stories are short visual scenarios that bring aspects of a forecast to life.

- Mentoring, reverse mentoring, or shadowing, where learners are immersed for a period of time in the life of another person from whom they want to learn. For example, some corporations have used reverse mentoring to help male managers get a taste of what female managers experience, to help white managers experience what managers of color experience, and to help older managers experience what new-hires experience.

- Ad hoc immersive experiences, where the goal is to help someone see the world from another point of view. Think of this as "anthropology light," since the goal is similar to what anthropologists would call ethnography, where a researcher immerses himself or herself in a culture to understand what is going on. Whereas an anthropologist goes deep for an extended time, an ad hoc immersive experience is just a quick taste—but it is a first-person and useful taste nonetheless. Ad hoc immersion experiences are similar to simulations, but they are much less ambitious since no imaginary world is created. An immersion is essentially an attempt to put the learner in someone else's shoes, so that they can better understand a different point of view and a different set of experiences. Special body suits have been designed with weights and awkward padding, for example, to give young people a sense of what it feels like to be inside an older body. Other special suits have been designed to give men some sense of what is like to have a menstrual cycle.

- Theatrical improvisation, where actors bring a future possibility to life in a vivid way while learners watch. These experiences can be more or less elaborate, as well as more or less involving for the learners. When the actors can engage with the learners, the learning opportunities are most profound. On several occasions, I have used actors in prototype homes or stores of the future to show how consumers might use them. In a more adventurous case, I was once involved in a business event with Shakespearean actors, where we compared our ten-year forecast with the basics of human life that are similar to the time when Shakespeare was writing. Even in times of great change, many things don't change, and it is important to understand those constants in life. The event was intriguing for me, but we were not able to connect very well with the audience. Clearly, it is important to blend the medium you are using with the audience you are engaging. Even knowing the difficulties of theatrical improvisation, I think that there is great promise in using actors to bring key ideas to life. Theatrical improvisation is like role-playing where the learners don't play the roles themselves—which means they are less engaged.

- Case studies, where a real-world situation is described in a third-person but engaging way so that learners can become involved with the case. Case studies have a long history and much current practice in business schools (with many different approaches), so most people have become comfortable with the case as a learning method. Case studies are engaging for the students who write them, but they usually are not as engaging for the readers. You can read case studies, but you can't experience them.

My purpose here is not to do a comprehensive review of immersion experiences or simulation gaming, but I do want to provide a sense of the many variations of this still-evolving medium for learning and how it can help leaders.

MILITARY SIMULATIONS

Recently, I was invited to the army's National Training Center at Fort Irwin in the Mohave Desert. During my experience there, I came to think of the center, which is roughly the size of the state of Rhode Island, as the world's largest video gaming parlor.

At the National Training Center, round-the-clock war gaming occurs, providing a simulation of contemporary urban insurgency warfare, in which the life or death challenges are vividly presented and experienced. The games are extremely intense and realistic, but death is only virtual.

I got to visit during a war-gaming exercise and talk with virtually dead soldiers about what they were learning from the experience. In each case, they described their experience with great emotion and vigor. The simulated experience at Fort Irwin is designed to be *more* difficult than real battle. A classic dialogue went something like this:

> "How long will it take before your unit is ready for an engagement with an enemy?"
>
> "We're ready right now, sir."
>
> "How long will it take before your unit is ready for a war game at the National Training Center?"
>
> "We can be ready in two weeks, sir."

War games at Fort Irwin are simulations of reality, but they also stretch reality to make the learning experience even more challenging than a real war is likely to be.

A war game allows a player to experience being killed without having to die. That's a big incentive to learn, especially since the players are going into a world of warfare where death is a very real possibility. Unlike their business counterparts, soldiers have a life-and-death incentive to play these games as part of their work. Simulation gaming allows first-person low-risk learning. It provides a practice field for future behaviors.

Our civilian-military exchanges with Columbia Business School at the Army War College often include a "staff ride" on the Gettysburg battlefield. The staff ride is part ad hoc immersion in history, part role-play simulation, and part context for discussion of strategic and leadership lessons.

Why study Gettysburg? What does such a long-ago battle have to teach regarding leadership and strategy today, let alone tomorrow? It turns out that the Gettysburg Battlefield is a rich learning environment where lessons of leadership and strategy can be drawn in a first-person and vivid fashion. In a surprising way, the fact that Gettysburg was so long ago and things were so different makes it easier to learn from it and draw lessons for the future. Even in a VUCA world, it is remarkable how many things don't really change that much—even in the midst of other dramatic changes. For example, issues of leadership and interpersonal relations have remarkable similarities. The key is deciding which things are really changing and which things are not.

Each participant in our Strategic Leadership Forums is given a role to consider as they go on a staff ride with a military historian on the Gettysburg Battlefield. The historians all have a flair for the dramatic. They shift into character as they approach the battlefield and act out each stage of the battle from varied points of view, drawing in the participants as they unfold each story.

> "What where you thinking at this stage, General Lee?"
>
> "When Lee told you that, Lieutenant General Ewell, what were the options that you considered?"
>
> "When you look out over this landscape, Brigadier General Buford, what opportunities and threats do you see?"

The staff ride takes the participants through each of the three days of the Gettysburg battle, moving among the varied places and perspectives. In each case, history provides a context for discussion of leadership, and strategy lessons for today. For example, Major General James Ewell Brown (Jeb) Stuart was Lee's favorite cavalry officer, who provided the eyes and ears for Lee by scouting the enemy's movements (what the military would call today the "fused intelligence" regarding the enemy). Stuart, however, rode off on his own just before and during the Gettysburg battle and didn't communicate with Lee until the battle was almost over, leaving Lee blinded as he considered his strategy against the North. Lee loved and respected Stuart, yet Stuart let him down dramatically at Gettysburg. At this point in the story, the historian asks business leaders:

> "Did you ever have a brilliant innovative thinker who acted in organizationally dysfunctional ways like Jeb Stuart?
>
> How do you engage with this kind of creativity without letting your bright star tear your organization apart?"

On every staff ride I've been on, every single participant quickly thinks of and painfully describes his or her incarnation of Jeb Stuart. I've had painful experiences with several "Jeb Stuarts" in my own leadership life.

David Ignatius, in a *Washington Post* column, drew a convincing link between Iraq and Gettysburg. The challenge in Iraq was not defeating Saddam Hussein; he was a problem that the U.S. military could solve. The real challenge was the dilemma-ridden world that followed the collapse of Saddam. Similarly, the North clearly won at Gettysburg and eventually won the fighting war, but Reconstruction posed severe tests because the South continued to resist the cultural changes implied by the Northern military victory. Slavery was the "great snake under the table at the signing of the Constitution" and the war did not kill the snake, it just drove it underground. Ignatius cites Colin Powell's famous Pottery Barn rule: you broke it, you own it; so how do you put it back together? Ignatius ends his column with these lessons, which are just the sorts of lessons that come out of a Gettysburg staff ride:

> First, what you do immediately after the end of hostilities is crucial, and mistakes made then may be impossible to undo. Don't attempt a wholesale transformation of another society unless you have the troops and political will to impose it. Above all, don't let racial or religious hatred destroy democratic political institutions as in the postbellum South. Giving up on reconstruction (as the North did after Lincoln was killed) led to a social and economic disaster that lasted nearly a century. That's a history nobody should want to repeat, least of all the Iraqi insurgents.[2]

Simulation gaming provides a practice field to develop both sensing and sensemaking skills. Simulation is a form of practice, like spring training in baseball where the point of the games is not to win but to create a realistic simulation of *gamelike* conditions. The best simulations are realistic but not real.

At the Army War College, there is an annual role-play simulation for all the generals-to-be, a few months before graduation. The entire faculty and all the students are involved actively in this two-week simulation of global crisis challenges—seventeen scenarios placed, for the class of 2007, in the year 2017.

A "puppet master" designs and adjusts the game each day, to keep it hard enough to be totally challenging for the students but not so difficult that it becomes impossible for them. (There is a debate in the world of simulation gaming about the virtues of hierarchical games with a puppet master, as compared to self-organizing and emergent games. Each has its advantages.) The global crisis simulation is a complex mix of role-play, computer-based problems, and other vivid lifelike engagement (like two daily CNN-like news reports, as well as participation by real members of Congress and other outside experts—some of whom play themselves in the simulation) that makes it a very intense experience. It is designed to be *harder* than the real world. In fact, the simulation is held several months before graduation in order to give the students time to recover.

Simulation forces people to engage with a forecast, not just read it. Simulation brings learning from the third person to the first person. "If this event happens, what would I do?" I expect that more organizations will use immersion experiences as a way of encouraging the kind of intense leadership-development experiences necessary to succeed in the VUCA world.

OTHER EXAMPLES OF IMMERSION EXPERIENCES FOR LEARNING

An Improvisational Acting Experience

In 2000, IFTF helped Mark Ciccone from Procter & Gamble organize an event on the future of retailing that was held at the Cambridge University business school. For this event, MIT's Auto ID Center worked with P&G to create a home and store of the future, including the use of RFID tags for products. We had twenty-five CEOs from all around the world at the workshop, and we wanted to give them a firsthand experience of the future. These were very senior executives from a variety of cultures, however, so we did not think we could do a simulation or role-play experience comfortably. Instead, we brought in improvisational actors and created vignettes that showed the CEOs how consumers might use the technology that was built into the demonstration area. The vignettes brought the technology to life and suggested how consumers will bring their own habits and practices to the technology. The CEOs clustered around the demonstration areas, where the actors performed the vignettes. Then, a dialogue ensued in which the CEOs could ask the actors what they were experiencing.

This was a kind of case study experience, but the actors animated the case and brought it to life. We drew from consumer research to create the vignettes, and the improvisational nature of the experience meant that unexpected things did happen. The CEOs were much more involved than they would have been reading a case or watching a PowerPoint presentation, but they could still stand back and watch without the anxiety of a role-play.

An Ad Hoc Immersion Experience

When full-scale simulation or alternate reality gaming is not possible, it is often still possible to create some kind of immersion experience that gives people a first-person sense of what's going on—beyond what can be done in a conference room or in a PowerPoint presentation. This is a story from an experience I had in Orlando, Florida:

I was doing a talk for the leadership team of a business that provides professional-grade cleaning products to hotels and restaurants. As part of their meeting, before my talk about the external future forces affecting their business, all the participants including me had an immersion experience to provide a firsthand experience of using their cleaning products in the field.

I was assigned to a group that went out and cleaned hotel rooms. We were briefed at the hotel, shown the laundry room, and introduced to the process of cleaning a room. Then, each of us was given a laundry cart loaded with cleaning products, clean towels, and other sundries and given a room to go clean. We got a bit of coaching, but each of us had to do the actual cleaning, remaking of the beds, and getting the room back in shape for the next guest. Typically, guest room attendants in this hotel are expected to take about twenty minutes to clean each room. We all took much longer, and we all learned a lot about cleaning hotel rooms that I had never known—in spite of the fact that I stay in hotel rooms regularly. It turned out that some of the products were mislabeled, some were diluted, and some were difficult to use correctly in that setting. It is important to realize that all of the participants in this conference were senior executives who were not at all used to hands-on cleaning experiences. Immersion provides a way to shift your point of view, to experience a world from the point of view of someone else, to see things you don't normally see.

I know of some U.S. companies that use immersion to teach executives moving to a country in the developing world about their new land. As part of their introduction to the country, they are required to live on an income level that is typical of the consumers they will be serving. Instead of moving to an upscale American enclave right away, as many executives on foreign assignment do, these leaders are immersed in the local culture, practices, and poverty right away. Immersion experiences are of the same genre as simulation gaming, but they are easier to organize and still provide a large part of the benefit.

A Mentoring Example

The personal career equivalent of simulation or prototyping is an old concept that is coming back into fashion: apprenticeships. The apprentice is an understudy to a skilled professional, a mentor, who teaches him a craft, an art, a trade, or another practice. In a complicated world, we all need mentors and reverse mentors. Mentoring is not a straightforward process of the young learning from the mature. Rather, all leaders have a perpetual learning challenge. Fortunately, if we are willing to engage as apprentices, potential mentors are all around us.

Deloitte, for example, has a "career customization" program that allows employees to try out various roles and customize their own career path to reflect their own priorities and their own strategy for work-private life navigation. In some parts of the world, secondments (temporary transfers of an employee to a different agency or business unit on an ad hoc basis) provide a way to taste a new work world without making a commitment.

"Shadowing" is a variant on mentoring, in which a learner follows a person around to try and understand what that person is doing. Typically, shadowing assignments are shorter and less intense than are mentoring ones.

Peter Drucker commented that in the first half of life one should work on many different tasks and with many different kinds of people, because he doesn't yet know who he is. In the second half of life, Drucker recommended working only on things one is passionate about and only working with people with whom he loves to work.[3] Young people who are just getting started often have trouble finding their passion. Apprenticeships allow a practical way to seek out and experience what might become your passion.

Some Examples of Simulations

The Serious Games Initiative.   The Serious Games Initiative (SGI) was founded at the Woodrow Wilson International Center for Scholars as a response to the emergence of an industry based on serious games, that is, nonentertainment games designed as pedagogical and educational tools. The SGI aims to "usher in a new series of policy education, exploration, and management tools utilizing state of the art computer game designs, technologies, and development skills."[4] It connects investors, companies, and game designers, fostering the field of serious gaming. It focuses on four main questions:

- What public policy and management issues or challenges are most amenable to computer-based gaming techniques?
- What existing and emerging game technologies (such as multi-user, virtual environments) might be particularly useful when applied to policy or management issues?
- How can we quickly expand the application of computer-based games to a much wider range of key challenges facing our government and other public or private organizations?
- How do we identify and proactively deal with any social, ethical, and/or legal issues that might arise through the application of game-based tools to public policy and management issues?[5]

People are realizing that the interactive and immersive nature of computer gaming can educate individuals about incredibly complex issues. Games also engage the next generation. As Henry Jenkins puts it, "The generation that grew up with Super Mario is entering the workplace, entering politics"[6] To them, games are second-nature, and the serious games movement is an attempt to introduce them to the complexities of not only the virtual world but also the real world—and the relationships between the two.

Deloitte's Use of Simulation. Simulation is an important learning medium, but even though it is a way of life in the military and other emergency service organizations, it is underutilized in business. There are signs of a shift, however, as more companies are using immersion experiences in creative ways. Deloitte, for example, is beginning to use simulation internally in its professional continuing education. But most interestingly, Deloitte is also using simulation in outreach to high school students. The company's work in this area grew out of dialogues that its representatives have been having on an ongoing basis with high school and college students. One of Deloitte's focus group participants said, "You need to meet us where we live, that is, with simulations and games, because that is where we spend much of our time." Deloitte is now using immersive experiences in a variety of ways to engage young people (future talent for them) in a businesslike way that also makes creative use of games, music, and the Internet.

Virtual Team Challenge, for example, is a classroom- and Internet-based simulation that has a community focus. It introduces high school students to the complexities of business and helps them explore how they might use their talents, interests, and skills in this world. Here's how Deloitte described the simulation experience to me:

> The simulation is introduced in high school classrooms over a four-week period. Teachers divide the students into teams of four students each. Each team is its own production company and competes with other teams in their own class, their school, and across the nation to stage a money-raising festival for United Way's Operation Graduation campaign.

At the beginning of the simulation, teachers introduce four core content themes that provide the base: business, ethics, money, and decision-making. Content for this curriculum was developed in collaboration with teachers and drawn from the Junior Achievement Excellence Through Ethics curriculum, underwritten by Deloitte.

After the introduction week, thousands of students from around the country simultaneously log on and begin the competition. The first step is to pick a personal avatar, an animated character that will represent each student in the virtual world. Players then go to their team office to get a business brief from their CEO, which says essentially: "We need to help our client, the town of New City, put on a successful event to raise money for the United Way." Each player adopts a role for the action, which involves choice, negotiation, and decisions.

As the simulation unfolds, players are introduced to an expert who gives them their vendor options and they need to decide among vendors. They access the real world to look for facts that will inform these selections. The players go off to vendors' places of business to interview them and negotiate. In week four, everything changes when it is discovered that counterfeit tickets are being sold in New City. Players need to apply what they've learned to solve the mystery and secure profitability for the event.

Winners are determined by the amount of virtual money raised for United Way, with reward certificates given out at regional ceremonies. Deloitte also contributes to the local United Way chapters where the high schools of the first, second, and third place national winners are resident.

Deloitte's explorations of simulation are aimed at creating collaborative online and in-person learning environments that educate, increase Deloitte's brand awareness, enhance awareness of accounting and business consulting as career choices, and facilitate communication between Deloitte and high-potential talent that might someday join them. The company is investing in new media to reach next-generation workers, while also engaging young people in the dynamics of its business environment. It is paying attention to young people with the expectation that young people will pay attention to Deloitte as they become adults and select colleges and academic majors. Opinions of careers are formed early, and Deloitte wants to be involved in that learning process in an engaging and accurate way.

The Simulation Game *PeaceMaker*. This online game simulation explores the Israeli-Palestinian conflict. Players assume the role of either the Israeli prime minister or the Palestinian president, and they must balance diplomatic negotiations, military attacks, domestic demands, and international pressure. The goal is to establish peace between the various powers. Players quickly experience the immense complexity of the conflict, realizing that a single head-on strategy cannot produce lasting peace. The many elements involved simulate a world of dilemmas in which clear answers cannot be found. *PeaceMaker* was developed at Carnegie Mellon University's Entertainment Technology Center in conjunction with ImpactGames studio.[7]

The Online Game *Darfur Is Dying*. In this online simulation, players attempt to keep a small refugee camp alive as long as possible. Assuming the role of a typical family member, players must deal with shortages in water, food, and medical supplies and prepare for Janjaweed attacks. Game play mostly consists of shuttling water to various parts of the village to ensure the villagers stay healthy. The most exciting component is harrowing runs to the well to get more water. During these runs, the player must duck behind objects to avoid detection by Janjaweed soldiers in Jeeps.

The game is short and blunt. As players wander around the village, they interact with families (and remnants of families) with awful stories of loss, hardship, and abuse. When the Janjaweed capture players, the game openly explains that the girls will likely be raped and killed and the boys abused and killed.

Darfur Is Dying uses gaming as a medium for engaging with people who might contribute to improving the situation in Darfur, or at least to give people a better appreciation of what is going on. It makes its point quickly.[8]

The Real-World Game Charles River City. For years, MIT has been developing educational "augmented reality" simulations that combine real-world experiences and information supplied in the field by handheld computers. One of the latest and most sophisticated of these is called Charles River City, a game in which players must investigate a simulated outbreak of illness in the Boston metro area.

In the game, a rash of disease has swept through Boston. A team of experts (the players) must gather and interpret data, plan and implement an investigation, assess risk, communicate with surrounding communities, and identify effective interventions.

A Pocket PC with GPS (Global Positioning System) makes it possible for the simulation to be complex yet manageable. The device also lets the game evolve over time, with patients' symptoms getting worse, environmental samples changing, and, most important, players working separately. The Pocket PC lets the team—usually around twenty people, each with distinct roles—form into subteams and still remain in close contact. The actions of one team may trigger simulated real-time consequences that another team must deal with. Information must be shared rapidly to keep pace with the sequence of unfolding events. The team must also manage myriad factors from public concerns over bioterrorism to officials seeking to quarantine patients. The simulation requires everything from data analysis to effective communication to strategy development to risk assessment. Players must think like clinicians, scientists, psychologists, sociologists, and politicians.

It would be a misnomer to say that the simulation *teaches* the players. Rather, it *immerses* them in a complex world and forces them to act and react. They must innovate and improvise based on their strategic goals. Such a simulation allows the players to learn to confront a complex dilemma, plunge in, and learn.[9]

The Cruel 2 B Kind Self-Organizing Game.   Jane McGonigal and Ian Bogost have designed an interesting game that is played in the real world, with people playing themselves. Playing alone or in teams, players must find other players in a busy area (the first large-scale playing was at Times Square) using mobile e-mail, text messaging, and other media support. In the game, people are "killed with kindness" and then form "benevolent mobs." The "weapons" that attackers use must match the other players "weakness."

This game is completely open and self-organizing, with a positive social intent. It is superimposed on everyday life and is collaborative in nature. There is no puppet master who controls this game, so the play is emergent and unpredictable.[10]

The Medical Training Simulation *Pulse!!!*   Another powerful example is the medical training simulation *Pulse!!!*, created by BreakAway, a company that has designed numerous simulations for the U.S. military and emergency response teams. In *Pulse!!!*, players must diagnose and treat a patient while responding to real-time symptom changes.

The first virtual clinical case involves a twenty-four-year-old male soldier from Iraq who is suffering internal injuries from an explosion. Players adopt the role of a health care provider and must interact with the patient to discover what's wrong. The process will eventually include subtle facial expressions, breathing rates, bleeding, and direct medical data. While it cannot train physical dexterity and movement, *Pulse!!!* can achieve kinds of realism, particularly rapid real-time changes in symptoms, that are impossible to simulate using a physical dummy.[11]

LEARNING TO BE COMFORTABLE BEING UNCOMFORTABLE

In the immediate aftermath of 9/11, novelist Rob Swigart suggested what he calls "satisfying ambiguity" as a way of learning to live with—perhaps even embrace—uncertainty.[12] In a VUCA world, prediction and control are impossible, but preparation *is* possible, and immersion experiences are the most efficient and effective means of preparation.

James Paul Gee, a professor of educational psychology who has studied simulation games, says that educational games should strive to build "morally ambiguous worlds," in which the way forward is not obvious.[13] The VUCA world is morally ambiguous, and games can capture that ambiguity so that it can be experienced in challenging but nonlethal ways. They can help players learn to navigate within the ambiguity to win in a world of dilemmas.

Immersion experiences allow players to learn to be satisfied and productive while they are in a state of ambiguity to be comfortable with the discomfort of dilemmas. Being satisfied while in a state of ambiguity means taking a centered stance toward the life: developing your own style of anticipation, with the ability to flex within the parameters of your committed direction, values, and intent.

The uncertainties of the future, especially in volatile times, can be energizing in a positive way, or they can instill fear and dread. Both are forms of anticipation. Eager anticipation is driven by vision, a belief that the world can be better in some way if only we can perform the right actions, make the right gadget, form the right kind of community. Such vision leans eagerly toward the future. On the other hand, anticipation driven by fear leans back from the future. Both the threats and the opportunities are real. Playing not to lose, however, is rarely a good strategy in any game—or in any aspect of life.

How might leaders use ambiguity creatively, in a more satisfying way? For example, the United States is intentionally ambiguous right now with regard to Taiwan-China tensions. Neither China nor Taiwan is quite sure whether the United States would intervene in a conflict if one started. Maintaining ambiguity in this case discourages Taiwan from being too aggressive about pursuing independence, while the same ambiguity serves to deter China from forcing reunification. If the United States were less ambiguous in this case, the clarity could shift the current balance of power and might trigger a war.

Simulation gaming gives the players lots of time to practice, and it takes practice to be comfortable with ambiguity—not just to be able to tolerate it. The best leaders will be able to thrive in a world of ambiguity. Fundamentalism denies ambiguity. Problem solving simplifies ambiguity as part of a search for solutions. In order to embrace uncertainty, leaders must build flexibility and sensibility into their leadership style.

Traditional approaches to leadership development, training, and education to prepare leaders will not be adequate for the dilemmas of the near future—or even for dilemmas of the present. In a VUCA world, there is little stable fixed content that can be transferred to new leaders. There is no script for leaders to memorize. Success will require flexibility and agility—like that of a great athlete or performer—within a firm structure of values and discipline. The best organizations will provide simulation gaming or other low-risk immersion experiences to allow leaders to rehearse in preparation for the future. We all *have* to perform, and we need practice time. The prepared will perform more effectively and efficiently over time.

One of the masters of immersion experiences for learning is R. Garry Shirts, who founded an educational simulation company called "Simile II" (now called "Simulation Training Systems") and designed a wide range of simulation games that are still in use in schools, government agencies, and businesses. IFTF worked with Garry in the early days of teleconferencing to design a simulation that introduced people to the new worlds of video, audio, and computer-based textual teleconferencing (which is similar to what we now would call a "wiki").

Our goal was to provide a low-risk way to try out and compare varied media for group communications, including in-person meetings. The simulation was published in a book that we did called *Electronic Meetings,*[14] and several teleconferencing suppliers used it for their introductory training. The big barrier to using this and other role-play simulations is that people—especially businesspeople—feel embarrassed to be playing games at work. Role-play simulations like Spinoff do require some time (several hours) and a willingness to step into roles and play the game in order to get a first-person learning experience.

Garry Shirts summarizes his experience with simulations as helping with the "Aha!" moment, "that instant when sudden, spontaneous insight cuts through the tangle of loose ends in a learner's mind to reveal a memorable truth." Here are some examples he gives from simulations that he has designed:

> Having spent nearly 40 years designing experiential simulations, I believe simulations are the most likely teaching method to create those "Aha!" moments. In a simulation called *Starpower*, the moment occurs when trainees, who might be police officers or corporate managers, unexpectedly realize that the only way to keep power over others is not to use it.
>
> In *BaFa, BaFa,* the moment comes when trainees suddenly grasp

the idea that good intentions can actually worsen cultural misunderstandings.

In a team-building simulation called *Pumping the Colors,* it happens when trainees abruptly comprehend that the rules a team operates under are actually the team's responsibility."[15]

Simulation gaming is growing increasingly sophisticated in its ability to teach the principles of life, including life in the future. For example, game designer Will Wright (the creator of *SimCity, The Sims,* and many other successful video games) is now working on *Spore,* which is a game that will allow players to create and live in an entire universe. Wright says, "The big underlying theme is creativity. We want to prove to players that they can make these real cool things that they never thought they could make. It's the computer as amplifier of your imagination."[16] Creating a new universe is beyond the "Aha!" moment that Garry Shirts imagined, but it is on the same evolutionary learning path, using the next generation of simulation gaming media.

Immersion experiences can add value at each stage of the Foresight to Insight to Action Cycle. At the front door of the Institute for the Future, we have a sign that defines the three basic elements of the cycle, all of which can be enhanced by the use of immersion experiences:

Foresight: perception of the significance and nature of events before they have occurred. Immersion experiences help learners imagine provocative futures that might never have occurred to them before.

Insight: the act or outcome of grasping or perceiving the inward or hidden nature of things. Immersion experiences encourage "AHA!" moments where learners see the world differently and imagine new strategies.

Action: the state or process of acting or doing. Immersion experiences allow for low-risk practice experiences, to try out new ways of acting and being.

Immersion experiences can bring a story to life and allow learners to experience the story firsthand. Immersion experiences allow leaders to get there early, before they actually arrive.

7 Sensing and Sensemaking

> To have, without possessing
> do without claiming,
> lead without controlling:
> this is mysterious power.
> —Lao Tzu, *Tao Te Ching*

I'm particularly impressed with the power of small-group workshops to kindle creative thought. This chapter shows how to use workshops to draw out insight from foresight.

Stories and immersive experiences are very useful for leaders, but you still need to draw your own conclusions and create your own strategy if you are going to get there early and compete. Both sensing and sensemaking skills are needed. First, you sense what's going on around you and what might be possible in the future. Then, you need to make sense of it all.

Sensing is basic to the "mysterious power" of leadership and the ability to "lead without controlling." Do you sense accurately what's going on around you? Are you sensitive to the right issues at the right time? Are you overly sensitive at the wrong times? Do you have good business sense? Do you have common sense? Are you sensible in your decisions? Are older workers sensitive to the wants, needs, abilities, and limitations of younger workers—and vice versa? Those who get there early are sensory wizards who are attuned to what is going on around them. Sensory skills and intuition are linked in most effective leaders.

Wayne Sensor is CEO of Alegent Health, a progressive health care provider based in Omaha, Nebraska. The first time Wayne came to Institute for the Future, I met him in our lobby and blurted out spontaneously: "Sensor! What a great name for a leader!" After trying unsuccessfully to hire him (we'd love to have someone at the Institute for the Future named *Sensor*), I kept thinking back to that day and to Wayne's wonderful leadership name: Sensor.

Leaders sense the future, drawing out insights and acting with informed sensibility. Leaders develop their own ways to sense dilemmas, engage with them, and develop flexible responses. Leaders also teach others about sensing. For example, how might older workers mentor next-generation leaders, and vice versa? Who teaches whom, in which situations? The art of sensing is fluid, like the martial arts.

Sensing and sensemaking are basic to innovative strategy. This centrality is because innovation is about conceptualizing and bringing new things into the world, a fundamentally creative endeavor that requires sensing, sensitivity, and common sense. Innovation requires a combined familiarity with analysis and intuition. Being able to identify what's most important or influential requires an ability to sense and make sense of both concrete information and qualitative experience. Fortunately, there is a multigenerational leadership sensibility starting to emerge in the midst of the dilemmas all around us. The mix of generations in the workplace can be a major resource if organizations can figure out how to leverage the strengths and minimize the weaknesses of each cohort. Workshops are a good way to pull together these diverse points of view.

Think of sensing as listening: listening to the world around you, listening to the signals you think are important for your organization, and listening for your inner voice of innovation. Sensing is listening for the future, hearing something that others don't yet hear.

FORESIGHT TO INSIGHT TO ACTION WORKSHOPS

Moving from foresight to insight is an intuitive search for "Aha!" It is a search for coherence in the midst of confusion. It is a nonlinear creative process best done in a small-workshop setting. What new strategy might be created—given the external future forces that are at play?

For somewhat mysterious reasons, small groups are particularly good at listening for the future in creative ways to generate insights and seed innovation. In an interactive workshop setting, a group of seven to twenty-five people can be amazingly productive—if they can learn to engage constructively with one another. My ideal Foresight to Insight to Action Workshop involves about twenty smart and engaging people from varied generations and backgrounds.

When planning a Foresight to Insight to Action Workshop, you need to do some assessment of where you'd like to focus. In our work with top executives, a typical workshop will have the following emphasis: 40 percent on foresight that is provocative for this particular organization, 40 percent on possible insight provoked by the foresight, and 20 percent on possible actions. This distribution can change, however, depending on why you are using the cycle and the organizational challenges that your organization is facing.

We worked with the president of a global business, for example, who set the distribution at 20 percent foresight, 40 percent insights for their business, and 40 percent on action steps, including a very specific discussion of who would do which tasks by when. With this guidance, we sent the forecast out in advance and designed a group process that emphasized a to-do list and schedule at the end. The Foresight to Insight to Action Cycle is inspired by foresight, so it is critical that a future view be included in some way, even if it is a very pragmatic way. However, the cycle can be adapted for action-oriented situations where you just don't have time for much foresight and have to act quickly.

Foresight to Insight to Action Workshops work best when they have the following ingredients:

- A meeting owner. Having a single person designated as a "meeting owner" gives focus to the workshop, provides a sense of urgency, and makes it more likely that the results will be used in practical ways. Even having a discussion about who the meeting owner is can be useful. The content facilitator works closely with the meeting owner to plan the process flow for the Foresight to Insight to Action Workshop. The meeting owner may need to make real-time decisions during the workshop regarding next steps. Of course, ownership can change—sometimes abruptly. I was once leading a workshop with the executives of a large retailer on the edge of bankruptcy. Our workshop was on the retail store of the future, thinking ten years ahead. Halfway into the one-day workshop, the newly appointed CEO (a turnaround artist) turned up by surprise at our workshop. I called a break to meet him, and when we returned, he became the new meeting owner. At his instruction, we shifted our sights from ten years out to three months out. What was a foresight meeting became an action meeting, in the face of survival and the presence of a new leader. The foresight was pro-vocative, but the emphasis was on action and who would do what by when. The company's turnaround literally began in our futures workshop.

- A target outcome. It is relatively easy to have an exciting conver-sation about the future, but it is very challenging to pull the threads together and make the conversation practical for the present. Having a clear outcome, a mantra for the meeting, gives everyone focus. I did a workshop in which our outcome goal was to reduce a large number of alternatives down to five priorities for action. We worked for most of the day on this task and were nearing our goal. About an hour before the scheduled end of the workshop, one of the meeting planners suggested that we change our out-come goal and widen the number of alternatives we would accept. At this point, in front of the group, I turned to the meeting owner and told her our alternatives—so that all would see her choice. If we opened up the discussion of alternatives, we would not meet our original outcome goal by the end of the workshop. She made the call to stick with the original outcome goal and keep rolling. (Sometimes it may be best to call a break and have this conversa-tion with the meeting owner privately, but other times it is impor-tant for the whole group to see the options and understand the choice.) The Iraq Study Group, which finished its report in late 2006, concluded with seventy-nine recommendations. As I facilitator, I think seventy-nine is way too many outcomes. Action-oriented strategic workshops need to focus their recommendations to not more than about five priorities. Seventy-nine recommendations may be a success in terms of consensus, because everyone agrees with at least some of them, but I view it as a failure in strategic convergence. As a facilitator, I'd be embarrassed to end a workshop—let alone an eight-month study group—with that many recommendations.

- A diverse group. Small-group conversations can be great, since people with different perspectives can stimulate one another's thoughts and draw links that are not apparent. Expertise is important, but the definition of *expert* needs to be considered carefully. Outside-in views are usually important, but it is also important to have key inside players who will own the outcomes and help bring them to action. Of course, diversity can create tensions that can be both positive and negative. Basically, you need diverse people who will play well together. Generational mixes and mixes of thought styles are particularly helpful. As a content facilitator I try to study the backgrounds of all the workshop participants in advance. If I know there are people who may be difficult in the workshop (that is, not play well with others), I try to meet them in advance and get a better sense of their views and style. You want to create a mood of high conflict around ideas but maintain respectful behavior toward others. Holding this balance can be delicate, particularly in high-powered groups with individuals who are under great pressure.

- A content facilitator. It helps to have a content facilitator leading a Foresight to Insight to Action Workshop to assist participants in drawing the links between the foresights, insights, and possible actions. By *content facilitator*, I mean someone with both content and group process skills—and with the instincts to be able to decide when to play which card. A good content facilitator should know at least enough about the content of the forecast being used to present it in a provocative way and then facilitate a conversa-

tion to identify insights—given the foresight—and then cluster
and prioritize them. The content facilitator should be friendly but
firm, a kind of pace car for the conversation. He or she is the real-
time weaver of ideas and of people in conversation.

- A chunk of provocative foresight. A big-picture forecast, such as
the Forecast Map inside the book jacket or the text summary in
Chapter 2, can be a wonderful stimulant for a Foresight to Insight
to Action Workshop, but it is also important to think through the
message track that you want to use to stimulate the discussion.
Foresight is based on outside sensing and an integration of facts,
observations, and possibilities, which should be presented in a
crisp and provocative form that engages the group without overwhelming the participants. A content facilitator must become
skilled at folding foresight into the conversations that occur
during the workshop. The Forecast Map inside the book jacket
contains a number of hot zones, which are intersections of driving
forces and impact areas. The content facilitator needs to be good
at telling provocative stories at these intersections, to stimulate
conversation about insights and possible actions. It is best if the
foresight gets folded into the conversation throughout the workshop, not just in a big chunk at the start. Artifacts and scenarios
can also be used as chunks of foresight, mixed in with the conversation to keep the insights and possible actions coming.

Each participant should feel slight off balance in a Foresight to Insight Workshop, never knowing when he or she might be called upon.
The mood should be relaxed but charged with energy.

I recommend taking a substantial block of time for introductions,
since they allow everyone to become oriented to the workshop and
build trust with one another right away. I've also learned through doing many of these workshops that it is very important for all participants to get individual airtime early. The longer it takes for a senior person to say something in a workshop, the more likely it is that when he
or she does say something, it will be dysfunctional. If you give every-

one space and a voice early, the chances for great group dynamics go up substantially.

I don't recommend simply going around the room and asking people to introduce themselves without any guidance. Rather, I think that a good content facilitator should move with an asymmetrical pattern and draw people out in introductions. What is the voice that each participant will be taking? The future will be asymmetrical, so why go around the room in a symmetrical way?

Introductions are not a *preamble to* the workshop; they are an important *part of* the workshop and a great opportunity for early engagement. A good content facilitator will be able to weave content from the forecast into the introductions, in dialogue with the background and interests of the participants.

The best workshops have a feeling of being at the edge, with a touch of urgency, punctuated by episodes of reflection. If there is no external source of urgency (hard to believe in these times), the content facilitator needs to create a sense of urgency. For example, I often facilitate with my colleague Susannah Kirsch, and we will sometimes switch roles every hour or so, with the timing paced by a countdown timer. Each time block has a goal of an aggressive outcome, with a handoff to the next time block. The goal is to stretch, with the countdown timer as a discipline and motivator. We strive for a sense of positive pressure to perform as a team.

When I co-lead Foresight to Insight to Action Workshops with Mark Schar, a former P&G executive and former chief marketing officer (CMO) for Intuit, I stand in the front of the room, and Mark stands at the back. I am the workshop leader, and I stay focused on foresight. Mark is a "color comments guy" who becomes the voice of insight and practical actions that are provoked by the discussion. Mark stays in tension with me throughout the workshop: the tension is between foresight and action. This front-back dynamic creates a different kind of energy in the room and keeps the participants spinning around the cycle from foresight to insight to action.

As forecasters—since nobody can fully know the future—we are always at the edge of our expertise. For workshop participants, we want people who get more comfortable as they get to the edge of their own expertise. This, of course, is not true of most people with graduate de-grees—who tend to get more comfortable in the center of their ex-pertise. We look for people who "fail gracefully" at the edge of their ex-pertise. Said another way, we look for people who can contribute usefully to a dialogue even if they don't know what they are talking about. And, of course, we don't want people who *pretend* that they know what they are talking about when they do not.

How can someone contribute usefully if they don't know what they are talking about? First and foremost, they can ask good questions—which are usually much more useful than answers when it comes to a forecast since nobody can know the answer. Second, they can use mod-els or frameworks to explore what is known and what is not known. The content facilitator is the guide as the workshop participants navigate the uncertain space stimulated by the forecast.

Venue and mood of the room are also important. For example, we once held an exploratory innovation meeting for a group of technology and human resources executives at the Explorer's Club in New York City, a membership club where only the world's leading explorers can join. For another workshop of technology executives interested in innova-tion, we chose the luxury box of a NASCAR raceway, with meetings in the pit area about technical innovation in NASCAR racing. In another case, we held a thought leaders workshop in the press box of a new foot-ball stadium. The point is to use your venue as part of your content, to help explore an aspect of the future with which you are engaging. The venue can be an immersive learning experience in itself or at least can be interesting and provocative. You can also bring the mood to your room with artifacts that reflect the topic you are exploring. For exam-ple, with brand-building workshops we will often have posters, videos, and other brand artifacts all around the meeting room in order to get the participants in the mood to be creative around brands. The quality of your room experience will have an impact on the quality of your out-comes, for better or for worse.

In our Foresight to Insight Workshops, we often use a graphic artist to record the insights and create a group memory in graphic form. The idea is to allow the workshop participants to think creatively, without

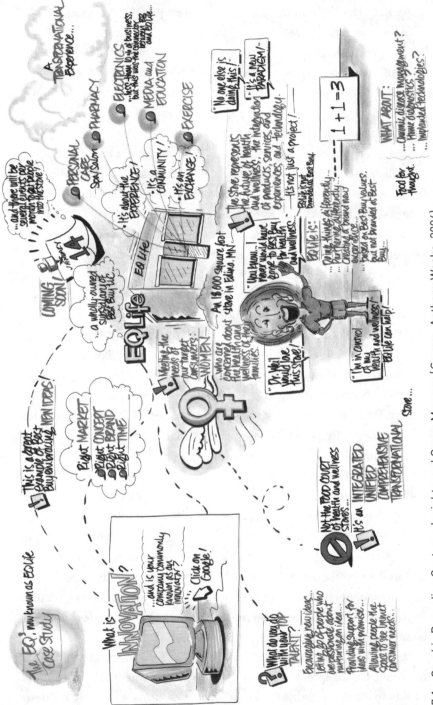

7.1 Graphic Recording Captures Insights and Group Memory (*Source:* Anthony Weeks, 2006)

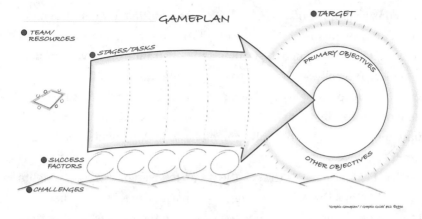

7.2   Group Game Plan by Grove Consultants International

having to focus on note taking. The artist creates a collage of key phrases and evocative images while the content facilitator uses the foresight to stimulate discussion, and works with the group to hone and cluster the insights to get them to an appropriate level of specificity—given the goals of the workshop.

I have worked with Anthony Weeks in many workshops, and I include an example of his work here (see Figure 7.1). Anthony created this graphic on a four-foot by eight-foot sheet of paper in real time, as the group talked. Group graphic recording is an unusual art form, and Anthony is one of the best. He is able to almost channel the conversation of the group, in a deep state of concentration, and then create a visual summary that is memorable for everyone who was there.

Once a level of specificity has been set (usually through one or two illustrative models of the types of insights that the group is seeking), then the artist can array the options in a way that they can be prioritized by the group. The graphic template in Figure 7.2 was developed by David Sibbet to help groups agree on a plan of action.[1] It is most useful at the insight to action stage of a workshop.

Sometimes we use electronic polling to do the prioritizing, but usually colored dots are more effective. (When we use the dots, participants are given equal numbers of dots and are asked to "vote" by placing the dots on the graphic display.) This process of sifting, grouping, synthesizing, and evaluating is very important to sort out what is possible and to begin to think through the virtues and constraints of the various possibilities. Typically, a Foresight to Insight to Action Workshop is not focused on deep consensus or decision making. Rather, the focus is on generating possible insights and beginning to prioritize them. Full evaluation of the insights typically comes later, with a smaller leadership group.

The facilitator needs to keep the group focused on possible insights or action steps that are stimulated by a particular forecast. There is a temptation within many groups to argue with the forecast, rather than accepting it as one possible future and drawing out insights or actions if this particular future should occur. Fortunately, you don't have to agree with a forecast to find it useful. It is most productive for a group to assume a particular forecast could occur (assuming it is plausible and internally consistent) and use it to stimulate insights. Then if you want to try another forecast, go back through the cycle again. This is where scenario development can come in to create a range of forecasts. Arguing with a forecast is always possible, but it is usually not very productive in providing input to strategy. It is much more valuable to go through the Foresight to Insight to Action Cycle first and then do another forecast if you question the value of the first one. Trusting the forecast usually leads to much better outcomes. Even if a forecast does not accurately predict what happens in the real world, it can still be useful to provoke insights. The ultimate criterion for a successful forecast is whether it helps people make better decisions.

A successful workshop depends on a good start, with prepared minds. Preparing your mind means asking questions like these:

- What are the current pain points for leaders and others in your organization? What pains keep your leaders awake at night? Although major change is occasionally prompted by compelling vision, change is more commonly prompted by pain. If you understand the current pains of an organization, you can figure out what kinds of foresight could be most provocative in generating pain relief. Typically, people and organizations are not motivated to change when things are going well.

- What is the intent of your leadership? If intentions are understood, then foresight becomes context around your intentions. Foresight is focused on external future forces. Intent always lives in a larger context, and foresight can help you understand—and possibly influence—that context. For Martin Luther King, the vision was the Promised Land, and his intentions focused on nonviolent direct action to get there. The intentions of leaders must be very clear, although leaders need agility to figure out on the fly how that intent can be achieved in the field.

- What is the destination of your organization? One of our clients did a ten-year vision of where the company wanted to be as a brand. The leadership team did a destination statement, refined the statement, and shared it widely as a target destination. Once the destination was clear and accepted, they used foresight to identify external future forces that either helped or hindered the steps toward their target destination. What are the waves of change that you could ride to reach that destination? What are the waves of change that could drive you off course?

- What is the biggest business challenge you are facing right now? How might that challenge be informed or influenced by external future forces?

- What outside forces are likely to influence you? What's going on in the lives of the participants, outside this meeting? Beware of people, including yourself, who may bring views to a meeting that don't belong there. Sometimes outside forces will influence a meeting, even if they have nothing to do with the content of a meeting. Foresight encourages people to step outside their normal routines, but the day-to-day pressures of life can still bleed in.

For a successful workshop you can also follow some of the tips and techniques that we have learned from doing Foresight to Insight to Action Workshops:

Challenge	Workshop Tools & Techniques
Introductions for a familiar group, where most people know one another.	Routine introductions can be short, but establishing a voice for each participant is important. For example, "Tell us something that your colleagues will not know about you."
Introductions for an unfamiliar group, where most people don't know one another.	Introductions should be longer in order to engage the group. Keep the introductions personal and draw links to content when appropriate.
Presentations where there is a lot of complex material that is new to participants.	Allow for very brief presentations to share material, and for discussion so people can ask clarifying questions and make links to their own work situations (individual learning), or to the situation or challenge under discussion (group learning).
Explore possibilities or stories, leveraging the group's experience to do so.	Use small-group work for scenario-creation activities. Provide clear guidelines and in some cases an example to stimulate people's thinking. Imaginative activities are usually most effective when people have had an opportunity to review new material before being asked to create scenarios or stories.
Focus on individual learning, rather than group decision making.	Provide tools such as learning journals and time to allow people to gather their thoughts. Allow time for individuals to work on their own to develop their ideas, and use small-group discussions and sharing to enable people to learn from one another.

Challenge	Workshop Tools & Techniques
Focus on group learning and decision making.	Use the time to go back and forth between sharing information and both large- and small-group discussion. When you break into small groups, allow time for reporting and discussion that builds on the ideas developed in the small-group setting. Small groups can leverage the diversity of expertise in the room to dig deeper into specific topics.
Focus on experience-based learning.	Use group immersive experiences with time to debrief and share the lessons. For example, consumer home visits or shop-alongs can be used to explore new product possibilities.
Prioritizing insights or agreeing on action steps.	Include dot voting on ideas or strategies once they are presented and discussed, and include both small- and large-group discussion to build shared understanding and consensus. Small groups can be effective at advancing complex ideas, particularly when you have a lot of material to cover.
Generating new insights or possible action steps.	Divide people up in small groups to maximize creativity. Use the large-group work to share new ideas and explore critical questions. If needed, use the large group to stimulate new discussion.
Going for actions, with signups regarding who will do what by when.	If participants are to be responsible for making sure the work gets done, use part of your session to sign people up for next steps. Encourage your outcome owner to have a list of people he or she believes could successfully implement any actions you agree to take.

During these workshops, there will be moments of intense conversational flow and moments of silence, when the conversation stops. Silence allows time for reflection, and a good facilitator will allow the silence to happen to allow participants to use the time to think more deeply. Conversational bursts are also important, since they can provide a new zone of creativity for a group to go places that the individuals cannot. The danger of constant conversation is that some important voices may not be heard because they are overwhelmed by their more vocal colleagues. The challenge is this: how long do you hold the silence as the participants process the complexity and try to make sense out of it? When do you interrupt an active conversation to do a process check, to refocus, or to allow the quieter participants to jump in? Content facilitators or meeting owners need to sense the group and make the call.

In any workshop conversation, leaders need to sort out what's important from what's just new. As I mentioned before, if a topic is really important, it is probably not really new. In the age of the Internet, everybody has access to what's new. The critical task now is to be able to sort through the newness and decide what's really important. When is the timing likely to be right? Many important innovations take years to emerge, usually in fits and starts and after many failures. Few successful innovations are truly new at the time they happen. Most are reimagined versions of an earlier effort that failed.

USE POWERPOINT FOR PROVOCATION

Brief, provocative PowerPoint images can draw groups into a conversation. In a Foresight to Insight to Action Workshop format like the one we are discussing here, however, PowerPoint can be a detriment if it is not used well.

First, the use of PowerPoint in a workshop room requires that you arrange the room so that it faces the projection screen. This arrangement takes the focus off the group and puts it on the PowerPoint slides. Having a PowerPoint screen involves a major tradeoff in small-group dynamics: people tend to look at the screen instead of looking at one another. The process of drawing out insights stimulated by foresight requires the participants to engage with one another as a group.

Presentations should be used for provocation only and should not look too finished. Consider this story from my experience:

In the 1980s, I helped to organize an industry workshop in Hakone, Japan. We brought together several hundred leaders from around the world, all of whom were major players in an emerging marketplace. The purpose was to share foresight about the emerging industry and draw out insights about how the various companies could collaborate to encourage growth in the field.

Apple Computer was the host, and the company had advanced presentation capabilities. At the time of this workshop, most of the participants were used to seeing 35 mm slides for formal presentations and overheads for less formal ones.

At the conference in Hakone, we did parallel workshop sessions with the participants on into the night, drawing on the many resources that were present to create a draft plan regarding how to grow this emerging market quickly. Those of us organizing and facilitating the conference met together to synthesize the workshop findings and get them ready to share with the large group the next morning.

At about 4 a.m., we shared the synthesized results—which were very impressive—with the top Apple executive who was present. He loved the conclusions and agreed to present them to the large group the next morning. Then came a serious mistake.

We debated how to share the draft conclusions. We had a good artist present, and one idea was to do a graphic summary of the evening's work and display it for the group. The hand-drawn feel, we thought, would be engaging for the audience as they considered the small-group insights and started to move toward possible action steps.

The Apple executive, however, was anxious to show off Apple's new capabilities to do high-quality presentations quickly. He made the call that we would present the workshop insights in a presentation format that would demonstrate Apple's presentation and artistic capabilities. Everyone would be amazed that Apple had done such a high-quality job so quickly, he thought.

Well, he was right that everyone was amazed. It was a beautiful presentation, and the Apple software and hardware performed with precision. The presentation was so amazing that many of the participants concluded immediately (though incorrectly) that Apple had prepared this presentation in advance.

Essentially, the presentation looked too good and too finished. Rather than drawing the conference participants into a conversation that reflected the small-group insights and beginning a synthesis process, the presentation planted seeds of distrust regarding Apple's intent.

We worked through these reactions and eventually made good progress going forward from the conference, but I took away a major lesson: any presentations, especially to a group engaged in a foresight-to-insight discussion, should not appear too finished. Presentations should be good enough to reflect the quality of early provocative thought, but not so finished looking that people feel they are being sold something. The presentation medium communicates something that is just as important as the content.

Imagine a world in which your PowerPoint library is organized like the playlists on your iPod. The basic unit of organization is not the linear presentation but the knowledge nuggets that are embodied in a particular image or video and captured in a PowerPoint slide. With a PowerPoint playlist, a workshop organizer can call up images spontaneously during a Foresight to Insight to Action Workshop, to provoke thought. We need to get beyond thinking of PowerPoint as a linear medium to replicate what we used to do. PowerPoint is designed as a linear medium, unfortunately, but there is great potential for it to evolve into a medium as flexible as an iPod, one that encourages users to think of their knowledge in terms of key ideas that can be rearranged as needed.

I compare PowerPoint use to drinking wine. Drinking wine in moderation is great; it is even healthy for you. If you overuse wine, however, you become an alcoholic. Similarly, if you use PowerPoint intelligently in moderation, it can be healthy for your meetings. It is not that PowerPoint is bad per se but rather that, like wine, it can be so easily abused. Many people in organizations behave as if they are addicted to Power-

Point, yet—like many alcoholics—they don't realize their addiction. The ease of PowerPoint slide creation subtly encourages sloppiness in thought that makes it harder to draw out insight.

The best PowerPoint presentation that I've ever seen is the one the Al Gore gives to discuss global warming, the presentation that is at the core of the movie *Inconvenient Truth*. Gore uses PowerPoint in a dramatic and yet human way to help audiences visualize complex data in support of a specific conclusion. This presentation by Al Gore may be the world's best PowerPoint presentation, but it is intended for large groups—not small-group workshops. A few of those images, however, could be used very effectively to provoke a foresight to insight to action conversation.

In this chapter we've seen how sensing and sensemaking are needed to bring together foresight and insight in a workshop setting. Chapter 8, about the transition from insight to action, provides specific examples of how foresight has provoked insight that led to inspired strategy.

ACTION

To Get There Early

Part 3 focuses on action with agility. Strategy is the bridge between insight and action and these final chapters will help you create strategy to guide your actions. Part 3 begins with successful examples of turning insight into action. Chapters 9 and 10 suggest principles for flexing and flexibility, plus a series of examples to bring the principles to life.

Action is a result, stimulated by foresight and insight, but action is also the beginning of a new learning process in which agility allows for course corrections as you go. Action creates real-world opportunities for learning from experience that can lead to new cycles of foresight and insight, as described in Chapter 11.

These final chapters are about the cycle from insight to action. Part 3 brings the threads of the book together with an emphasis on how to blend the fuzzy potential of foresight and insight together to make things happen. (See Figure 8.1.)

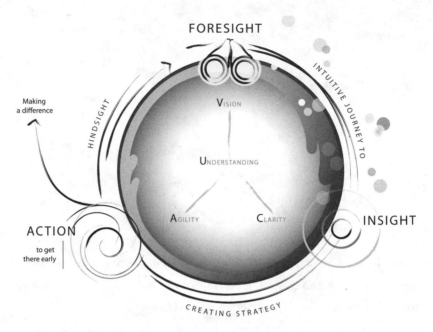

8.1   Foresight to Insight to Action Cycle: Insight to Action

8 From Insight to Action

Have deep roots, a strong trunk.
Live long by looking long.
—Lao Tzu, *Tao Te Ching*

In high school and college, my life revolved around basketball. I was taught from an early age that when I got a rebound, I should "look long" down the court. If a pass wasn't possible, the next best option was to look for an outlet pass to someone on my team moving down court rapidly in order to get the ball to the goal early—ahead of the other team—at the other end of the court.

In basketball, it is always easier if you get to the goal with the ball ahead of your competition. By looking long, you can sense the play as it is taking shape. If you get there early with the ball, you score—unless you miss an easy shot.

Looking long in basketball is, essentially, foresight—but it is foresight in the moment, linked closely to action. Looking long gives you a better chance to get there early, ahead of your competitors. Looking long demands an ability to sense what's out there, just as a basketball player senses the court and what's taking shape. Looking long is built into any great strategy.

Looking long does not mean you have to predict the future, even though anticipation is important. Great basketball players sense where their teammates will be—not just where they are; they lead them with passes. They don't know exactly what will happen on the next play, however. Great players see the game as it is taking shape, and they prepare to take advantage of the opportunities as they develop, as well as respond to threats. Great players think strategically about what is likely to develop in a particular game, and they practice so that their movements become instinctual. Great players use their practice sessions to get there early. They think in practice so they don't have to think during a game.

Great leaders, like great players, "live long by looking long," as the *Tao Te Ching* advises.[1] Looking long worked 2,500 years ago when the *Tao Te Ching* was written, it works today, and it most certainly will work tomorrow. Foresight is a particularly good way to stimulate strategic insight and to inspire new strategies.

This chapter is focused on insight to action, the action zone on the Foresight to Insight to Action Cycle. Action is the culmination of any successful foresight to insight process. This chapter emphasizes the transition from insight to strategy to action.

Once you have a compelling insight, the seminal ingredient in a winning strategy, how do you go about putting it into action? There are many methodologies to bring insight to action (many of them with acronyms and trademarks), and there are many consultants practicing with those methodologies. The process of turning insight into action is essentially good common sense, executed in a consistent, timely, and competent manner. Good consultants can play a useful role in this transition, helping to turn insight into strategy and action.

In his analysis of business strategy across a wide range of corporations, Willie Pietersen, who is a professor of management at Columbia Business School, observes that every winning strategy is based on a compelling insight.[2] Competitors strive to "win the battle for insights," which come from recognizing what is important before one's competitors or from seeing it better than one's competitors. He refers to this process as "strategic learning" to emphasize that it is an ongoing process in which you have to keep learning to keep winning. The planning is what's important, not the plan.

On our Foresight to Insight to Action Cycle, notice the pixie dust between foresight and insight, to symbolize the intuitive thinking that must happen in this zone. Although such breakthrough thinking can be done on one's own, small groups are particularly good at stimulating this kind of creativity. Insight is often based in an "Aha" that leads toward a great strategy.

Southwest Airlines, for example, had the insight of providing low-cost airline travel that was competitive with automobile travel, plus providing a touch of fun. "We will operate at the lowest industry costs, and provide fun-filled travel that competes with the cost of car travel."[3] This compelling insight has driven the company to success since its founding, while most airlines—with the exception of Singapore Airlines, Virgin Atlantic, and a few others—struggle with vague strategic mandates. Southwest Airlines has also demonstrated that success requires not only a compelling insight but also a persistent and incredibly intense focus on driving that insight every day, in every aspect of their business. In addition, Southwest (unlike most airlines) has good labor relations and relatively happy employees who, in turn, have an interest in providing good experiences for passengers.

INSIGHT TO ACTION: A CLEAR DIRECTION

The transition from insight to action is more straightforward than the transition from foresight to insight, as the solid line on the Foresight to Insight to Action Cycle suggests.

In a military context, strategy is the calculated relationships among ends (objectives), ways (underlying methods being used in the pursuit), and means (resources that are available and resources of choice for a particular situation). Basically, strategy is about what you want to accomplish and how you want to accomplish it. Strategy implies having a clear direction, even though there may be more or less obvious answers regarding how that strategic direction will be achieved.

Still, many people want—and some people need—fixed and obvious answers. Strategy is hard work. Even when the direction is clear, the implementation of strategy typically is not. Consistency in strategy is very useful, but overpackaging is not. Strategy must include flexibility as well as clear direction.

Military strategy, like other forms of public policy strategy, often requires a consensus and a checks-and-balances process that is different from that of most corporations. In the United States, our forefathers had a deep distrust of central power, so checks and balances were designed into the government to slow down the decision-making process in a complex maze of hurdles and challenges—all in the trust that a more thoughtful and wise decision will come out in the end. The result of such a strung-out process, however, can be a least common-denominator strategy, rather than an insight-driven strategy. The resulting debate invites polarities and name calling, as well as a resulting strategy that is aimed at appeasing the various powers that be. As a Washington insider told me, "In our world, focus is not an option."

Generally, public policy strategy in democratic societies is much more difficult than corporate strategy is. In most corporations, strategic decisions can be more centralized and less consensus-driven than in the public sector. The key to effectively creating and implementing strategy, whether in the private or the public sector, is to focus on the decisions that must be made, including decisions about direction and decisions about execution. Both clarity and flexibility are required for strategy to succeed.

Ian Morrison, a president emeritus of Institute for the Future, observed some years ago that the purpose of forecasting is not to predict the future but to make better decisions in the present. The action stage is where forecasting pays off.

Action is aimed at results, at making a difference. But action does not necessarily mean final action. Action unfolds. In the world of design, for example, prototyping is low-risk exploration but, unlike simulation, prototyping takes place in the real world. In prototyping, you expect to fail in the early stages, and you learn from those failures on the fly. Bob Sutton, a Stanford professor who has studied IDEO (one of the world's leading design firms), points out that designers at IDEO actually argue for their point of view through prototypes. If a designer disagrees with another designer, she builds a prototype that embodies a different approach. Leadership in design requires this kind of learn-as-you-go style.

In business, making a difference can mean making a certain amount of money within a designated time frame, but *making money* can be defined in many different ways, with different processes: Outcomes. Return on investment. Implementation. Shareholder value. Rollout. Change. Commercialization. Institutionalization. Execution. These are all outcome oriented, but even outcomes often come about in stages.

The ultimate basis for evaluation of a forecast is not what you got right in the forecast but whether the forecast helped leaders make better decisions that led to action that made a difference. Before illustrating with some examples, let me inject a caveat, a dangerous carryover from the world of problem solving.

Beware of the Operational Problem Solver

Action is great, unless it is the wrong action. Those who are problem solvers also want to get there early, but they are more likely to get there early with an answer that is wrong—even if it is right in the short run. Action is the home court of the problem solver. Problem solvers love to act, and they especially love to act quickly and decisively.

Modern strategic dilemmas require new kinds of leadership, however, and new kinds of leadership development. Even solvable problems can be embedded in dilemmas, and the dilemmas can be nonlinear— like global warming—with real potential for large-scale sudden or long-term impacts that can rearrange entire systems.

Leaders need to think twice about problem-solving actions in order to engage constructively in a landscape of insolvability. They must attune themselves to the challenges they face to have the kinds of complex emergent response capabilities that will be a match for those challenges. Strategy and action must change when even perfect problem solving is not enough.

Thought leader on strategy Roger Martin says, "Great design is characterized by deep user understanding, visualization of creative resolution of tensions, collaborative prototyping to enhance solutions, and continuous modification and enhancement after launch."[4] Most dilemmas cannot be resolved within the framework of operational problem solving. Great strategies require looking long, beyond operational problems.

The key here—in the midst of action—is to recognize the difference between a problem and a dilemma as early in the process as possible. When you are confronted with a situation, how do you recognize whether you are dealing with a problem or a dilemma, or some combination of both? In many situations, you don't have much time to think or reflect, even if you do get there early.

If in doubt, assume you are dealing with a dilemma. If as the situation unfolds, it turns out that you are dealing with a solvable problem, all you need to do is solve it and move on. On the other hand, if you mistake a dilemma for a problem, you can dig yourself in very deeply before you realize what's going on—and before you figure out that no solution is possible. By this time, there may be no way out, or at least no face-saving way out.

Sometimes, solving a problem will only aggravate the larger dilemma in which the problem is imbedded. Joe Fox, an internal strategy consultant at Procter & Gamble, has a motto that he uses in his strategy workshops: "Beware of the operational problem solver." He has many colorful stories to support this motto, and he encourages people to stretch their thinking beyond the operational—while still remembering the importance of operational excellence.

The following stories illustrate how foresight has provoked strategic insight and action in a wide variety of settings:

Sustainability Strategy

> FORESIGHT: *Long-term financial performance won't be possible without changes in environmental practices*
>
> INSIGHT: *Wal-Mart needed a new approach*
>
> ACTION: *Create the Wal-Mart Business Sustainability Strategy*

Consider this question: What would it take for your company to continue growing at its current rate for the next twenty years? Wal-Mart executives asked themselves this question and decided that they could not continue to grow without changing the company's approach to natural resource use.

At the suggestion of a key board member, Wal-Mart's executives looked twenty years into the future, and they didn't like what they saw. Sober forecasts about energy and the environment provoked insight for Wal-Mart regarding the company's own strategy and the impacts it is having and could have. Wal-Mart is now engaging with the dilemma of growth and sustainability, even though the case is still out as to whether it can win. Certainly, the Wal-Mart business sustainability strategy will be important—no matter how it turns out. Wal-Mart, as the world's largest company, has rippling impacts on almost everyone. If Wal-Mart changes, its suppliers and customers change, too.

Wal-Mart has always been all about growth and "everyday low prices." In October 2005, however, CEO Lee Scott entered into new territory with his focus on "business sustainability," which he defined as including the goals of environmental sustainability and robust business performance. Scott said, "We need to look differently on the way we run and conduct our business." Business sustainability, for Wal-Mart, is focused on "our ability to replenish natural resources at a rate that is sustainable over the long run" and on "improving quality of life for us and for future generations."

Many people were amazed when Wal-Mart embraced environmental sustainability. And, of course, many are skeptical and think that this is just a public relations move ("greenwashing," some say)—not a true shift in business strategy. How can Wal-Mart continue to grow and manage its massive scale while performing in a way that is environmentally sustainable? This is a fascinating move, by the world's largest retailer, into the intense dilemma zone of growth and sustainability.

Wal-Mart's business sustainability strategy has three core elements, each of which involves dilemmas within which it will be trying to win:

- **Climate and renewable energy.**   Wal-Mart's first green prototype stores were in McKinney, Texas, and Aurora, Colorado. The company has specific goals for fuel efficiency in all the stores, as well as the distribution centers and fleet of trucks. It also has a prototype green truck with improved aerodynamics, fuel-efficient tires, emission reduction technology, and auxiliary power unit for idling in hot or cold weather. It is investing heavily in energy-saving technologies.

- **Zero waste.**   The goal here is to "close the loop" of waste in Wal-Mart stores, Sam's Clubs, and distribution centers. For packaging, for example, the company is using the following slogan: remove, reduce, reuse, renew, and recycle.

- **Sustainable products.**   Wal-Mart's goal is to sell products that are made from sustainable resources and that still keep customers' costs low. The goal is to have at least 20 percent of product inventory aligned with this goal within the first three years.

These aggressive environmental goals are all being pursued within the context of aggressive business and financial goals. Wal-Mart is doing a range of things across what it thinks of as the "Sustainable Value Network," from quick wins that improve things immediately to innovation projects that take awhile longer, to big game-changers that will take longer to implement. Wal-Mart executives realize that they face an uphill climb from today's business practices to sustainable business practices.

Notice the term *Sustainable Value Network*. Wal-Mart is now organizing itself in a series of these networks that include people in various parts of the company as well as—in some cases—members of other companies and even of NGOs. Although Wal-Mart still has a core hierarchy, it is increasingly a network-style organization. This shift was made partly to improve the company's readiness to respond quickly to crises such as Hurricane Katrina.

Wal-Mart is aiming to do good while doing well, that is, without compromising its financial goals. It is aggressively pursuing the economic benefits of improved sustainability. The open question is whether it can win within the zone of this dilemma of sustainability when no other company of the gigantic scale of Wal-Mart has done it.

In 2006, I visited Bentonville, Arkansas, to learn more about Wal-Mart's strategy. I left convinced that Wal-Mart executives are taking sustainability very seriously. Wal-Mart is in charge of the supply chain, and it can set standards in a way that is almost like a government agency. For example, a few innovative companies tried concentrated detergents in the1980s, but most consumers did not like the smaller packages because they felt they were getting less value. Now, Wal-Mart is requiring all of its suppliers— including its own private-label brands—to reduce their package size with concentrates. Wal-Mart can dictate changes like this that are difficult to make in open-market settings or in climates such as we have in the United States, where government is not willing or able to make strong environmental regulations.

Perhaps Wal-Mart's years of bad press—certainly, it is facing a public relations dilemma—influenced its decision to deal with the environmental dilemma. Dilemmas tend to interlace with one another.

The turning point may have been Wal-Mart's response to Hurricane Katrina: Wal-Mart responded much more quickly— and with more compassion—than did any government agency. Sheriff Harry Lee from Jefferson Parish in New Orleans said, "If the federal government would have responded as quickly as Wal-Mart, we could have saved more lives."[5] Even the company's enemies know Wal-Mart as an organization that can move mass volume very efficiently through its logistics and supply systems. In the case of its response to Katrina, this core business skill yielded great social value. As Lee Scott himself said, "This was one of the few times at Wal-Mart when we did the right things and actually got credit for it."[6] It appears that Katrina was a turning point for Wal-Mart, but the next few years will be extremely challenging for the company and for its suppliers— who are bound to carry a big portion of the organizational and financial burden of this strategy.

Perhaps the Wal-Mart business sustainability strategy will break new ground more generally in terms of how companies develop winning strategies for dealing with dilemmas. The Wal-Mart approach was to do careful, quiet research (more than one year of research was done before the public announcement), but then to mount a bold public campaign. Lee Scott is calling for a mind-set change at Wal-Mart; he has taken a stand. The current Wal-Mart leaders seem to be inspired by the Peter Drucker insight "Every single pressing social and global issue of our time is a business opportunity."

Wal-Mart chose a sustainability strategy because it made a judgment that the company cannot grow at its current rates over a twenty-year period unless it changes its environmental practices now. Foresight inspired a strategic insight. How can such a massive retailer grow its revenue and profits and have environmental sustainability at the core of its strategy—all without increasing its everyday low prices?

Wal-Mart committing to sustainability could be like Richard Nixon going to China. If a liberal democrat had gone to China instead of Nixon, the positive impact on trade would have been far less than it was. Similarly, Wal-Mart is not the sort of company that anyone expected to be a sustainability leader. Wal-Mart's business sustainability strategy was a surprise to almost everyone, including many people inside Wal-Mart.

If Wal-Mart succeeds, the impacts will be huge. Stories will ripple from this decision to engage with the dilemmas of sustainability, even though it is not yet clear whether this will be a winning business strategy for Wal-Mart. The company is leveraging its unique advantages in creative ways that could result in both doing good and doing well.

The Story of Wikipedia's Encyclopedia for the World

FORESIGHT: *Much of the world will have limited access to knowledge*
INSIGHT: *The world needs a free, open-source encyclopedia*
ACTION: *Create Wikipedia*

Jimmy Wales, the founder of Wikipedia, has a vision of reaching everyone in the world with a free encyclopedia. His ambitious goal is to include "all human knowledge."[7] His foresight was to see a need for knowledge that extends to everyone in the world. Faced with the volatility of the world, he created a compelling vision and then figured out a way to bring it to life and grow it. Now, he is well on his way to reaching his amazing goal of creating a free encyclopedia for everyone.

Jimmy Wales has commented that the big challenge for Wikipedia now is "scaling the community." Wikipedia is large already, but it faces recurring challenges with scale thresholds as it continues to grow. Wikipedia is an open-source encyclopedia that has grown to be what Jimmy Wales calls a "community of thoughtful users," who now call themselves "Wikipedians." For Wikipedians, Wikipedia is a space where they are empowered to contribute and engage as a volunteers contributing to the growth of human knowledge globally. Being a Wikipedian has become a personal identity for a growing number of people. As Jimmy Wales says, "The design of Wikipedia is the design of a community. Wikipedia is a social innovation, not a technology innovation. It is a human dialogue and conversation: all the rules are social, all about dialogue and about humans making decisions. We don't use any automation of the voting process."[8]

Wikipedia is breaking new organizational ground as a network organization that is fostering community as it grows. As Wikipedia communities grow, some are reaching a threshold where the community has difficulty "enabling and facilitating positive behavior," as Jimmy Wales describes it.[9] There are times when the core community faces tough choices and decides to say, "We appreciate your work, but you just cannot continue to behave this way." This form of leadership is tough, but it is necessary to keep the community's core values intact. The ability to flex includes the courage to decide that some behavior just doesn't fit and some forms of flexibility are too flexible. The values of Wikipedia are firm, but the structure is flexible.

Managing networked communities like Wikipedia means dealing with dilemmas. When Wikipedia was small, Jimmy Wales was the single decision maker when the hard choices had to be made, and he referred to himself as a "benevolent dictator" in a networked world. Now, with its incredible and rapidly growing scale, Wales thinks of his leadership as more like a "constitutional monarchy," where he rarely needs to intervene and almost all of the tough decisions are made by the core communities. Staying flexibly firm is an ongoing challenge.

A Story of Cell Phones in Caracas

FORESIGHT: *People who are poor need connectivity*

INSIGHT: *An expensive service can be reimagined to be affordable in poor regions*

ACTION: *Create an affordable cell phone for text and voice*

I was in Caracas in 2006, doing home visits and shop-alongs with low-income people in the barrios—which are essentially slums. How might a company provide products or services to areas like the barrios in Caracas in a way that helps the local area *and* provides a sustainable model for ongoing success (for both the local community and the company) beyond just a short-term contribution? Gifts to the developing world are wonderful, but they are usually not sustainable over long periods. How might corporations help seed long-term positive results?

There is a growing literature and experience focusing on the "bottom of the pyramid," as this segment is starting to be called by the business world. Low-income consumers and shoppers are a potential source of long-term growth for companies, but they also offer an opportunity to do good while doing well. C. K. Prahalad is best known for his writing and activities in this area.[10] There is a research center at the University of North Carolina business school that does case studies of bottom-of-the-pyramid business innovations.[11] Ashoka is an ongoing program that provides seed money in support of innovative ideas in social entrepreneurship.[12] The Grameen Bank, which I discussed in Chapter 3, is perhaps the best known, and it has had a dramatic impact. My purpose here is not to review this growing stream of literature and impact of the programs but to provide a taste of this intriguing market, using Caracas cell phones as an example.

Local people from higher socioeconomic levels and visitors from the north tend to glance up at the Caracas barrios and see them as one large slum. However, local people told me that there are over three hundred distinct slums in Caracas, not just one big one. The barrios of Caracas cling precariously from hills surrounding a sprawling central city that has no apparent center. The wealthy people of Caracas are sharply separated from the much larger population of poor people. When encountering the barrios, Northern eyes tend to see poverty, decay, and danger. Although these strongly negative perceptions of the barrios are accurate in a way, more perceptive southern eyes see much more, and they see more completely. Local people see vibrancy, emotion, love, and growth. Of course, they also experience the poverty, decay, and danger— but with a very different frame around what they see.

Ed Jardine, the leader of the Andean Marketing Development Organization for Procter & Gamble and the leader for the company's Latin America low-income consumer strategy, uses a photograph of the barrios to introduce the area to company employees, as well as to visitors from the north. He asks people what they see, and they usually answer with words like *poverty, unrest, instability, decay*, and *risk*. He then reveals that the picture they have been looking at is upside down. Northern eyes frame this picture as one mass of poverty, so undifferentiated that they cannot even see that the picture is upside down. We don't see the details at first glance, yet the details are the source of energy in the barrios. There are many things going on in the barrios, but rich outsiders tend to see only a mass of poverty.

In the barrios of Caracas, about 75 percent of the people have no access to banking as we know it in the north. It is a day-to-day, mostly cash economy. Many of the homes in the barrios are constantly under construction, one room or one small improvement at a time, with unplanned growth, governed by family needs or by money coming in or going out. One family I visited, for example, had to choose between cement and food during an urgent family race to beat the rainy season. They chose cement and lived on less until their new room was covered.

Basic infrastructure (conventional landline telephones, water, electricity, sewage treatment) is crude and cannot be counted upon. The people of the barrios live in a demanding world, but they figure out ways of living, growing, and being happy in a world of constant personal and family risk. (Yes, there is considerable evidence of joy—in spite of the intense poverty.) In most of these cramped homes, there's not much money, and there is not much room to stock anything. The turnover is rapid. People in the barrio can't afford to make mistakes, and when they do, the mistakes can cost them dearly. Tangible benefits and immediate results are valued highly. Risk is everywhere. Nothing is sound or solid in the barrios.

Entertainment, however, is a big part of life in the barrios. A frequent saying I heard during my visit: "Venezuelans celebrate everything." If you scan the hillside, you see satellite dishes—reaching out to the wider world—sprinkled among the partially built structures. If you look in the homes, you see televisions and boom boxes—sometimes more than one of each in the same household. When I was there, the World Cup was underway, and interest, especially in the Brazil team (Venezuela did not qualify), was intense. Although baseball dominates sports in Venezuela, football fever takes over at World Cup time. Most households and most stores had live links to the World Cup, the news from which fed ongoing conversations about the beautiful game.

Kids are the future, and children are a source of constant hope in the barrios. While many people in the barrios seem to be at peace with their own lot in life, they want better for their kids. In the households I visited, the mother is the bedrock of the family, and the dreams are about the children. Their focus is on children and family—in the midst of a daily world where many things can go wrong. It's a day-to-day world, except with respect to the children.

Presently in Caracas, as in many parts of the developing world, there is strong anti-American sentiment. This political environment adds tension to the dilemma of reaching low-income people with products or services that they will value. The local government does not trust American companies, yet trust is critical to reaching potential consumers. In a situation like this, it is difficult to know just where to start.

What might a company do to develop a viable ongoing business in a place like the Caracas barrios, while still contributing to the social good in the community? I'm intrigued by the example of cell phones. Cell phones were initially bought mainly in the wealthy north, and not so long ago, cell phones were a status symbol, even there. Now, just a few years later, cell phone sales are raging in Latin America, Africa, China, and pretty much all parts of the developing world. Quite to my surprise, nearly all of the households in the Caracas barrios already have cell phones. Nearly all of the people in the barrios have access to cell phone calling, at a rate they are willing to pay.

Cell phone providers have redesigned their service plans to reach low-income people. Payment schemes in the form of advance payment, sometimes on cards, allow poor people to pay what they can, to chunk the cell phone service into smaller, more affordable pay-in-advance pieces—without reliance on credit, banking, or monthly billing accounts. In addition, all around the barrios, street corner vendors with cell phones on tables fill in the mix, offering one call at a time for a fee to passersby. These vendors provide the local equivalent of a pay phone on a street corner, since pay phones are rare in Caracas. And, of course, cell phones are more than phones for calling: most are used for sending and receiving text messages, and some of these devices are also used for Internet connection. At this time, most of the potential Internet services are unused or underused in developing countries, but the platform is there—once the needs, wants, and services are matched.

Cell phone services have an inherent emotional attraction in the barrios: they enhance human connections, and human connections are what the barrios are all about. Social networks, especially family networks, are critical to the local culture. Emotional connections have always been most important in the barrios—a sense of linkage to family and friends—and cell phones help people feel connected to one another, often with a very high rate of frequency. If you experience a downturn in your life, and there are many downturns in the barrios, an emotional connection to friends or family means a lot. Cell phones are a new technology supporting an ancient social networking need: the need for a sense of human connection.

Cell phone services in the developing world are growing rapidly, and very profitable businesses are taking shape. Of course, it is still not clear how the "doing good" and "doing well" dimensions of these businesses will balance out. It is always possible that there will be exploitation of poor people by some companies. But there is also the real potential to provide constructive social connectivity, as well as connectivity to the global Internet world, at a fair and affordable price for people in the barrios—people whose lives will be enhanced because of these new services.

What other products or services besides cell phones might be offered to low-income people like those in the Caracas barrios, using a business model that works through the dilemma of doing good while doing well? Foresight about poverty is vivid, and insight about what companies might do is growing—with a growing number of interesting actions to consider.

The Story of the Omidyar Network

FORESIGHT: *The gap between the rich and the poor is growing*
INSIGHT: *People who are poor can create sustainable markets*
ACTION: *Create a unique investment strategy*

The conditions in the Caracas barrios highlight a crucial dilemma zone in our forecast: poverty in the developing world. Whereas many looked at the poorest of the poor and saw hopelessness, Pierre Omidyar, like Muhammad Yunus, saw opportunity. However, Omidyar wasn't interested in making small low-profit loans to individuals. He didn't share Yunus's social vision of helping the poor one by one. Rather, he wanted to create sustainable markets that ultimately would benefit everyone. Omidyar's launch into fame began in 1995, when the young software engineer created what became eBay. Omidyar has great faith in free markets, as conceived by Adam Smith, and he envisions a "perfect market" of complete transparency that will create a sustainable *and* just economy.

Omidyar's vision for the poorest of the poor is economic self-empowerment, whereby acting in a free market, the poor can realize their potential to make a difference. As this is happening, the local economy grows, stabilizes, and connects with other burgeoning economies, ultimately supporting the poor and making profits for outside investors. In this way, everyone wins. "We believe that business can be a tool for social good. Microfinance has already shown that enabling the poor to empower themselves economically can be good business."

He founded the Omidyar Network, which makes for-profit investments in companies and organizations. It aims to support local economies at a structural level, monitoring the health of the economic system. It tries to ensure equal access to information, rich connections, and a sense of ownership among participants—conditions necessary for people to assume control of a healthy economy. Meanwhile, as the economy grows, investors profit, which encourages further investment in a cycle Omidyar envisions as revolutionizing the developing world and its connections with the developed world.

Omidyar saw a slightly different dilemma than Yunus did. Omidyar focused not on individuals but on the community and its surrounding economy. The economy needs financial support and a clear strategy for sustainability. The opportunities bring top investors and attention. They also encourage innovation.

When Tufts University—Omidyar's alma mater—came asking for donations, Omidyar gave a hundred million dollars. However, he added a crucial condition—the principal must be dedicated to investments in microfinance, and the university could collect all the profits. As Omidyar says, "Kill two birds with one stone — support the alma mater and support the mission [of microfinance]."[13] Like Omidyar, many companies are exploring ways to tackle in one strategy the two goals of doing good and doing well.

The Story of a Healthy Food Dilemma

FORESIGHT: *Health will be an important filter for food-purchase decisions, but taste will still be important.*

INSIGHT: *Campbell's should focus on nourishing lives*

ACTION: *Implement the Campbell's Strategy*

In 2005, Campbell's Soup executives looked at the marketplace for their products and thought ten years ahead. As part of this process, they concluded that healthy, portable, and nutritious eating will be an important driver for the food industry. They also concluded that Campbell's should be at the center of this space.

The future of food will go to those providers who do not view taste and nutritional value as either/or choices. Rather, the most successful foods will be both tasty and nutritious. In the health economy, more and more consumers will use health as a filter to evaluate products and services for purchase. Food companies must engage in the dilemma of creating healthy foods that taste good.

Campbell's Soup has a strong brand, and most consumers already expect the Campbell's products to be nutritious. Campbell's wants to keep growing, however, to reach a wider range of consumers with portable, nutritious, and easy-to-prepare food. In some cases, it has products that are perceived as healthy but not very tasty or not much fun. In other cases, it has products—such as those with high sodium content—that present health questions, which are an important factor for some consumers.

The Campbell's introduction in 2006 of a sea salt that contains half the sodium—but still has the same taste—is a major improvement in the eyes of many consumers who are watching their sodium intake but still want tasty food. Salt intake is not a major health issue for most people, but it is a critical issue for some—and it is not easy to know whether you are sensitive or not. It is clear, however, that salt improves the taste of soup. Consumers say they want less salt, but if the taste is not there, they don't buy as much soup.

For example, one of the key strategic choices regarding winning when faced with the dilemma of healthy or tasty food is whether to emphasize bold new products or to go slowly and gradually improve the health criteria without making major taste tradeoffs. This choice is a delicate one for companies. Bold new products usually fail unless they can offer new health benefits without changing the taste—as with the Campbell's sea salt innovation. Gradual improvements, such as the gradual reduction in sodium that has been going on with salty snacks for more than a decade, may not be recognized.

The Campbell's USA leadership team developed a destination statement, thinking ten years ahead. The focus was on where they wanted to be as a brand and as a product line in ten years. The essence of this destination is the slogan "Nourishing people's lives everywhere, everyday." Around this core statement, specific dimensions of success were developed, including measures that could be used to track their progress. This process was a useful approach to strategic foresight, where Campbell's began with a careful analysis of where they wanted to be in ten years. From that destination statement, they could work backward to figure out what they needed to do between now and ten years from now in order to reach their destination.

The forecast of external future forces happened next: what are the external forces of change that could have major impacts on the company's destination? Basically, this is a matter of evaluating which waves of change it should ride and which waves of change it should avoid getting hit by. The following are some of the driving forces that will affect the challenge of creating portable healthy food:

- Empowered people are more likely to take charge of their own health, to make decisions about which foods are best for them while still looking for foods that taste great.

- The grassroots economy provides new opportunities for products and services that appeal to consumers with individual needs, consumers such as those with chronic diseases that they must manage over long periods of time.

- Empowered consumers will want to share their insights about food and their actions, and they will use smart networking to do this exchange. Brands can benefit from these exchanges but are also vulnerable to them if consumers perceive that the brands are not performing. Smart networks also extend the R & D process for large firms, to provide new opportunities for innovation.

- Health values will be basic to consumers' decisions about food as food comes to be seen as an important ingredient to health, as well as a possible response to illness. For example, generations of kids have grown up with a trust that chicken soup is good for colds.

- Advocacy groups at the polarizing extremes will be pressing for easy answers to the complicated dilemmas of tasty and nutritious food. Food companies need effective ways to engage with advocacy groups across a wide spectrum of concerns. These groups circulate both sophisticated information and misinformation.

Food is basic to health in ways that are not fully understood. Over the next ten years, the food marketplace will contain many more choices that mix nutrition and taste. Foresight can provide a context that helps companies create their own particular role in this marketplace.

A Carbon Tax?

FORESIGHT: *Our vehicles are contributing to global warming in massive ways*

INSIGHT: *Citizens would like to "be green" if they can do it without giving up their cars*

ACTION: *Offer the TerraPass service*

TerraPass allows people to purchase carbon offsets. The carbon offset compensates for the CO_2 emissions of driving and flying—two specific ways that consumers contribute directly to global pollution and warming.

The average American driving a Honda Civic puts close to 8,000 pounds of CO_2 into the atmosphere every year. A round-trip flight from San Francisco to Chicago puts close to 1,500 pounds into the atmosphere. Are you worried at all about your impact on the environment?

Most Americans would answer yes. Are you willing to give up your car or forego your flights? Almost everyone would answer with a resounding NO! We like the environment, but we can't live without our cars. TerraPass mediates these conflicting desires. It also generates revenues that can be used to counteract the negatives. You can purchase a small pass to offset your pollution. Your money supports clean-energy programs that reduce CO_2 levels in the atmosphere.

In an experiment, TerraPass has even partnered with Ford to create an environmentally conscious drivers program, a partnership that flies in the face of typically antagonistic relationships between environmentalist groups and car companies. Rather than seeing each other as enemies, both saw an opportunity to do good while doing well.

Many people, however, doubt the long-term viability of TerraPass. How can the company be "offsetting" pollution? Do its investments actually translate into environmental impacts? TerraPass is still a work in progress, but it is an interesting effort—even if it doesn't succeed.

TerraPass presents itself as socially responsible, affordable, and effective. TerraPass capitalizes on the fact that people are beginning to understand themselves as part of a wider economic and environmental system. Behavior has consequences, which should have responsibilities attached to them. TerraPass essentially takes a practice currently used by governments and major corporations (carbon offsetting) and brings it directly to the consumer level. People like convenience, and TerraPass is an easy, straightforward way to absolve pollution guilt, if nothing else. We expect more efforts like this as foresight about global warming leads to insight and action.

The examples in this chapter show that foresight can provoke both insight and inspired strategy. The specific ways in which this insight emerges is, of course, both varied and unpredictable but there are many models from which to learn.

9 Flexing and Flexibility

> Climbing the organizational hierarchy is no longer
> like climbing stairs in a stable structure. The stairs
> have become rope ladders, with managers clinging
> desperately for balance. Organization Man is changing
> into Spider Woman.
> —Robert Johansen and Rob Swigart,
> *Upsizing the Individual in the Downsized Organization*

Leaders need new abilities to flex in response to challenges they cannot predict. Among these are the abilities to use flexible organizational networks and to create new ones if necessary. Organizations must be flexibly firm—flexible, but guided by a firm understanding of their own beliefs, values, and responsibilities. This chapter introduces, describes, and advocates for flexing and flexibility—for both leaders and for organizations. Chapter 10 provides real-world examples of flexible firms.

Economies of scale (where bigger is almost always better) are giving way to economies of organization, where you are what you organize, inside—and especially outside—your organizational boundaries. This chapter focuses on the organization of workplace and workspace, where dealing with dilemmas will actually happen.

Flexing is necessary to be able to respond without a script, to be able to keep your balance and direction—even when there is no order around you. Flexing is the process of engaging with dilemmas by stretching (as in exercise) and sensing what is happening and what could happen.

Organizations are essentially networks of people. Kathi Vian, IFTF's leader for the annual Ten-Year Forecast, usually puts it this way: "In a networked world, you have to take very good care of your relationships." We've always had social networks, but now our networks are amplified and are increasingly virtual—in addition to being physical. Flexing is largely about relationships in a complex mix of media. These days, we all have many more people than before with whom it is possible to establish and maintain relationships. Of course, not all of these many relationships will work for all the parties involved. The new media world introduces new possibilities for close relationships at great distances, but new toxic relationships are also possible. We need new skills to "take care" of our positive relationships while we still "take care" to stay away from those that become toxic.

Corporations are often referred to as *firms,* even though they are becoming increasingly less firm and more *flexible.* The organizational context is shifting and twisting—but most organizations still consist of a network of contributors, a social network that can support the flexible firm. Even though social networks are not new, what is new is the flexible network environment within which social networks can be discovered, nurtured, and grown. The tools for social networking are coming of age; tools with powerful capabilities.

The organizational form for the future will be more like a network than a hierarchy, although hierarchies won't disappear. There is no single center in the network organizations; there are as many possible centers as there are network nodes. The action is at the intersections and the edges. Such a structure is just right for dealing with dilemmas.

Leaders must have the ability to flex: the wherewithal to maintain a clear direction and then to decide where, when, and how to work. Fortunately, the next generation of workers wants even more flexibility and more choice—and they are ready to navigate the work/private life dilemmas implied by this increasingly networked world.

Leading requires an ability to flex, to draw new connections with new media as well as to stretch the boundaries of what we think of as a firm. Nobody controls organizations that function like networks, but they can be woven into varied patterns and flexed without losing strength. We introduced the concept of the "fishnet organization" in 1994,[1] but this kind of organization (now called many different things) is much more widespread now than it was then.

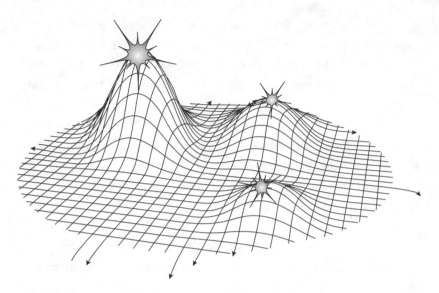

9.1 The Fishnet Organization

All the many forces of organizational change are having one major seismic effect: they are flattening the corporate structure. Hierarchies haven't gone away, but they are changing in fundamental ways . . . what replaces the monolithic corporation is what we call the fishnet organization.

Imagine a net laid out on a dock. If you grab a node and lift, the rest of the net lattices nicely under it. A temporary hierarchy appears as long as you hold up the node, with layers consistent with how high you lift the node and the width of the mesh. The hierarchy disappears when you lay the net down. Pick up another node, another soft hierarchy appears.[2]

Since 1994 the tools for growing fishnet organizations have improved dramatically. The fishnet organization is becoming the basic medium for organizational innovation and strategic leadership. Leaders must now develop their own abilities to flex and to create organizations that can flex with them. (See Figure 9.1 for a graphical representation of the fishnet organization.)

DEVELOPING YOUR ABILITY TO FLEX

Flexing is like the freedom that a musician has to improvise within the rhythmic structure of a particular song. Music in most genres is more structured than it sounds: there are clear patterns within which improvisation can happen. Usually, there is a clear direction, as well as someone (usually the drummer) who is setting the beat. But there can be lots of room for improvisation, even in highly structured arrangements. In music, what I call "flexing" might be called "riffing" or "going on a ride."

In most organizations, there are distinct values and legal requirements. Organizational structures and responsibilities are both explicit and implicit. The outside world, however, is not necessarily governed by the same principles. Organizations cannot assume that their ways of working will be followed by others. Often, organizations—particularly those with high values—have to struggle to sustain a responsible and orderly practice in a chaotic world. Flexing skills need to be tempered by an organization's sense of direction, similar to the way that musical improvisation happens within a melodic direction of keys, chords, and progressions.

In a corporation, people have at least some mandatory direction that comes from the corporation's legal responsibilities, its principles, and its management. Individuals often have great flexibility, however, with regard to how their daily work is conducted within the firm's direction and intent. The more senior an individual is, the more freedom he is likely to have to set direction and interpret the way that direction applies in a particular situation.

How can we help one another be more successful—to tune for the world of mixed generation dilemmas, to move from problem solving to engagement with the dilemmas of our marketplace and society?

Institute for the Future's ongoing research on cooperative systems has yielded a useful set of "tuning levers" that can be used to design and evaluate organizational structures.[3] Each of the seven tuning levers is employed below to help understand flexing and flexibility:

STRUCTURE.   Like the cord on a fishnet, network structures are strong but they are flexible. The number and pattern of the nodes on the net are critical to its strength and flexibility. Insurgents in Iraq, for example, use loosely structured networks that are like fishnets and are extremely resistant to attack. "Attack any single part of it, and the rest carries on largely untouched. It cannot be decapitated, because the insurgency, for the most part, has no head."[4] Paul Baran is an engineer who helped develop packet switching, the core technology of the Internet. Curiously, Baran's initial assignment at Rand Corporation was to develop a network architecture that would resist nuclear attack. At the time, telecommunications networks were centralized so that if any part of the network was attacked, the entire network would go down. Packet switching, still the core technology of the Internet, is an architecture that continues to live even if parts of the network are destroyed. The Internet has no center, and it grows from the edges. Network organizations—especially those that make heavy use of the Internet—reflect a similar networked structure.

RULES.   Flexible firms work best with only a few rules, but those rules must be followed religiously. Principles, rather than rules, work best in the context of network organizations, since they provide both clarity of direction and intent and are delivered with flexibility. The most successful networked organizations are principles-based, but they do have a few strong rules. In Dee Hock's "chaordic" organizational structure (part chaos, part order), principles provide the primary glue that holds the network together, but there can be a small number of central rules that can never be violated.[5] The small number of rules are firm, but the principles allow for flexing.

RESOURCES.   The key resource need in network organizational structures is for dependable, strong, and flexible infrastructure — to make communication possible across the network. Typically, information technologies and electronic networks provide the (usually virtual) "cord" that connects the nodes on the network together. The Forecast Map inside the book jacket highlights the wide range of cooperative technologies now available for use by network organizations. I first used what was then called "computer conferencing" in the early1970s, in the early days of the Internet, back when it was called the ARPANET. For more than thirty years, scientists, and now others, have developed, tested, and redesigned a wide range of tools to link interpersonal networks across wide distances. What we used to call "computer conferencing" is similar to what is now called a wiki. Electronic networking tools, while still challenging, are more powerful, easier to use, and cheaper than when these networking experiments began.

THRESHOLDS.   Scale thresholds are critical in the life of network organizations, since small groups are typically more cohesive than large ones. Thresholds of organizational scale allow networks to grow and amplify their impacts, but they also create critical challenges as the network grows. Wikipedia is now breaking new ground in terms of global network scalability.

FEEDBACK.   Network organizations need feedback to learn what is working and what is not. Feedback often comes informally by word of mouth, but the lessons need to be shared across the network in order for organizational learning to occur. Networks often extend over the boundaries between work and private life, and individuals need feedback to set those boundaries. Ellen Galinsky, president of the Families and Work Institute, has concluded that work life balance is an impossible goal. Instead, she coaches people to develop their navigation skills, to find their way through the fixed and variable forces all around us, within the firm and outside it.[6] Feedback should contribute to navigation for network members, just as navigation instruments guide a sailor through an archipelago.

MEMORY.   Network organizations are challenged to know what they know, to remember and share what someone in the network has learned. Memory in network organizations is often decentralized, and formal methods for organizational memory (like databases) often do not capture the vitality of the knowledge being stored. Memory needs to be fluid in a network organizational structure. The army and some nonmilitary agencies use After Action Reviews (more on AARs in Chapter 11) as a discipline for learning from experience, but a key finding from that long experience is that informal exchange of lessons learned is much more effective than a formal central database.

IDENTITY. Network members may or may not have shared collective identities: some networks are formal, with a clear collective identity; others are informal with dispersed identities. Sometimes, group identities are present but decentralized in network nodes or patterns of nodes. Identity can leverage and magnify growth of the overall network, however, as well as provide a sense of meaning and belonging for the network members. "Cellular churches," for example, are network-style organizations with a religious purpose. Evangelist Rick Warren uses small groups to nurture a large network-style organizational structure from the bottom up "to create a church out of a network of lots of little church cells—exclusive, tightly knit groups of six or seven who meet in one another's homes during the week or worship and pray."[7] These small groups become nodes on the larger network, but the vitality is sustained at both the small-group and large-group levels. Although his approach is controversial, Warren offers a clear identity for members, apparently without the sense of self-righteousness that is sometimes found in conservative religious groups. He also provides the direction of a "purpose-driven life." The energy starts and is sustained at the level of the small-group network cells. The sense of identity comes from personal, small-group, and large-group experiences. In a chaotic world, a purpose-driven life is attractive but difficult to sustain.

FLEXIBLE PLACES

Flexing and flexibility emerge from answers to these questions:

- **Where** does the real work of network organizations get done?
- **What** is the role of our offices and other physical places?
- **When** are we "working" and when are we "not working"?
- **How** might we work in the future, and how can we prepare ourselves for network flexibility?

Organizing, nurturing, and sustaining a network requires basic skills that begin with deciding which medium is best for the situation. In-person, face-to-face meetings in the office (or the church or the home or the community center or any other physical place) are only one option, and the array of alternatives is growing increasingly rich and attractive. Indeed, our definition of *office* is changing within the firm—and in the world around the firm. As the firm becomes more flexible, the role of the office is likely to change. Gradually, organizations are coming to think of *office* as a flexible array of activities—not necessarily a fixed place.

Perhaps we need to change office from a noun to a gerund: officing is perhaps a better word for the activities that are necessary to create a strong organization.[8] Officing is flexibility. A fixed office—especially an expensive office with permanent walls and a long lease—has little flexibility. Officing is all about connectivity and culture. An office reflects the culture of an organization, but it also shapes that culture. Offices provide a place for in-person communication, which can be great, but they also have limitations.

Many organizational cultures still implicitly assume that most work gets done "at the office," which is either a physical office location or a client's office location. Many senior managers still think they know that their employees are working because they see them working. There are new models, however. An extreme example is the consulting firm Accenture, with more than 100,000 people but no operational headquarters and no formal branch offices. The chief executive has neither a permanent desk nor a permanent office.[9]

Offices tell a story in subtle and explicit ways: traditional offices in prestigious downtown locations used to be clear statements that your company was successful and that you were in it for the long run. But office stories are changing. Will the next generation of workers be less anchored to offices and more committed to flexibility? Will next-generation clients be less concerned about where the work gets done and more concerned about different measures of success?

Might some customers decide against any firm that "wastes" its resources on what they perceive as fancy offices in high-rent districts? Rising real estate costs are bringing this issue to a head, but so are the increasingly viable and proven options for virtual work. Network flexibility is now becoming both attractive and affordable. Expensive property and elaborate physical offices are becoming increasingly hard to justify for many organizations. It is much easier to get there early and compete if you can be flexible regarding where you work.

Sometimes, external events force a change in how organizations consider their own in-person and virtual identities. In the 9/11 attack, Deloitte suddenly lost use of a New York office, a major location, for more than one year. The resulting period of forced virtual work is having major effects on how Deloitte now chooses to work with clients, effects it is only now beginning to realize. It is learning new ways of working virtually and at client sites, and it is reconsidering what would constitute the ideal Deloitte office. Now it has new office designs—none of which look much like a traditional office. Deloitte recognizes several dilemmas regarding virtual and physical work identities, and each has its own challenges:

- It is difficult yet extremely important to find optimal mixes of media to connect people in useful ways, both in person and through virtual media, for a variety of different tasks.

- Managers need to focus on ways—other than physically seeing them working—of evaluating output from employees as they work in a variety of different media.

- Managers must recognize that the way works get done is as important as what work gets done. Especially in a regulated industry, it does matter how work gets done, so output cannot be an exclusive measure.

- The firm needs to develop people in an ongoing way using a variety of media, with the choice of media depending on personal lifestyles and needs—in addition to regulatory requirements for in-class training.

Deloitte does not require workers to choose whether to work in an office *or* through virtual media. Rather, it assumes that most workers will work through *both* in-person and virtual media using firm-approved criteria for choosing which medium is best for a particular business application. Deloitte communicates its principles of flexibility and choice as well as the tools that it offers to help people work that way.

One external factor that could accelerate the growth of flexible places is the discomfort of travel. In the VUCA world airline travel is much less convenient and is sometimes downright uncomfortable. How much worse does travel need to get before companies say "enough!" and start to emphasize alternatives for at least some of their travel. Of course, many people will still want to meet in person, but online media offer many new possibilities to be present without being there.

FLEXIBLE MEDIA

IFTF first developed an early version of Figure 9.2 more than twenty years ago, when teleconferencing and groupware were just becoming practical. This simple map displays the basic options of place (same place or designated place) and time (same time or different time). A physical office is a place where face-to-face meetings (same time, same place) are possible. This foursquare model summarizes our basic choices, which are richer, more reasonable, and less expensive than just a few years ago. Figure 9.2 illustrates the basic options for working in a network organization in terms of place, time, and tools.

Our research suggests that most executives travel more than they need to, and they often travel at the wrong times. This chapter will suggest rules of thumb for deciding which tools are best for the purpose, including one of the most important decisions a leader must make: when do I travel to go there in person? Leaders today (and even more so tomorrow) must be able to nurture and sustain trust through multiple media—not relying only on in-person presence (although both will still be useful on occasion).

Place plays an important role in this media mix. What does place offer? What does place constrain? Adjacency is a scarce resource in physical architecture, since space limitations don't allow everyone to be adjacent to all the good things they would like to be near. In a seamlessly mobile world, however, more flexible adjacencies are possible, since

wireless
seamless mobility

blogs
wikis

IM
video chat
voice-over IP

24 hour offices
virtual work

offices
cafés

Different Time
Designated Place

Same Time
Designated Place

Any Time
Any Place

Different Time
Same Place

Same Time
Same Place

9.2   Options for Communicating in a Networked Organization

DEFINITIONS

blog   short for "Web log," where one individual puts his or her views out and invites others to read or sometimes comment on them.

wiki   a group version of a blog.

IM   short for instant messaging, which allows simultaneous text messages in a corner of your screen.

video chat   a sort of video IM, where you can see someone on your screen and talk with him or her.

VoIP   short for "Voice over Internet Protocol," audio (like a telephone) carried over the Internet and increasingly easy and high quality.

seamless mobility   a concept developed by Motorola to describe the vision of wireless interconnection in a seamless and painless way.

wireless connectivity can allow people to be "next to" resources, even if the resources are physically distant.

Most people older than thirty still assume that face-to-face is the medium of choice whenever possible. As media richness has improved and the difficulties of in-person contact have increased (especially with globally scattered workforces), the unexamined assumption that face-to-face is best is being called into question.

The workforce of the next decade will be a rich and challenging mix of backgrounds and styles of work. Three needs are likely, all of which will affect choices regarding which medium to use in what situations:

- **Workers will need meaningful face-to-face engagement, in parallel to intense virtual communications.**   Paradoxically, the more time we spend communicating with others by way of machines (such as the phone, computer, or handheld), the more important face-to-face experiences become. In more than thirty years of research on travel/telecommunications tradeoffs, I have found little evidence that virtual media replace the need for in-person meetings—unless there is an intervening crisis or policy mandate. In short, the more people are linked electronically, the more they want to communicate in person. Electronic media extend human communications, but they rarely if ever replace the need for in-person exchange. In addition, the more time we spend working with distributed global colleagues, the more important local connections become.

- **The workforce will be characterized by deep diversity, on many dimensions.**   Most organizations will have an increasingly heterogeneous workforce in terms of age, nationality, race or ethnicity, and lifestyle. Immigration is changing the ethnic composition of the country, particularly the western and southern regions. Women are having children later in life, and the number of "traditional" households is declining. The aged live and work longer and more independently.

- **Network communication skills will become critical for leaders to master.**   Most of today's leaders lead through their abilities to communicate in person. Many have charisma and great ability

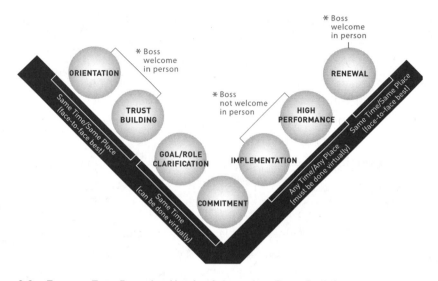

9.3   Face-to-Face Remains Key for Orientation, Trust Building, and Renewal (*Source:* IFTF, IFTF Team Performance Model, Alan Drexler and David Sibbett, 1999)

to bring people together—if they can be there in person. In a networked world, leaders need to present themselves electronically, through interactive media (in addition to mass media), and engage with their network members in a compelling fashion. These are not just new technologies; they are new media, and they require new communications skills.

A more peoplecentric office strategy can be designed to promote communication, engagement, and community among a company's workers. The challenge is to design the strategy for a labor force with increasingly diverse needs, expectations, and demands—from incoming digital youth to returning senior alumni.

Certainly, in-person meetings have great value for orientation, trust building, and renewal, as we summarize in Figure 9.3, a graphic that was first developed when we studied high-performance cross-cultural teams for the IFTF book GlobalWork and updated based on our recent research.[10] Electronic alternatives are improving rapidly, and it is becoming apparent that many forms of productive work can happen without people being together in person or in an office. The key decision is which medium (including face-to-face) is good for what purpose. Do you really need to be in an office to do this work? Is it desirable to be in an office to do this work, even if you would like to do so? Making intelligent choices like this is key to flexibility.

IFTF research, from across all our research domains, suggests an emerging transformation of work practices over the coming decade:

- The way workers will relate to space and place will be enabled by mobility, connectivity, and location-based services.

- The way workers will relate to one another and to clients will be shaped by increased collaboration, multilayered communication environments, and globally distributed work and talent.

- The ways we learn and create knowledge will be augmented by social software and collective intelligence.

Motorola's concept of "seamless mobility" is an inspirational vision of what anytime, anyplace work will be like in the future—perhaps the near future if everything comes together the way the Motorola and other providers are advocating.

The new Stata Center at MIT is an example of reimagining work space to include the notion of seamless mobility. William Mitchell, the dean of the MIT architectural school, describes the Stata Center this way:

> One of the important things about the Stata Center is that it explicitly takes advantage of the fact that a lot of work is mobilized. It understands that people are carrying around their laptops, everything is wirelessly connected, and you can sit down anywhere and work. So it provides a huge amount of unassigned space that can be appropriate in ad-hoc ways as needed for particular purposes. The whole point of that is the space has variety so you can find a quiet space when you need it, or you can find a more public space when you need it. Serendipity really depends on that. You don't get much serendipity if people are all sitting locked in their private offices staring at their computer screens!
>
> So the idea is to make a kind of ecosystem of diverse spaces where people are just encouraged to sort of grab a workspace wherever

they may need it—grab a working cluster, cluster around a white board, cluster around a café table, etc. And they can do it without losing connectivity.[11]

All of these shifts will take place within the context of a larger economic move toward the "sharing economy."[12] The growth of the sharing economy portends new ways of supporting network organizations.

In most organizations, it is not clear who "owns" media choice. Who decides which media are available for whom, in what situations? Several organizations are likely to be involved, and everyone has a stake in media choice. The information technology (IT) organization provides IT support. Real estate provides office space. Human resources (HR) organizations provide people and organizational development expertise—both of which are critical to media choice. And the organization's strategy implies media choice, because particular media configurations are best suited to particular strategic choices. Ideally, the choice ought to be made on criteria roughly in this order:

1. **Strategy.** Given the organization's strategy, which media mixes will provide optimal support for execution of the strategy? Strategy should be most important in guiding media choice.

2. **People.** Which mix of people can best carry out the strategy, and which media do those people prefer in order to perform at their best? HR should be involved in choosing people who can support the strategy.

3. **Media.** What physical and virtual media resources should be provided in order to support the people who will carry out the corporate strategy? In this sense, information technology and real estate should work together (ideally, they should be part of the same organization, reporting to the same executive) to decide on the appropriate media mix to provide. Office space is just one medium in an array of electronic and in-person possibilities.

Of course, in most organizations, Strategy, HR, IT, and real estate exist separately and rarely work together. The expanding powers of the new media give organizations a chance to rethink how they are organized.

DIGITAL YOUTH ARE TUNED FOR FLEXING

Baby boomers tend to see technology as either tools or toys or both. Digital youth see technology as an extension of themselves, and they often don't *see* technology much at all, they just assume it as a part of their being. Three underlying trends will shape the American workplace in the next decade, with the next generation of workers who are just now beginning to enter the workforce:

- **The digital youth are different.**   After more than a decade of widespread Internet use, studies indicate that youth are developing a wide attention range and a short attention span. That is, these youth are accustomed to a multimedia and multichannel learning style with frequent interruptions. On the positive side, they are skilled at sharing knowledge and creating social networks online. These skills are the basis for new forms of business practices and client services.

- **Many organizations will experience a shortage of young, skilled workers who are willing to work at wages they are willing to pay.**[13] Demand for a smaller pool of top talent will intensify at the same time that youth will bring new ways of working and learning into the workplace—challenging old models of work.

- **All players will have access to an increasingly robust infrastructure for support of virtual organizations on a global scale.**   Network organizations can be created easily now, with options for participation from all over the world. The technology is functional, proven, and cheap. Differentiation will come from the organizational skills with which these new media are used. Anyone can now go virtual, but the challenge is in how you go virtual, with what results.

Today's young people are indeed growing up with distinctly different formative media and technology experiences from those of previous generations. Their influence, in combination with other social and economic factors, will shape their workplace demands in the next decade. Corpo-

Digital Youth	Impact on Flexing and Flexibility

Workers have multimedia, multitasking, and flexible work styles.

The younger the employee, the more likely he or she is to favor a flexible work style.

Percent who do an activity all or most of the time while doing routine homework:

    Go online 60
    Listen to music 42
    Watch TV 32
    Chat via phone calls,
    IM, or e-mail 27
    Work with friends/
    classmates 23
    Play video/online games. . . 7

These workers will do best in lively, multifaceted workspaces that provide multiple channels of communication, including face-to-face.

Spaces are needed for real-time collaboration, both impromptu and planned.

Quiet spaces are needed, spaces that support focused work as well as private phone conversations.

The best spaces will highlight the presence of colleagues. Examples include open work environments and glass walls to enhance visual proximity.

Ubiquitous wireless Internet and phone access are needed.

Places are needed where television and music are appropriate, with and without headsets.

Workers want to set their own schedules, even if they have to work more.[14]

Most workers (58 percent) prefer a flexible work schedule, even if it exceeds forty hours a week, while only 42 percent say they would prefer a regular nine-to-six job.

Younger students (those eighteen to twenty-one) are even more likely to favor flexibility.

Deloitte's internal research findings suggest that a flexible work schedule is a key factor in employee retention, especially of women.

Work happens at all hours, in different places. The office is only one choice among several. Office must leverage its key advantage over other workplaces: it is the only place where colleagues congregate frequently.

Systems are needed that signal the presence of colleagues so that people know where others are — in or out of the office.

Spaces are needed that highlight the work community, with places for socializing, human warmth, and central meeting places.

continued on next page

Digital Youth	Impact on Flexing and Flexibility

Workers are more ethnically diverse and youth-oriented than before.

Physical environments should communicate diversity of the workforce and work processes; for example, spaces are needed that can be repurposed for different work needs and staff configurations.

Spaces should communicate the collaborative nature of the work process; for example, shared space rather than private space should be emphasized.

Family and private life is important, and workers have a commitment to making time for both work and fun.

Organizations should provide diverse spaces with zones for informal, ad hoc social interactions as well as zones for quiet, focused work.

Support is needed for work/life navigation decisions.

rations have the choice to be a step ahead in providing next-generation workers with the spaces and tools for productive flexibility and engagement. For example, the chart to the left and above summarizes recent research that Lyn Jeffery has done on the characteristics of entry-level professional services employees in the near future:

How might a *firm* become more flexibly firm, using physical offices as just one focal point among many possible focal points? Certainly the places where work gets done are already changing, as are the times at which work gets done. Leaders and managers will still supervise the outcomes of an individual's work, but seeing their employees working is not likely to be either possible or important.

Navigation of work and private life boundaries is becoming more difficult, especially since we have crossed the Blackberry Threshold—where the reach of "the office" is anyplace, anytime. Starbucks is a vivid example: it has created a "third place" (not home, not office) that reflects important elements of both work and leisure. One of the most provocative alliances in the past five years was the joint venture between Hewlett-Packard, T-Mobile, and Starbucks to create WiFi hot zones at most Starbucks locations. Now, a Starbucks café can for some customers be a mobile office, a flexible yet comforting and functional place. You can order your favorite drink and be relatively sure it will be prepared the way you like it while you connect to the WiFi world.

Of course, unintended consequences are lurking. For example, there has been a series of laptop robberies in San Francisco coffee shops. Thieves innovate, too, and they've learned that someone concentrating on a screen—often a very expensive screen—on an unattached device is a very tempting soft target. One San Francisco laptop theft occurred in a total of fifteen seconds, and when the surprised laptop owner stood up instinctively, he was stabbed. The thief was out of the coffee house before anyone noticed him, and he was never caught. We live in a world that is often threatening, even in—maybe especially in—our comfort zones.

Comfort zones can be virtual, and sometimes the virtual will be safer than the physical. Leaders of network organizations can create islands of coherence: bases for flexible and sensible action, with a feeling of comfort. Place plays an important role in coherence, but a fixed place—a comfortable fixed office that reflects success—is only one kind of comfort.

Will corporate offices become more like Starbucks cafés and less like the formal offices that still dominate our office landscape? Next-generation workers are certainly more likely to be comfortable and productive in a café atmosphere than an office atmosphere. Is there an alternative to "offices"? Cafés or play spaces perhaps? Something else we have yet to imagine?

The new flexibility clearly involves space, technology, and protocols for working. It exists at the functional intersection of real estate, IT, and HR—all linked by business strategy and customer needs. Leadership development will be played out at this intersection, since this is where we will work, where we will learn, and where we will grow. A critical element of leadership development is workspace design to optimize the ways in which that learning occurs, as well as the way in which our work is performed.

Network organizational structures are now being employed by a wide range of organizations, from corporations to NGOs to churches to terrorist networks to national and insurgent military organizations. Which are most advanced? Although performance is difficult to measure in this network world where many networks are invisible or only partially visible from the outside, it seems to me that the extreme groups are more network savvy than the moderate groups. This result makes sense because commitment provides the shared values, purpose, and meaning that can hold a network structure together. Without commitment from members, networks become limp.

As I argued earlier in this book, the VUCA world requires that we learn to be comfortable being uncomfortable. Offices as we know them are part of our current comfort zone, but the ground is shifting beneath our offices. We are already in an anytime, anyplace world.

Great leaders can make things look easy, but things rarely are. Leadership flexing is tough work—with a fun element on the good days. The mother of all flexing dilemmas is how to lead a network organization without getting tangled up in it.

10 Flexible Firms

Nothing in the world
is as soft, as weak as water.
Nothing else can wear away
the hard, the strong,
and remain unaltered.
Soft overcomes hard,
weak overcomes strong.
Everybody knows it,
nobody uses the knowledge.
—Lao Tzu, *Tao Te Ching*

This chapter builds on Chapter 9 and describes how the flexible firm is beginning to emerge. I include several real-world case studies of flexible firms and a vignette that stretches current experience into the future. This chapter gives a taste of what organizations and leaders can do to deal with dilemmas in creative and useful ways.

My purpose here is to bring the idea of the flexible firm to life. This chapter is only a beginning, of course, since the flexible firm is still being created, and new models are appearing all around us.

An Open-Source Flexing Story

IBM realized that the world was changing. What had worked for the company in the past was not going to work in the future. As IBM's hardware and software business declined, it began a dramatic transformation that has allowed it to become a different kind of company. While it still supports hardware and software businesses, it makes money off of services. It used to sell computers, but now it sells computer services. In order to go open source, you have to think with foresight and flexibility.

IBM learned that it can't make money from each new idea right away, but it is figuring out ways to leverage its ideas later in the process. Openness fuels innovation, with the potential for direct links to new business development. Open source for IBM includes:

- Co-production of value between competitors and users

- Celebration and incorporation of user-generated innovation

- Discovery of communities of interest and efficiencies among users, producers, distributors, partners, and employees

IBM has been able to create or participate in open-source or free zones where it gives away software in order to create a higher value competitive zone where it can offer services. It is cooperative and open in hardware and software but competitive in services. Essentially, it gives things away in order to grow a level playing field on which it is confident that it will win most of the time.

IBM faces a constant dilemma of both cooperating and competing with the same companies, depending on where they are in the cycle. Instead of being commoditized selling software and hardware with smaller and smaller margins, IBM shifted to licensing or even giving away basic platform tools (or co-developing them with competitors), but creating a high-value zone where it can compete in a world of much higher margins. In recent years, IBM has become much more collaborative and cooperative with its competitors and customers—as well as much less secretive. Big Blue has become much more of a network-style organization, providing a wide range of services.

IBM has now mounted a program to create a new academic discipline in services arts and sciences, in much the same way that it did in the late 1960s and early 1970s to help create the computer science discipline. This visionary move has value for both the economy and for IBM, since the new graduates from these programs will also become a labor pool for IBM to hire from.

IBM is creating new ways to win in the dilemma-laden world of computer services and systems. It went from selling customers a box to helping them manage the ongoing dilemmas of computer systems operations. It still positions its services as "solutions" but is interested in living solutions—not just one-time solutions. One-time solutions do not last for long in the world of computer systems and networks, because most solutions come with a need for ongoing support. Computers do solve specific problems, but they also create much larger dilemmas that need ongoing support.

The driving force of grassroots economics that was part of the Chapter 2 forecast will fuel growth of open source, as will smart networking. The future favors open source as a strong direction of change. Empowered users want open source; they want to influence the direction of the fields in which they are playing. IBM is a dramatic example of a slow-moving company of the past that saw change coming and transformed itself into a flexible firm in an impressive fashion.

An External R & D Flexing Story

Procter & Gamble's CEO, A. G. Lafley, has said publicly that more than half of P&G's new-product ideas should come from *outside* P&G. Chief Technology Officer Gil Cloyd is advocating a "connect and develop" strategy to draw on outside resources and innovations.

> When I began working with P&G in 1977, my first project was to assess how the Internet (then called the ARPANET) might be used to grow what was then called the "invisible college" of R & D scientists within P&G worldwide. P&G was then, and still is, one of the largest science-based companies in the world. In 1977, the assumption was that innovation needed to occur mostly inside the firm, with a proprietary orientation that protected new ideas and new products from competitors.
>
> It is remarkable indeed that, between 1977 and 2006, P&G has

moved from an internal orientation toward innovation to one
that is both internal and external — with an emphasis on outside
sources of innovation. The strategy is even discussed in an article
in the Harvard Business Review.[1] In 1977, it would have been
impossible to imagine P&G publishing its "new model for innovation" in the Harvard Business Review. Yet, in 2006, P&G's more
open strategy is completely consistent with the directions for
change summarized in Chapter 2. P&G's strategy is demonstrating
flexibility. Its innovation networks are flexible, but its corporate
values remain firm.

We are moving toward a much more open world. It is a both/and
world where intellectual property is still important, but the intellectual property is generated and managed in different ways from
the much more proprietary days of the past. Networks fuel this
new world.

In 1977, the ARPANET was still oriented toward defense contractors at university and government agency research sites. Most of
what went on was secretive, and some was classified. P&G wanted
to learn from this experience and apply it internally at P&G.

Over the past thirty years, network structures have made it
possible to create new networks for innovation, like the connect-
and-develop strategy suggested by P&G. Hierarchies haven't gone
away, and they still play a useful function, but they come and go
and are more flexible than before.

In a world of empowered consumers (the P&G mantra is "The consumer is boss") who are also deeply networked, innovation needs to be
connected to those networks—not isolated from them. Connect and develop is essentially a flexible networking strategy mounted by the
world's largest consumer products company to better link to its consumers and to outside sources of innovation.

A Geoweb Flexibility Story

As discussed in Chapter 2, the geoweb is the mixing of virtual and physical media to extend both our experience of the physical world and our

access to online resources. Walt Disney World is already mixing the physical experience of the park with virtual links and is focusing attention on both the technology and the human efforts to work with the technology to provide great experiences for guests (Walt Disney World customers). Certainly technology will play a role, and many kids already come to theme parks as digital natives who are deeply at home in digital worlds. This is a story of my experience with an early geoweb innovation at Walt Disney World in Orlando:

> Pal Mickey is a small Mickey Mouse stuffed animal that has a radio frequency (RF) reader in its nose and an ability to "talk" to the person who is holding him. As a guest goes around Walt Disney World, Pal Mickey gives updates on where the lines are shortest and points out local attractions that might be interesting to a guest. Pal Mickey also has jokes for the kids and a number of other verbal offerings that are only occasionally annoying for parents and almost always entertaining for kids.
>
> When I carried one of the early Pal Mickeys at Walt Disney World in Orlando, however, mine stopped working. I brought my sick Pal Mickey to a nearby Disney stand to see if they could help. The cast member (Walt Disney World employee) told me, "No problem, I'll give you a new Pal Mickey." I responded that I had developed a personal relationship with this Pal Mickey and was hoping she might be able to heal him—rather than giving me a new one. The cast member was taken aback at first, but then she smiled, winked at me, and said she'd take my Pal Mickey and be right back. She went behind a curtain and returned a few minutes later with a fully operational Pal Mickey.
>
> "We're in luck," she said, "I was able to find a doctor, and we were able to heal your Pal Mickey right here!"
>
> I realized that she may have replaced my Pal Mickey behind the curtain, but I was charmed nonetheless. She had lived up to her challenge as a Disney cast member: to provide each guest with a "magical experience." She also demonstrated that introducing virtual technology in a theme park is not an either/or choice

between technology and human interaction. As a guest, I had an experience of technology with a human touch.

Pal Mickey is a small and interesting step toward a geoweb-enabled theme park, a progression that will move from episodic interactions with guests to always on within the park (if the guest chooses) and the potential for immersive interactive experiences as a guest moves around the park. In this scenario, the theme park becomes like a game board, with amplified everything in a physical and virtual reality that is only beginning to be imagined with today's multiplayer games that combine virtual and physical worlds.

Kids are impatient and are used to working with multiple channels simultaneously. Theme parks are already stimulation rich, but the geoweb theme park could multiply and personalize the richness. A child, for example, could have one experience while the parent walking next to him has a very different experience.

Theme parks present new opportunities for all sorts of transformative entertainment. Just as massive multiplayer games are becoming the learning ground for workplace behavior in the future, geoweb theme parks could become the learning ground for creative linkages between the virtual and physical worlds. A large complex theme park will be able to offer both connected and escapist experiences—all in the same park at the same time.

The best technologies will become part of the landscape, part of the experience that is both reassuring to the parents and stimulating for the kids. The dilemma will be figuring out how to create magical theme park experiences that *also* employ virtual media as appropriate—without taking the guests or the cast members out of the park experience. How might technologies provide a great sense of safety for the parents while also providing thrills for the kids? We expect the linkages between physical and virtual to develop and become more engaging over the next decade.

This dilemma will be shaped by the geoweb, which will allow new possibilities to reimagine a theme park as a physical-virtual blend. Pal Mickey is just a beginning. Combine the geowebbed theme park with empowered and networked guests, and the experience could become even more magical. And theme parks may be the prototyping ground for experiences in other physical environments outside the park.

A Flexible Identity Story

In the emerging mix of physical and virtual worlds, corporations develop brands and online identities—but so do the people who work for corporations, either as full-time employees or as part of the broadening web of consultants, suppliers, alumni, and contractors that form the increasingly porous boundaries of the firm.

Most of all, leaders need to lead in both the in-person and virtual worlds. Each leader needs an online persona. The online persona is becoming increasingly important as our organizations become more distributed and leaders cannot "be there" in the traditional sense of being there in person most of the time.

An increasing number of employees—especially the twentysomethings or younger—are creating an online persona to go along with their real-world persona. What are the boundaries between a person's "work self" and his or her "personal self"? When you Google someone, you begin to see his or her online presence, and it may or may not be consistent with the self-image that person projects in the real world—or the image that his or her employer would like to see projected.

In the online world, of course, someone can adopt alternate personalities, avatars, handles, or presences that express another aspect of their personality that they may or may not want to share with others in other worlds—such as the world of their employer. The employer's dilemma is how to sort all of this out, not just in terms of potential problems for the company but also in terms of leadership and innovation opportunities. How does a company manage (you can't control) work and personal identities that are associated with your brand? The personal dilemma here is a tension between a person's virtual self (or selves) and their physical self. One does not solve this dilemma, since the worlds keep changing, as does the person and the organization(s) with whom they are working.

I offer a story from the near future, about a job interview and the personal dilemmas that are faced by this next-generation applicant for a job at a professional services firm as well as those faced by the baby boom partner who is interviewing him and trying to figure out what's going on. Notice the multiple identities that the job candidate demonstrates, in a context that is more complicated than it seems. Notice how the partner doing the interview gets increasingly confused, since he is not comfortable with virtual identities and doesn't know what to make of the job candidate. Still, the partner is intrigued:

> The partner produced his card. "Steve Argyce, rhymes with 'nice.' Which I'm not," he added. This was designed to throw the potential recruit off. "Sit down."
>
> The recruit, whose name was Winton Feyer, sat down and relaxed. Good. Steve approved. No reaction to his standard opening. He would be able to handle clients, who could easily turn demanding.
>
> Winton did, however, have spiked hair and an earring. Nothing ostentatious, nothing vulgar. No spikes through the chin, no safety pins in the eyebrows. Probably that fad was over, but the iPod earphones draped around his shoulder suggested long use, in a habitual manner.
>
> Warning flag, Steve noted. He probably spends most of his time playing *Everquest* or one of those other online games.
>
> Well, he'd majored in philosophy. There was nothing wrong with that, per se.
>
> Steve tented his fingertips and leaned forward slightly. "What philosophers do you particularly like?"
>
> "None," the boy answered. "Too much head-in-the-clouds, too much muddy thinking. I understand them, most of them, but I don't really like them."
>
> "Really?" Steve made it sound skeptical, even critical.
>
> "Really," Winton stated, glancing around the room.
>
> Steve suddenly felt self-conscious. It was such a typical hotel business center meeting room, with its neutral tones and paint-

ings of sailboats on the wall. He quickly suppressed the feeling. He was the interviewer. "Do you play computer games?" he asked.

Winton almost smiled. "Of course. Doesn't everyone?"

"Ah." Steve made a note on the file. "Which one?" Not that he would know the difference. Already the candidate was losing ground.

"Well, it's not really a computer game, but I'm into *Second Life*."

"I see. *Second Life*. You don't consider that a bit too much head-in-the-clouds, as you say? Muddy thinking, I believe was your term."

"Not at all."

"Why is that?"

"Because I have a small business there."

"Business?"

"Yeah. I offer financial services."

"I don't think I understand. This is a game we're talking about?"

"People have businesses in *Second Life*, and most of the online games. Some of them are very successful. They have bars, design clothes, the make things other players buy. But to build a business there you have to earn money, and it takes time to build up capital, just like in the real world. Sure, you can buy *Second Life* money online for real money, of course. But it seemed to me that for it to be realistic people should be able to borrow money in the game world, same as in the real one. So I started a financial services company. I started with small business loans. Did pretty well. Now I have an investment company."

Steve was leaning forward and had to force himself to relax. "An investment company," he repeated. "In the game?"

"Sure. We do venture capital, leveraged buyouts, mergers and acquisitions, that sort of thing. And of course we offer accounting services. If we didn't, I wouldn't be here, would I?"

"I suppose not. But you said we?"

Winton shrugged. "Sure. Business got too big for one person, especially one who had to write a senior thesis on Kierkegaard, so I took on some partners and started a network."

Steve chewed on his lower lip and read a few lines of the file while he considered how to continue. It wasn't that the interview was out of control, not really, but it was taking some surprising turns. Should he ask about the partners, or ask about Kierkegaard? He closed the file. "How many partners do you have in your network?"

Winton smiled. "Honestly, I don't know."

"You don't know how many partners you have?" Steve asked absently. He had already closed the file folder and begun planning to gracefully terminate the interview.

"No. It depends on whether you mean in the real world, or online."

In spite of himself, Steve said, "I don't understand."

"Well, most people, though I'm not one of them, have more than one identity in the virtual world. They may have several avatars in there, each a different character with different interests, maybe different genders. So some of my partners may in fact be the same person in the real world. I suspect three are at least doubling. One I'm pretty sure is a triple. So if in *Second Life* I have fourteen partners, in the real world there are likely many fewer. By doubling like that, they make more money."

Steve was trying to imagine one of the partners in his firm having a double or triple career. The image made him smile. "How is that possible?"

"They can sell into the different markets, the various communities where they have a presence. Really, Mr. Argyce, I imagine at your firm two partners make a great deal more than one. Same thing, except in the real world it probably isn't as easy."

Steve didn't bother to reply to this. "If your business is too much work for one person, how can the others double up, as you say?"

Winton laughed. "They just sell into the various groups where they have identities. Some people spend way more time in there than I do. And I don't sell, I just create product and advise. Really, the business pretty much runs itself these days."

"And you make money on this?"

Winton shrugged. "Last year about a hundred twenty thousand."

"Game money, of course."

"No, no, I cash in. That's dollars."

Steve reopened the file folder. He now wasn't sure he would be able to make an offer the boy would accept. When he finished his thesis on Kierkegaard, of course.

In-person and online identities already mix, in ways that are difficult to sort out. The world of this story is almost here already, and some would argue that it is here for a few serious players. The mixes of real-world and virtual identities, however, are about to become much more complex—with many more creative possibilities and many more risks. The ability to flex will be mandatory, for the firm and for the players in the firm of all ages. Each leader will need to manage his or her own virtual identity, in addition to his or her real-world identity. For example, Jane McGonigal, one of the bright stars of gaming and immersive experiences, came to IFTF recently to do a seminar. I met her afterward and gave her one of my cards. In response, instead of giving me a card, she said, "Just Google 'Jane' and 'games.'" Her virtual identity is so well established that she really doesn't need business cards. Her identity is linked to gaming, so her "business card" is the search engine link between her first name and games. This association sends an important message that accurately reflects her professional identity.

The foresight in this vignette suggests that we are moving toward an increasingly anytime, anyplace world, where work gets done at many places and at many times. In an anytime, anyplace world, flexibility is a good thing for workers and for the firm, but there are downside risks. If it is possible to work anyplace, anytime, some people will try to do it, and some managers will try to require it. Leadership in the mixed-media world will be different from leadership in a physical office alone. Immersive environments, as suggested in the vignette, are the training ground for the leadership style of the future.

Social Venture Flexing

The Social Venture Network (SVN) was started in 1987 by a handful of visionary leaders seeking to promote socially responsible and sustainable businesses. The network champions the "triple bottom line" of business — people, planet, and profit. Member companies are committed to doing good while doing well, or as the SVN puts it, "value healthy communities and the human spirit as well as high returns."[2] Recognizing the importance of information access, especially in an environment of experimentation and innovation, the SVN connects different enterprises and creates a community of collaboration. Member companies strive to influence public policy for the common good, make markets beneficial and economies ethical, and ensure that their values inform their actions.

For example, consider how the Social Venture Network addressed the dilemma of youth in prisons:

Imprisoned youth face a sea of difficulty—frequent abuse, little support, and sparse if any rehabilitation services. Eighty percent transition to the adult prison system. A group of SVN members, all approaching this issue from different angles, created a series of better alternatives.

By rallying activist parents, developing a documentary, and lobbying in the California legislature, SVN helped bring about a one-third drop in the state's youth prison population.

The prison dilemma has no absolute solutions, but progress is possible. The reality is that youth commit crimes, and prison funding is low. Most people don't want to face the reality of prisons, much less youth prisons. Media has been saturated with stories of prisoner abuse; these stories can both raise awareness and desensitize people to the facts.

Mobilizing parental support (a section of the population clearly interested in the prison situation) and an organization focused on human rights documentaries (to confront the public and policy makers with the facts), members of SVN mounted a comprehensive multidisciplinary approach to the dilemma of youth incarceration. They navigated between the various factors to target the core issue: the unnecessarily negative experience of incarcerated youth and their lack of support.

The Social Venture Network understands that networks of people bound by common values and connected through technology are vital in this VUCA world. Members are applying the practices of venture capital to the higher principles of social change.

Principles for Flexibility

Leaders have a special role in creating islands of stability and coherence that workers will expect in workplaces—both physical and virtual. The new flexibility clearly involves space, tools, and protocols for working.

At Institute for the Future, we created our own core principles in the mid-1990s, stimulated by the work of Dee Hock, who believes that principles-based organizations have much more flexibility to be able to respond creatively to uncertainty.[3] If you have strong principles and strong people, you don't need many rules. Rules are more rigid and brittle than principles. Of course, it takes a long time to develop a consensus and belief around core principles. Once the principles are established, however, they can grow into a sustainable core. I offer these principles not because they will be right for every organization but to share a real example of principles that are specific enough to guide behavior yet are open-ended enough to allow for flexibility and individual creativity. These are operational principles that guide the work of IFTF as we interact with one another and with the outside world:

1. **Get There Early:** We pursue research topics early, before others move in. We focus three to five years into the future, as far as ten years when we can, and as far as twenty years or more in the future occasionally. We work just beyond the normal thought horizons of our best clients. Getting there early means acceptance of high uncertainty. Getting there early also means we meet our

project deadlines, we keep our promises, and we start and end meetings on time.

2. **Pursue Public Good:** IFTF is an independent nonprofit research group, and we have a responsibility to our clients, since we depend financially on organizations that value our research. We are professional bystanders, honest brokers between the known and the unknown, the imagined and the unimagined.

3. **Courageous Opinions, Humbly Expressed:** Diversity of perspectives is mandatory if we are going to understand multiple futures and distinguish between what is new and what is important. We use many methods to explore the future. We seek provocative forecasts and strong points of view, but ones that are expressed with humility, respect for others, and thoughtful reflection on alternative views.

4. **Give Generously, Ask Respectfully:** We work as teams, and we need one another. We need to be direct with one another and express our opinions honestly, not through back channels. We value silence, listening, and reflective abilities as much as we value speed.

5. **Work Less, Learn More:** We each design our own training and educational programs so we can growth within IFTF. As an organization, we enable, encourage, and require such continuous personal growth. Since we encourage long-term continuity in staff, we must facilitate serial "careers" for everyone while they continue working at IFTF. We foster an intense work environment, but one that is family-friendly and respectful of the spiritual sides of life.

6. **Honor Essential Processes:** We are committed to a few simple core business practices at IFTF, which, if they are *unanimously* followed, allow great freedom for individual researchers and project teams. We minimize administrative and management procedures.

It is the responsibility of all leaders at IFTF to make sure that these principles are put into practice in research and administrative work and that

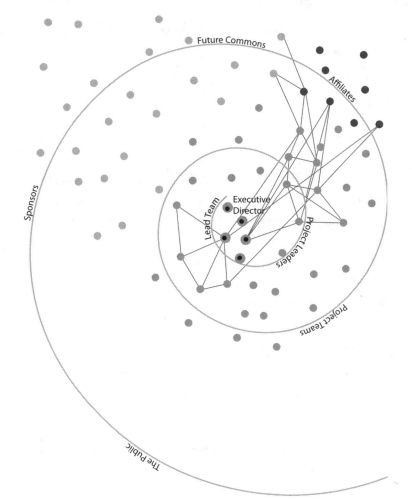

10.1 IFTF's Organization Chart: Organic and Circular

all new staff members understand them, both in concept and in practice. The principles are reviewed periodically to make sure that they continue to represent the best wisdom of the group and that there is a common understanding of them, but the principles don't change often.

It is the responsibility of the executive director to ensure that the basic principles continue to express the best wisdom about how IFTF aspires to operate and that the principles form the basis of performance reviews at all levels in the organization. If any staff member consistently violates the principles, it is the responsibility of the executive director to correct the problem or terminate that person's connection to IFTF's network.

Since the structure of IFTF is a network, not just a hierarchy, we wanted to have a different kind of organization chart. (See Figure 10.1.) I expect many new models will take the place of traditional organization charts that are arranged in hierarchical fashion. Again, I doubt that the IFTF model will apply to your organization, but I hope it stimulates thought about alternatives to the traditional organization chart.

This structure is intentionally organic and circular, ringing out in a network structure from a core group in the center. We are an independent nonprofit, so we need a public orientation while being independent from our sponsors. In our case, the core group of full-time people is about thirty, the next ring out (what we call "the Affiliates") is up to about a hundred less-than-full-time people, and the "Future Commons" is up to about a thousand fellow travelers around the world. Hierarchies come and go at IFTF, usually in the context of projects. In a sense, the highest-ranking person at IFTF is the project leader, and many of the teams are formed on an ad hoc basis. This organizational model gives a basis for making decisions about where work gets done.

The examples in this chapter provide an early hint of what is possible as firms learn how to stretch their own abilities to flex. The next ten years will be critical, with a whole new range of options for flexible work as the geoweb unfolds and as our networking skills improve. The vision of being flexibly firm is possible, and in many cases it will be required.

11 Foresight from Hindsight

All greatness
is improbable.
What's probable
is tedious and petty.
—Lao Tzu, *Tao Te Ching*

"Improbable greatness" is, essentially, what we call innovation today. Any great strategy is improbable. Greatness often lies hidden in an experience, and sometimes it is only revealed in the context of action. This chapter explores how agile approaches to action can yield both success in the present and lessons for future success.

On the Foresight to Insight to Action Cycle, the activities between action and foresight are those of observation, measurement, induction, and learning from experience. What can we learn from our actions to identify new approaches for the future? Thoughtful foresight should include hindsight: our rule of thumb at IFTF is that you should look at least twice as far back as you are looking forward. For example, our ten-year forecasts usually include a twenty-year look back.

In applying the cycle to your own organization, you should periodically do a re-visioning (reconsidering your view of the future), based on your experiences in the field.

After Action Reviews

One of the most effective disciplines for learning from experience that I have seen is the After Action Review (AAR). The army and a number of other military, fire service, and police agencies use AARs as a regular discipline for debriefing and documenting lessons from every significant event. Each soldier, firefighter, or staff person develops his or her own personal practice that includes daily use of AARs to learn from personal and group experiences.

The army keeps a database of AAR lessons, but the primary value of AARs is not in the database; it is in the personal discipline of learning that is ingrained in daily life. Lessons from AARs are fleeting, and they are best understood in a real-life context. The insights are fluid, but a database is fixed. Everyone has to learn in his or her own way, and relearning is necessary in the field, but AARs speed up the relearning process and the spread of learning. The army defines an after action review as "a professional discussion of an event . . . that enables [participants] to discover for themselves what happened, why it happened, and how to sustain strengths and improve on weaknesses"[1] The structure of an AAR is simple but profound: What was our intent? What happened? What worked? What could have been more effective? What did we learn?

The army believes that it took at least ten years to embed AARs into its culture. The roots of the AARs track to Vietnam, a war that many in the army believe was lost because of a failure to learn from experience. The transformation of the army that began after Vietnam is in many ways a transformation of learning styles. Senior leaders must buy into a basic culture shift like that implied by AARs, and it must become a natural part of the everyday environment for everyone, a state of mind.

A big challenge for the army, and a bigger challenge in business, is to distinguish performance evaluation from learning. At many companies, managers talk boldly about "learning from failure," but the common wisdom among employees is that there is a strong — usually unspoken — cultural pressure to produce and not to admit failure. Some business leaders talk about failing early and cheaply, but the pressure to perform is extreme, and it is stronger than the pressure to learn. Of course, the pressure to perform is still critical, but the pressure to learn is even more important. The sweet spot is found in both performing in the short term and learning for the long term.

The important thing is to develop some daily discipline for learning from experience, whatever that discipline might be. In debriefing sessions for the navy's Blue Angels pilots, for example, each pilot is asked to assess his own performance and to volunteer "safeties" that he will correct in the next flight. A "safety" in this sense is a little like a mulligan in golf, where you get another chance. A safety is a self-admission of a mistake before the external evaluation is reported. In this way, self-assessment becomes part of the routine, and pilots are encouraged to point out their own mistakes before others point them out. At the end of his opening statement, each pilot adds, "I'm glad I'm here."

If people are worried about being evaluated, they won't talk about what's important, and they aren't as likely to admit their mistakes — let alone learn from them. If people are worried about being evaluated, they aren't likely to point out the mistakes that were made by their superiors. Corporations have a great deal of trouble applying AAR logic in the world of business because they just cannot separate an after action review from a performance evaluation.

For most companies, failure is still taboo. Silicon Valley visionary Alan Kay, when he was at Xerox PARC, observed, "The purpose of research is to fail, but to fail in an interesting way." The army and other organizations that use AARs seem to have gotten this logic, but most corporations — not even Xerox when Alan Kay was there — have not.

The army talks about using the AAR to search for "ground truth" (what actually happened). An AAR focuses on finding truth, not fixing blame.

Many AARs are facilitated, but the process eventually becomes natural, and groups are often able to do it themselves as part of their daily practice. AARs are a learning discipline and learning is key to development. Futurist Alvin Toffler said it very well: "The illiterate of the future are not those who cannot read or write, but those who cannot learn, unlearn, and relearn." Those who cannot learn from their own mistakes are most vulnerable and sometimes most dangerous.

Users of the AAR seek to create a culture of grassroots learning. The AAR has become an on-the-spot coaching and team-building discipline. When it works, learning becomes routine.

The AAR is meant to be a dialogue, not a lecture. Openness and honesty are critical, so a climate of trust must be established. Leaders must not dominate, and that is why some critical AARs are conducted by an independent outside facilitator. Leaders must acknowledge their own flaws and participate with humility in these sessions. The current Army War College guidelines call for an AAR to

- Be conducted immediately
- Focus on the intended objectives
- Focus on individual, leader, and team *performance* (rather than fault finding)
- Be facilitated (either internally or externally)
- Be linked to subsequent training
- Involve everyone
- Have an open climate
- Have recorded results
- Maintain morale[2]

After Action Reviews are an example of content synthesis, which was described as a tool for foresight in Chapter 1. The key to the AAR, as well as to any other form of experience synthesis, is to learn from what's happened and apply that learning to one's understanding of future possibilities. I have seen that this kind of learning can occur in companies that do not have a formal AAR discipline as well.

For example, synthesis workshops can bring together experiences across a large corporation and draw out principles that can be applied to spread an innovation or learn from failure. By bringing a well-informed, highly experienced group together, stimulating them with case studies, and then facilitating a process through which the group arrives at key principles for success or failure—essentially lessons learned—one can develop an accurate content synthesis. This can be a good way to sift and sort through the explicit and tacit knowledge inherent in an organization that doesn't know what it knows, in order to feed that knowledge back for continued success or avoidance of old mistakes.

Whether formal or informal, the key is to have some process for learning from experience in the field, as well as to reapply those lessons going forward.

Learning in the Field

The stories in this chapter are all focused on lessons derived from action. Each story reveals dilemmas that become clear only in the field, in the midst of experience. Each story shows how insight can emerge from action in organizations with enough agility to reapply the learning.

Learning from what people buy.   Tesco, one of the most innovative grocery and multicategory retailers in Europe (and now expanding to other parts of the world), is one of the leaders in loyalty cards. Customers can sign up for a Tesco loyalty card at one of the company's stores or online and get special benefits when they use the card. The card also provides Tesco with a way of linking specific buying behavior to specific people. Consumers vote with their purchases.

As buying behaviors become better understood, Tesco hopes to improve its ability to serve those customers and provide personalized services that are consistent with the kinds of things customers have purchased in the past. Loyalty cards have been around for a long time, but most companies have not been able to figure out what to do with the massive amounts of data that the cards generate. Loyalty cards are a vision of the future that has not yet come to pass beyond a few innovative retailers like Tesco. Experience in the field with early prototypes, however, is leading to some very promising developments.

> Tesco teamed with Dunnhumby, a small London company that has now become the premier data-mining company in the world. Tesco has become a major investor in Dunnhumby, and Kroger has made a similar investment in Dunnhumby U.S. The more a retailer knows about its individual shoppers and households, the more it should be able to serve their needs. Tesco in the United Kingdom and Kroger in the United States are leading the way, but many other retailers will likely join this movement as the methods of data mining are proved.

Meanwhile, some consumers and some vocal NGOs have expressed concerns about privacy regarding buying cards. Perceptions of privacy are at least as important as the technical reality of privacy. Corporations are trying to develop ways of understanding and becoming close to the people who buy their products and services. Consumers, however, define in their own minds what is close and what is too close. If a large corporation is perceived as being too close, it won't matter if the company is able to make a technical argument that the customer's privacy is still secure. Trust is the core issue here, and once trust is violated, it will be very hard to restore. If an appropriate balance can be struck, the value for both retailers and customers is obvious.

Some years ago, large corporations started talking about "intimacy" with their customers. Intimacy, however, is just not easy for a large company to achieve with a single customer or a single household. Sure, customers are sometimes brand loyal, but intimacy is an almost impossible goal for large companies seeking to bond with individual people. Most people just don't want casual intimacy with a large corporation. The exception could be situations of danger, where the corporation can assist in an emergency. For example, the General Motors OnStar service connects drivers of GM cars with emergency services anyplace, any time. If your car breaks down in a bad neighborhood and you need help, or if you have a heart attack while driving, intimacy with OnStar is exactly what you want. If OnStar comes through for you, as it usually does, a bond is created.

The forecast in Chapter 2 provides encouragement for corporations that want to understand more about consumer needs, but there is reason for caution. The personal empowerment driving force means that consumers will both expect more and be more sensitive to corporations that go over the line—and the consumer gets to draw the line. The existence of smart networking and sophisticated NGOs means that consumer perceptions will be shared widely and rapidly, whether it is good news for a brand or bad news.

Polarizing extremes will play a role as well, as watchdog groups with strong opinions, strongly held, will be out to expose any corporate behavior they find inappropriate, and some groups (perhaps many) will not be fair. Advocacy groups and government agencies will attempt to define what is too close when it comes to data collected by large corporations, especially if there are indications that the corporations are abusing their access. On the other hand, corporations have a chance to provide personalized products and services if only they can better understand what people need and want.

The dilemma for retailers is how to use the depth of the data they have about individual households while still protecting the personal privacy of their loyal customers. They must *both* provide great personal value and protect personal privacy.

Learning from your adversaries.   In many areas of global commerce, organizations can be both adversaries and alliance partners. An organization can be extremely focused on a goal yet willing to cooperate with enemies for some shared value. Consider this example:

> At one time, one part of Oxfam was boycotting Procter & Gamble for its free trade coffee policies while another part of Oxfam was teaming with P&G for distribution of its water purification product. When I was in Cincinnati to speak at an internal Procter & Gamble educational event, I was surprised to meet several members of various NGOs who had been invited to this internal meeting.
>
> The dilemma here varies, depending on your perspective. For large companies, the dilemma is figuring out how to get close enough to NGOs to engage with them while realizing that you cannot please all of them. For the NGOs, the dilemma is how to get close enough to corporations so that you understand what they are doing and have a chance to influence them while not getting co-opted in some way. NGOs and corporations are typically adversaries, but an increasing number are seeing potentials to engage in the dilemma of being both adversaries and (at least sometimes) collaborators.
>
> In May 2006, I participated in a two-day meeting in Germany, hosted by P&G but gathering about thirty consumer associations from across Europe. Procter & Gamble hosted this meeting of consumer and parent associations from all around Europe at its

Pampers plant. The group visited the Braun R & D facilities and the Wella consumer research and R & D facilities.

In this case, P&G is working to build bridges between itself and local concerns. This was one of the first times that a large company had invited NGOs to meet and discuss, while also giving them an inside view of three P&G sites.

Many large corporations want to open channels of communication that are focused on consumer needs, knowing that they will not always agree with all of the consumer associations. At a minimum, corporations and NGOs should understand one another's positions. If corporations and NGOs must fight, at least make it a good fight where there is honest disagreement—rather than misunderstanding one another's positions.

Learning from field locations.　Alegent Health in Nebraska has led the way in creating storefront cardiac care units much closer to the places where its patients live—and away from the big-city hospitals. New technology has made this decentralization of care possible, and the cost of technology is dropping while the capabilities are increasing. Doctors, still important in the process, can move around among remote locations to service patients. The doctors have flexibility and can increase their earnings by moving among locations. Operational staff members are also important in these distributed centers, but they tend to stay at one place while the doctors move around.

Dilemmas are arising as decentralization of cardiac care clinics continues to the point where some of these centers have fewer patients and fewer opportunities to learn in the field. In large hospitals, there is so much action that learning opportunities abound—without compromising the quality of care for an individual patient. In the small outpost clinics, however, there is less action and—potentially—less learning. It is becoming easy to imagine a situation in which the best care is not given at the remote site, simply because the staff at that site had not experienced anything like the case they encountered. The rotating doctors help resolve this dilemma, but the doctors are not always there.

The definition of winning in this dilemma all depends on whose perspective you take. For the doctors, having lots of outpost clinics among which they can navigate is attractive. For patients, having close-to-home access to clinics is great, as long as the quality of care is as good as the convenience. For staff at each outpost, being close to home is a plus, but so is the opportunity to learn and grow—so they are ready when emergencies arise. This is a dilemma fueled by technology and by the scattering of population across wide areas.

Learning from employee experiences.   As I mentioned in the Introduction, UPS is very sophisticated in its approach to the future. As part of its work with scenario planning, it realized that its workforce is going through fundamental shifts that will affect the company—as well as many others in the transportation industry—over the next ten years. The driving forces discussed in Chapter 2 will have specific impacts on the UPS driver of the future.

> Ten years from now, the drivers will be much more diverse ethnically, and most will come from urban areas. Over the next ten years, an ethos of deep diversity will emerge in the United States as people encounter others from different backgrounds, as we move "beyond ethnicity" in the narrow sense of the term.
>
> Networked youth tend to excel at social network and dilemma management skills. UPS and other elite companies will likely attract a rich crop of high performers. Many of the future drivers will be digital natives, having grown up with video games and complex media plots. Growing up online is facilitating entirely new skills sets for forming, managing, and leveraging distributed online teams of young workers—as well as for cross-generational mentoring and reverse mentoring.
>
> In multiplayer online games like *World of WarCraft*, knowledge repositories like Wikipedia, and social networking tools like Meetup, young people are pioneering new practices for distributed work and for learning about work.
>
> There will be other generational differences as well, and this

generation of workers appears to be concerned with navigating the boundaries between work and private life. UPS drivers have considerable flexibility, and they have an inherently healthy job, because they are moving around a lot. They also work very hard, however, and they have a constant pressure to get there early— as UPS's commercials emphasize.

Over the next ten years, the UPS driver's role will become a complex mix of knowledge and manual work. The distinction between blue-collar and white-collar work is already fading, but the UPS driver may be one of the first to have a true mix of these skills.

The new media will provide new kinetic learning opportunities to learn on the go, using flexible learning media that are rooted in the worlds of video gaming and simulation. Combinations of voice, instant messaging, location sensitivity, and the interface options of immersive environments will become possible.

As visual learning and simulation are reshaping education, learning on the job will become more possible and more robust. Drivers will be able to learn while they are in the field, sometimes just in time as they are encountering challenges on the job.

UPS has looked to the future and decided that its current methods of training will not be enough. It is now prototyping a wide range of learning media and working with the U.S. Department of Labor to better understand workforce trends and training opportunities.

Learning from citizen journalists.   Reuters has the world's largest network of professional journalists, a network of people with varied specialties based in all parts of the world. Reuters has 2,000 professional reporters around the world and is known for having some of the world's best resources to get there first with accurate news. Reuters is an international news organization with a focus on financial services news and analysis.

Looking ten years ahead, Reuters has realized that both smart mobs and dark mobs have kindled a new wave of citizen journalism where almost anybody (not just trained journalists) can be a reporter. The London "7/7" bombings of July 7, 2005, for example,

were captured in vivid detail by cell phone cameras in the sub-
ways—not by professional photographers, who did not happen
to be nearby when the crisis happened.

Citizen journalism is potentially a source of grassroots innovation in the news business. Professional and amateur reporters
are becoming collaborators in the networked world. How might
professional journalists cooperate with amateur citizen journalists
to create better news products and services?

Already, there have been cases where citizen journalists have
altered photos to make them more attractive to sell or more expressive of a particular point of view. Still, on-the-spot amateurs
have eyes, ears, cheap-but-sophisticated cameras, and network
connections. Combined with professional journalistic resources,
citizen journalists could contribute to a new generation of news
reporting. Rather than looking at citizen journalists as competition, a news agency might be better off viewing them as resources
and possible network partners.

Reuters is already engaging with the growing and widely
distributed network of amateur photographers to create an
exchange (and perhaps a marketplace) for photos. At the same
time, Reuters is convinced that there are some areas where
professional photography and professional reporting will still
be highly valued. The challenge is in finding attractive mixes
of amateur and professional resources.

The Reuters vision is to get there first with trusted stories.
Trust is key for Reuters, which is already a highly trusted source
for news, particularly financial news. In the emerging world of the
Internet, metadata for sale (that is, access to information through
some sort of finder and filter) is becoming more valued than the
information itself. Google and other more specialized services are
selling access to information. The dilemma for Reuters is figuring
out how it can maintain and grow its position as a trusted source
of expert reporting—while still engaging with the new journalistic
resources of a much wider (but also much less expert) pool of
citizen journalists.

The driving forces we highlighted in Chapter 2 will fuel the trend toward citizen journalism, which is essentially smart networks of empowered people (some with very high networking IQs) engaged in a grassroots economy of news, photographs, and other resources. In some situations, there will be clear differences and clear choices between professional and citizen journalism. In many other cases, however, it is the mix that will be attractive. The dilemma for news organizations is how to succeed in this complex mix of professional and amateur resources.

Policy lessons in the field.   Long before the introduction of carbon trading, Bill Drayton fought to reform Environmental Protection Agency (EPA) policy and implement a program governing factory emissions. Appointed as assistant administrator to the EPA in 1977, he was possessed by a vision of reforming the fundamental framework of environmental policy. He felt that the field was built on a flawed and failing foundation, a condition leading to recurrent (and unproductive) tensions between environmental advocates, who constantly fought polluting factories without satisfying results, and factories, which resisted the costly restrictions on their practices. In fact, many factories found it cheaper to fight the EPA in court rather than implement environmentally safe practices. This wasn't just a problem—it was a messy dilemma. Everyone involved faced a complicated set of factors, and the existing framework that mediated the interaction between the EPA and businesses only created further frustrations.

Drayton's vision was to restructure this framework by introducing an entirely new way of thinking about pollution emissions, based on experiences from the field. Under the existing system, regulations applied to every polluting stage of a plant's operations—spray-painting, degreasing, and so forth—and each stage was required to reduce its emissions. Each regulation involved its own administrative procedure, usually overseen by its own team of people.

The net result was a jungle of paperwork and many uncoordinated regulations. Factories hated implementing all the changes, especially given the costs of some of them. This system clearly couldn't sustain itself, and everyone was losing. Drayton went back to the basics: the

EPA wanted fewer emissions overall (it was protecting a common space), and the factories wanted to save money. One of his big insights was the concept of the "bubble," by which regulation policy looks at the factory as a polluting whole rather than as a set of individual polluting parts. The goal of regulation was just to reduce pollution coming out of the entire bubble.

Under the new framework, the EPA let factories decide how to reduce their own emissions, as long as overall emissions were reduced to an acceptable level. Factories suddenly had economic incentive to develop their own efficient emissions reduction practices, whereas previously the last thing they wanted was for someone to develop another emissions reduction regulation that they would then be required to implement. Each factory could have its own methods. In fact, the bubble concept could be extended to groups of factories, even entire businesses—a possibility that opened the door for credit trading.

Drayton saw that the EPA and polluting businesses were playing a lose-lose game, so he changed the rules. The existing system wasn't going anywhere good, and his foresight told him that further costly frustrations awaited everyone. He understood on a deep level the situations of both the businesses and the EPA (and all the environmental groups behind it) enough to imagine a policy outside of the current situation. In the new framework, everything fell into place. He saw with clarity how all the different factors could be rearranged to create a win-win policy.

He also saw that the new policy was both clear and agile—the bubble concept could be applied across the board and could accommodate numerous revisions (including credit trading). It also encouraged factories to be agile and learn from their own experiences. It took time for Drayton's passion to pay off, but the 1990 Clean Air Act and the Kyoto Protocol, to name two examples, bore the stamp of the original idea. Drayton then began a new chapter in his story: Ashoka.

> Drayton demonstrated his abilities again in conceiving, creating, and nurturing the nonprofit association Ashoka: Innovators for the Public, in the process becoming one of the creators of "social entrepreneurship." As Drayton imagined decades ago, social

entrepreneurs were ambitious and persistent individuals with solutions for society's most pressing problems. History is full of them, from Mahatma Gandhi to Susan B. Anthony to John Muir— people possessed by a social mission and committed to realizing it. Drayton merely gave such people a name, and he built an organization to identify and support them around the world. Ashoka currently supports the work of over 1,800 fellows, who are developing innovative, sustainable, and replicable solutions to social problems.

In building Ashoka, Drayton displayed remarkable vision— based on real-world action and experience. The nonprofit sector and NGOs around the world were consumed with addressing social issues, and they still had substantial funding (Ashoka was founded before the major government budget cuts of the Reagan administration). The word *entrepreneur* smacked of corporate profit chasing and free-market ideology, which was classically considered apathetic toward, or even opposed to, social causes. Drayton's vision was to blend the two approaches, to find the champions who pursued social causes with the zeal traditionally admired in business. As Drayton explains, "Social entrepreneurs are not content just to give a fish, or teach how to fish. They will not rest until they have revolutionized the fishing industry."[3]

Drayton didn't think he had the best approaches to innovation, but he wanted to find people who did. Rather than set out with a clear plan for how to construct Ashoka and carry out its mission, he met with and listened to countless people who fit the bill. His team dug up information on people who had revolutionized their industry, whether it was child care, low-income housing, or women's rights. Holding discussion after discussion, field experi-ence after field experience, Drayton began to understand a little more clearly what his champions—the social entrepreneurs— needed. One major requirement was freedom. Ashoka wasn't investing in a specific approach—it was investing in a person. It didn't need to review plans or pore through proposals. Its fellows received Ashoka's support with full faith in their abilities.

Ashoka let the fellows be agile, and in so doing, Ashoka itself could be agile, free to innovate and expand its own operations. Ashoka could then focus on what it does best—identifying and supporting social entrepreneurs. Ashoka firmly sticks to its mission of supporting these change makers, but it is inherently flexible in realizing it.

Drayton is a master with social dilemmas. He successfully navigates the classical dilemma of being confident without being egotistical. Drayton is a man of indomitable will *and* humility. He doesn't think he has all the answers. As his work with Ashoka has shown, he looks to others to be the champions. He has a vision of social change and is inspired by other social visionaries, particularly Gandhi. His actions are informed by a deep understanding of field experiences. He sees the world from others' points of view, a skill that has helped him develop a win-win scenario for the EPA and businesses. Once he finds a point of clarity, he focuses all his energies. Finally, he strives to create inherently agile solutions that can themselves accommodate further innovation. He changed the rules of environmental policy. He evolved a new, sustainable, and flexible way of thinking about social policy and economic performance, with impressive elements of foresight, insight, and action. His work is grounded in action.

The Foresight to Insight to Action Cycle is, most of all, a cycle. Foresight is a starting point, but hindsight is just as important. Both the past and the present can inspire the future.

Often, the best foresight happens in real time, in the midst of the action. The best leaders develop an instinct for response, a discipline of readiness, not just a plan. The best strategy emerges from the flow of experience and events. The deepest insights arise in the field, as a mystery is revealed just enough to suggest new insights and action. Often, an initial insight suggests a first action, but as the action unfolds the insight gets deeper. That's what prototyping is all about, a kind of learn-as-you-go style for strategic action.

Conclusion

Making Your Peace with the VUCA World

> But going beyond thought is not reserved to men of
> genius. It is open to all of us in so far as the mystery of
> life is not a problem to be solved, but a reality to be
> experienced.
> —Alan W. Watts, *The Wisdom of Insecurity*

This Conclusion draws out lessons for leaders, lessons for moving from the book to implementation. I use stories of leadership to sort out how you can use the Foresight to Insight to Action Cycle in a practical way to get there early and compete. These stories pull together the core ideas in the book, but they also suggest approaches you might take as a leader.

I start with a personal story about an unlikely leader.

When the Seattle Mariners still played baseball at the Kingdome in Seattle, I took my young son there for our annual baseball trip. At our first game, I was impressed with a peanut vendor named Rick. He dazzled me with behind-the-back, on-target peanut bag tosses up and down the long rows of seats. He didn't just toss peanuts; he trick-tossed the peanuts.

Rick smiled his way up and down the aisles, trading jokes about peanuts and life in general. Rick seemed to be something of a folk hero in that stadium. I asked around and learned that Rick had been featured on television showing off his long throws and pinpoint accuracy. Local fans recognized him in and out of uniform, inside and outside the stadium. Kids asked for his autograph.

I found out that before Rick became a peanut vendor, he had been a basketball point guard and a football quarterback. In these sports, he learned to sense people at his periphery and sting them with no-look passes from any angle. Now, he throws softball-sized bags of warm peanuts for a living—a much better living than most peanut vendors make. Rick had made himself into a leader, a very special peanut experience provider.

I tracked down Rick the peanut vendor before our next game and learned more about him. I gave Rick $10 for a $4 bag of peanuts and asked him to throw the bag behind his back to my son from about fifty feet away down a crowded row of fans. My son was up to the challenge, and he caught the peanuts—to the great relief of the frightened lady sitting next to him. We got a bargain when I spent $10 for that bag of peanuts.

When I was a kid, my parents taught me that it didn't matter what I did for a living as long as I was able to do whatever I did very well. My dad used to say: "If you end up being a ditch digger, be a great ditch digger." My mom's motto is "I'll bloom where I'm planted," which conveys a similar sentiment. Rick the peanut vendor figured out how to bloom in a job that few people lust after: hawking peanuts at baseball games. This remarkable peanut pitcher reminded me of my parents' wisdom regarding how to make the best out of a life situation. I hope my son learned that night in Seattle what I had learned from my parents years before. We will never forget that night at the ballgame, and most of our memory is about the peanut vendor, not about the game. Rick the peanut vendor seems to make some money too: my $6 tip was not the largest that he received that night.

Rick had the foresight to see that he was in a very limiting job if he followed the standard instructions for peanut vending, but he had the insight to figure out a way to win anyway by redefining and adding to the role—building on his own skills. He decided that he could rebag his peanuts to a size that was easier to throw with accuracy. He figured out how to heat the peanuts, so he could charge more for them. He realized that people who go to ballgames are open to experiences—especially if the experience involves giving a treat to a kid. Rick figured out a way to add to the fan experience with his own skills, for a price. His actions reflect both his foresight and his insight: he still sells peanuts, but he also sells experiences. The peanuts are still a product, but the experience is seeing him throw the peanuts to you or to others in exotic ways. The value of the experience is more than price of the product.[1] Rethinking of product, service, and experience can work well if you are able to stretch the system but still stay within the limits of your particular capabilities and not overstep your bounds.

Interestingly, Seattle is also home to the fish throwers at the Pike Place Market, near the water in downtown Seattle. The fish throwers work together to pick up each fish and throw it with great drama to a fish catcher (the really hard part) before it is finally wrapped up for the customer. The routine process of purchasing fish is transformed into an experience where crowds gather around to watch the excitement of fish throwing. And, of course, a fish that has been thrown costs more than a fish that has not. Whether throwing fish or throwing peanuts, there is value in entertaining experiences. What will they throw next in Seattle?

In a grassroots economy with empowered and networked people, expect more people like Rick the peanut vendor and the fish throwers from Pike Place Market. Leaders will create new experiences, new ways to turn boring jobs into more interesting and higher paying ones. Rick figured out how to win in what many would think of as a no-win job. Looking ten years ahead, the mix of jobs will include many at the low end of the spectrum, jobs that few people will crave. But the winners will be those who turn boring jobs into interesting and profitable ones. Of course, some jobs are hopeless in this regard, but most are not. Leadership opportunities are hidden in strange places.

Leaders of organizations face the same kind of challenge as Rick the peanut vendor. Leaders need the foresight to anticipate external future forces that might affect their own organizations and their own jobs. Leaders need the insight to figure out unusual ways to extend their own job descriptions, using the unique skills that each leader brings to his or her role. And leaders need to act in ways that allow them to have an impact and learn from their experiences. Rick learned what tricks drew the largest tips. Leaders need to do something similar in the much wider and unstructured world of leadership in the flexible firm.

I got to spend an afternoon with Peter Drucker in his living room, late in his long and rich life. We were meeting with A. G. Lafley, and the focus of the discussion was on organizations. Peter Drucker commented that afternoon that most large organizations focus in performance reviews on weaknesses, not strengths. Thus, "people don't usually understand what they're good at, even though they do understand their weaknesses." Rick the peanut vendor has a very good sense of what he is good at, although I doubt that he had a manager to help him discover his strengths. Managers need to look at what people have done successfully and weave together the unusual strengths of each person. And organizations, of course, are the combination of all the personal strengths and weaknesses of their people. As we departed, Peter Drucker left us with one final thought that has never left me: "Great managers help eccentric people produce."[2]

I believe that each person is eccentric in his or her own way. There is no simple moral equation for leadership in a world of dilemmas, and I think that is good news.

LEARNING FROM AMBIGUITY

Frank Stockton's short story "The Lady or the Tiger?" is a tale of dilemmas and ambiguity.[3]

> In this story, a "semi-barbaric king" devises a unique system of criminal justice whereby those accused of committing a serious crime are given the choice of two doors in an amphitheater in front of a large crowd. Behind one door is a beautiful lady, to whom the accused will be immediately married in celebration if he choses that door.
>
> Behind the other door, however, is a ferocious and hungry tiger. The lady or the tiger? A beautiful life or a certain death?

The accused has no idea what is behind each door. He faces his life-or-death dilemma in a large arena full of screaming people, there to watch this intense human drama of justice play out. Which door to choose?

The plot thickens when a handsome young peasant falls in love with the king's daughter. The king is appalled and immediately orders a "trial" in the arena, where the offending young man will be forced to make his choice.

Meanwhile, the king's daughter somehow learns—secretly of course—which life form (the lady or the tiger) is hidden behind which door. The king's daughter also discovers that the mystery lady behind one of the doors is a beautiful young woman who has already shown herself to be attracted to the handsome peasant now facing his life-or-death choice.

Thus, if the king's daughter reveals the secret of the doors to her lover, she must choose between either giving him up to death by tiger or giving him up to a competing woman—a woman toward whom she already feels considerable hostility.

As he comes into the arena, the peasant looks up at his lover—the king's daughter—and he senses immediately that she knows which door she wants him to choose.

Stockton, however, turns to us as anxious readers in his closing paragraph: "The question of her decision is one not to be lightly considered, and it is not for me to presume to set myself up as the one person able to answer it. And so I leave it with all of you: Which came out of the opened door—the lady or the tiger?"

Seek out and read this story carefully. It is a story that teaches us to live with dilemmas, to enjoy the uncertainty of life and engage with it. Hollywood endings almost always seek to draw everything together at the end. Hollywood endings play well with problem solvers. The real world is not a world of clean endings, however. We need to learn to live with ambiguous outcomes. We all need to read and create more stories like "The Lady or the Tiger?"

DISCIPLINES OF READINESS

Action is not just about doing, it is about being prepared to do. The most effective action will come from a state of readiness, and foresight helps create readiness. We all need to accept uncertainty, not avoid it or pretend that it is not there. Strategy and plans are great, but surprises should be assumed. If you get there early, you are more likely to be prepared for a threat, an opportunity, or a mix of both.

In aikido and other martial arts, mental preparation is the most important quality a practitioner can have. Attacks are unpredictable; hence, being ready for an attack means being comfortable not knowing what the attack will be or from which direction it may come. Mental preparation means being in a state of relaxed anticipation, with what the masters call "soft eyes" or "centered attention," a kind of unfocused awareness. Novices often put all their attention on the weapon they face. A weapon by itself does nothing, however: it is inert, mere matter. The intent of the person holding a weapon is far more important and dangerous than the weapon itself, but the intent is hidden. Attack first? Retreat? A dilemma, certainly.

A great aikido instructor named Terry Dobson used the example of a man in a bar who suddenly knocks the drink out of another patron's hand. The man who has lost his drink is naturally angry, and his instinct is to respond. But what if the first man knew the drink was poisoned? He didn't have time to give warning, only to knock away the dangerous drink. What is an appropriate response from the person who had been holding the drink? Certainly not throwing a punch at a man who just saved your life! What skill does the empty-handed former drink holder need in that moment? It would be helpful if he understood how to protect himself while managing the situation, by redirecting aggression and rendering it harmless to both. This may mean immobilizing the other man until he has had time to calm down, or at least trying to figure out why the drink had been knocked out of his hand. Quick judgment in situations like this is dangerous, but so is deciding too late to act if you are indeed being attacked.

HINTS AND HOWS

Below I have summarized some key leadership lessons from this book. I frame them as hints, since I don't believe this is a time for absolutes or packaged answers. I believe that these hints are true, but you will experience variations in your own world. I've also included some suggestions regarding how to bring these hints to life in your own organization.

HINT: **Nurture your own sensing and sensemaking abilities.** Sensing is the critical leadership skill for the future. For sensing to occur, you need an open mind that resists premature judgment.

HOW: **Explore provocative futures and learn how to prepare.** The VUCA world rewards readiness.

HINT: **Be clear without being simplistic.** The VUCA world rewards clarity, but clarity should not be achieved by oversimplifying truth.

HOW: **Be clear about your strategic intent but flexible in terms of how your team might execute your strategy.** Your people need the agility and organizational slack to respond and adapt to the environment in which they are working — all within the context of the leader's strategic intent.

HINT: **Be flexibly firm.** Flexibility does not mean being free to do anything you want, anytime, anyplace. Be firm on values as well as intent but flexible within those frames.

HOW: **Develop your own virtual persona, your voice of leadership through multiple media.** Collaborate well in a variety of media, with your own style for in-person and online engagement.

HINT: **Be confident and humble.** Leadership confidence will still be important in anytime, anyplace workspaces, but the indicators of power will be different than in the old days, as will the potential for control. You also need the ability to pause and reflect, to slow down and listen.

HOW: **Communicate, but listen more than you speak.**

HINT: **Create a mood of high conflict and high respect.** Encourage a culture of high conflict around content, strategy, and alternatives—but high respect for individuals. Kindness toward individual people is always possible, even in the midst of conflict.[4]

HOW: **Communicate the ground rules for dialogue and engagement within the team.** Provide opportunities for full debate of ideas, leading to the best decision possible and buy-in once the decision is made. Acknowledge differences, but pull together when a decision is made.[5]

HINT: **Nurture a culture of urgent patience.**[6] Maintain a delicate balance between urgency and patience. When things get too comfortable, introduce urgency. When things get too hectic or people are striving too hard, ease off and encourage patience.

HOW: **Sense where your team members are and decide what they need, at each given time, to be high performing.** Focus on recognizing what each person needs for peak performance, not on coddling people. Great leaders can make things look easy, but flexing is tough work—with a fun element on the good days.

HINT: **Use organic language and avoid mechanical metaphors.** Avoid the mechanical metaphors of problem solvers and use organic metaphors, which are much more accurate and expressive for a world of dilemmas.

HOW: **Check your language as you create new strategy and innovations.** Pick the right words to describe a possible future, and they will help draw you toward that future; pick the wrong words, and you will fight them as you go. The next decade will see a gradual shift from the language of engineering to that of the life sciences.

In the United States, we are now tending dangerously toward highly polarized points of view—with many leaders stuck in problem-solving polarities. One pole is characterized by a vapid optimism that the United States will win out, optimism that is independent of global crises, global warming, or global criticism. True believers trust vaguely that all our problems will be solved, with little idea how that might happen. There are no set, fixed, or obvious answers. But many people want and some people need absolutes.

Another polarized view is characterized by corrosive pessimism that varies only on a relative cynicism scale. For these counter advocates, our dilemmas cannot be addressed successfully—no matter what we do.

Leaders need to get beyond either/or perceptions. We are already in a both/and world. We need hope, but it must be a flexible hope that engages in the dilemmas all around us. Hope can be vitalizing. Hope can be resolute. Hope can accept the tough road that lies ahead, while holding to the promise. Our industrial culture is rooted in problem solving, but there is no need to be stuck there. We can win—and others can also win—in a world of dilemmas.

The future will be laced with dilemmas, some of which will look like problems that can be solved—especially to problem solvers. Recall that the way of the problem solver is to consider many options, pick the two best, choose a solution, and run—with the expectation that one will be evaluated by how fast he or she runs. The future world, however, will be dominated by dilemmas. There will be no place to run. Although it is impossible to predict, it is relatively easy to provoke. The more constructive the provocation, the more likely that you can create a strategy that allows you to get there early.

I think future sensing, strategy, humility, and a sense of humor should all go together. "I don't know" is the only honest response in some situations, and it is perfectly acceptable, as long as you don't walk away in a huff after you say it. "I don't know" can be the starting point for a constructive conversation about what you can do within the constraints of what you know and don't know. Humility is engaging; arrogance is not.

PUTTING FORESIGHT, INSIGHT, AND ACTION TOGETHER

The Foresight to Insight to Action Cycle is fueled by visionary foresight and clear insight, but it creates value through action. Leaders need to sense and understand the future context for the decisions they make in the present. Hope is assumed in the cycle, a hope that things can always be better—and in some cases they have to get better if we are to survive. The hope is based on a belief that preparing your mind with thoughts about the future will provide value when it comes time to make a decision in the present.

Leadership requires a discipline of sensing, but it also requires the ability to understand and make sense out of what you are gathering. Foresight is of limited value by itself, but it is extremely valuable if it stimulates insight about what to do—given the pattern of future forces you are seeing.

The Foresight to Insight to Action Cycle, when applied in a disciplined and consistent way, helps leaders become comfortable being uncomfortable. Discomfort can lead to fear, and fear begets more fear. Expectations and preparedness lead to a feeling of comfortable discomfort, a sense of centered readiness.

Some aspects of the VUCA world are not optional. We all must learn to make peace with vulnerability, uncertainty, complexity, and ambiguity in our personal lives. When tragedy hits, we are challenged to respond. We all need our own vision, understanding, clarity, and agility if we are to succeed.

Typically, there will be no single best path. In fact, the best leaders will resist when they are shown only one path. If you see only one option, you must be missing something. If everyone agrees, you all must be leaving something out. Great leaders will want to consider multiple paths and multiple options. We must learn that our focused problem-solving skills still have value in limited situations, but the real challenges are the dilemmas that cannot be solved, that won't go away.

Here is a final story that combines foresight, insight, and action:

Alegent Health in Omaha, Nebraska, is working with Chip Davis, the founder of the musical group Mannheim Steamroller, to create a hospital experience of the future that turns around the personal VUCA world that so many patients experience when they come to hospitals. Chip Davis is writing music for this experience, music that is played over natural sounds that he records digitally on his farm near Omaha. His music evokes nature and employs natural sounds, in natural cycles.

The prototype hospital room of the future that is being developed has digital color displays in the ceiling that are synchronized with the music—which is coordinated with the waking and sleep cycles of the patient. The developers' hypothesis is that natural sounds and a soothing environment can speed the healing process.

Before surgery, almost everyone in recovery has an anxious mind-set laced with volatility, uncertainty, complexity, and ambiguity. These hospital rooms, however, create an atmosphere that is conducive to natural healing. The experience has been designed with an understanding gained through deep research with patients and caregivers.

The experience is personalized for patients: the hospital could become a zone of natural serenity and calm healing—an image that is far from what most patients have or that most hospitals today would claim. Finally, the caregivers who deliver the experience will be agile enough to adapt to varied musical tastes, varied stages in the recovery process, and individual differences that often come up as a person heals.

The hospital room of the future is being prototyped and tested with musicians, doctors and other caregivers, and patients. Chip Davis and the leaders of Alegent are in listening mode, to understand what might be possible and to create a holistic healing experience that works for patients.

Creative efforts like this are practical attempts to engage with a chaotic world and make peace with it. Following are some rules of thumb to follow as you figure out how to make your peace with your own VUCA world:

Volatility yields to vision.   Vision does not have to be grand, but it works best if it is compelling. In the face of volatility, people need a sense of direction, and leaders have a chance to provide intentionality and purpose. The vision in Chip Davis's hospital room of the future is of ambient natural and music therapy to speed the healing process and make it more enjoyable. It doesn't take much foresight to see that hospitals are not very pleasant places to be for the foreseeable future. Also, patients in modern hospitals are likely to be more and more disconnected from nature. Chip Davis combines high-tech methods of audio recording with natural sounds. His vision is to reunite patients with nature in the context of a modern hospital.

Uncertainty yields to understanding.   Listening is the first step to achieving understanding. Chip Davis did his best to design the hospital room of the future, but then he stepped back and let people use it and tell him what they thought. He developed trust and used field experience as a way of gaining additional insight. Authentic gestures of trust demonstrate understanding and allow for ongoing relationships. In the later stages of his career, my dad had a few vending machines in a factory, machines that he bought and serviced himself. At holiday time, he set the vending machines so that they would dispense free drinks as a gift for the factory workers who bought his products all year long. In many years of doing this, the number of drinks given away never surpassed the number usually sold during a comparable period. His gesture of trust was rewarded by customers who did not take advantage of his good will — even though they could have easily done so, since nobody was watching the machines. Leaders need to listen, understand, and act in ways that show trust in their workers and their customers. That trust is likely to be rewarded, and it will be even more valued in times of great uncertainty.

Complexity yields to clarity.   Framing a message is critical, as we learn again and again in the world of politics. Framing is a first step toward clarity, and clarity is so important for people who have exceeded their own personal thresholds for complexity and understanding. The insight for Chip Davis was realizing that natural sounds could speed the healing process, as well as make it more pleasant. This vision is, for most people, both attractive and believable. Chip Davis's explorations of ambient therapy for healing are still in the early stages of development, so they cannot yet be stated with great clarity. In a few years, with greater experience, a clear compelling statement will be possible. Most people long for clarity, but clarity is elusive.

Ambiguity yields to agility.   Even after an action plan is decided on, it must be carried out with flexibility. The experience of the real world will shape what actually happens and what should happen in response.

Dealing with the VUCA world requires time to reflect, and taking time to do that is not easy in a time-starved world. Most leaders experience time as a deficit, not an asset. If you get there early, you earn more flexibility. Getting there early is not about more rushing around; it's about more wisdom. We need time to consider our options, time to understand. We must, as hard as it is, reconsider how we experience time. It's not just about time; it's about timing.

Leadership will be defined by how we "take time" or "make time" to reflect and understand what's going on around us. In today's corporations, few people feel that they have time to reflect. Reflection is demanded, however, to think through your options and strategies, as well as to refocus on those core values that should *not* be flexed.

Like "The Lady or the Tiger?" this book will end by leaving the responsibility for action up to you, the reader, to make your own peace with the VUCA world. Getting there early, the Foresight to Insight to Action Cycle, and the creative combination of vision, understanding, clarity, and agility can help leaders resolve the continuing challenge that opened this book, the tension between judging too soon and deciding too late.

Notes

Some chapters begin with a brief quote from Ursula K. Le Guin's new English version of the *Tao Te Ching*. My intent is to link thought about the future to wisdom from the past. As Le Guin says in her introduction: "I wanted a Book of the Way accessible to a present-day, unwise, unpowerful, and perhaps unmale reader, not seeking esoteric secrets, but listening for a voice that speaks to the soul. I would like that reader to see why people have loved the book for twenty-five hundred years. It is the most lovable of all the great religious texts, funny, keen, kind, modest, indestructibly outrageous, and inexhaustibly refreshing. Of all the deep springs, this is the purest water. To me, it is also the deepest spring." Ursula LeGuin, *Lao Tzu:Tao Te Ching* (Boston: Shambhala, 1997), 3.

Introduction

1. Michael Lewis, *Moneyball: The Art of Winning an Unfair Game* (New York: W. W. Norton, 2003).

2. Although the Foresight to Insight to Action Cycle was developed at IFTF, we are not arguing that this is the first learning cycle. Certainly, there have been many other learning cycles that take similar approaches, including David Kolb's Kolb Learning Cycle, OODA Loops (for Observation, Orientation, Decision, and Action) by Colonel John Boyd, and the PDCA Cycle (for Plan, Do, Check, and Act) that was first developed in the 1930s by William Shewhart and later adapted by W. Edwards Deming in the Total Quality movement. The big difference in our approach is that we add a ten-year perspective to provoke strategic insight and innovation. Our approach can certainly be used in concert with other learning cycles. There is a basic truth in learning cycles: learning is an ongoing process.

Chapter 1

1. Roy Amara's initial idea was to regularize the institute's base forecasts, to provide grounding for the more specific forecasting projects that had been done by IFTF since it began in 1968. Gregory Schmid, a globally oriented economist who joined IFTF from the Federal Reserve, became the leader of the Ten-Year Forecast, and he continued in that role until 2003. Kathi Vian is the current leader; she is a communications researcher and an information designer. It was Kathi and IFTF's digital graphics lead, Jean Hagan, who made the Ten-Year Forecast visual, adding to its grounding in text, analysis, and data.

2. Herman Kahn was a very provocative guy. I met him once when I was invited to a weekend workshop called "Prospects for the Year 2000," held in 1972 at the Hudson Institute in Croton-on-Hudson (aka "Herman-on-Hudson"), New York. At the time, I had just finished my PhD and was teaching introductory sociology, sociology of religion, and sociology of the future. I was intrigued by this 300-pound giant of a man, Herman Kahn, who had a mind that was as large as his size. In talking informally with his staff that weekend, I learned that the draft program for Prospects for the Year 2000 weekend workshop had Herman Kahn presenting all the lectures, in spite of the incredible range of the topics. In the end, he backed off on playing such an all-inclusive role, let other researchers lead some of the sessions, and did only about half of the lectures—which was still amazing.

Herman Kahn was provocative in many ways. I felt his provocation personally that weekend, since he argued that shallow thinking by young untenured sociologists had caused the student revolts of the 1960s, and I was the only young untenured sociologist present at the workshop. I squirmed in my chair, fumbling with what I might say in response. I cannot even remember what I said, but I doubt that it was very profound.

Herman Kahn's most influential books are *Thinking about the Unthinkable* (New York: Horizon Press, 1962) and *On Thermonuclear War* (Princeton, NJ: Princeton University Press, 1960).

3. The Myers-Briggs Type Indicator (MBTI) was developed by Katherine Cook Briggs and Isabel Briggs Myers and was first copyrighted in 1943. For information on the MBTI visit www.myersbriggs.org or see Isabel Briggs Myers and Mary H. McCaulley, Robert Most, ed., *Manual, A Guide to the Development and Use of the Myers-Briggs Type Indicator* (Palo Alto, CA: Consulting Psychologists Press, 1985).

4. Institute for the Future, *Science and Technology Outlook: 2005–2055* (Palo Alto, CA: IFTF, May 2006).

Chapter 2

1. *Beyond ethnicity* is a term coined by David Hayes Bautista from the Center for Latino Health and Culture at UCLA. Intermarriage is the big driver taking us beyond ethnicity, and this shift means that ethnicity becomes even more important. The population cannot be segmented in traditional ways, since there are so many mixes of ethnicities. Los Angeles County and the Houston metropolitan areas are two of the most likely models for future ethnic mix in the United States.

2. Peter Drucker, interview by author, Claremont, CA, July 26, 2001.

3. Robert D. Hof, "The Power of Us," *BusinessWeek Online*, June 20, 2006, http://www.businessweek.com/magazine/content/05_25/b3938601.htm.

4. William Gibson, *Neuromancer* (New York: Ace Books, 1984).

5. Institute for the Future, *2006 Map of the Decade*, SR-997 (Palo Alto, CA: IFTF, 2006).

6. Chris Anderson, "The Long Tail," *Wired Magazine*, October 2004; Chris Anderson, *The Long Tail: Why the Future of Business Is Selling Less of More* (New York: Hyperion, 2006).

7. Howard Rheingold, *Smart Mobs* (Cambridge, MA: Perseus, 2002).

8. The terms *connected core* and *nonintegrated gap* come from Thomas P. M. Barnett's book *The Pentagon's New Map: War and Peace in the Twenty-First Century* (New York: G.P. Putnam's Sons, 2004). The central argument is that the connected core regions have great economic and social incentives to cooperate, or at least to not go to war. On the other hand, the nonintegrated gap regions are characterized by unbalanced extremes.

9. Institute for the Future, "Extended Self," *Technology Horizons Fall Exchange* (Palo Alto, CA: IFTF, 2005).

Chapter 3

1. The idea of reframing the dangers of the VUCA world in a positive way first arose in a workshop I was leading at George Lucas's Skywalker Ranch. This was a workshop on external future forces around learning, hosted by the George Lucas Educational Foundation. I believe it was Milton Chen, the George Lucas Educational Foundation's executive director, who first suggested reimagining *VUCA* as a positive acronym.

2. J. R. R. Tolkien, *The Hobbit* (New York: Ballantine, 1937), 60.

3. Alan Jolis, "The Good Banker," *The Independent*, May 5, 1996.

4. Ishaan Tharoor, "Q&A Muhammed Yunus," *Time* (October 23, 2006), 20.

5. Tom Shanker, "A New Enemy Gains on the U.S.," *New York Times,* July 30, 2006.

6. Joe Pine and James Gilmore, *The Experience Economy: Work Is Theatre and Every Business a Stage* (Boston: Harvard Business School Press, 1999).

Chapter 4

1. Lao Tzu, *Tao Te Ching,* trans. Ursula Le Guin (Boston: Shambhala, 1997), 52–53.

2. *Towne v. Eisner*, 245 U.S. 418, 425 (1918).

3. *Webster's Online Dictionary*, s.v. "dilemma," http://www.websters-on-line-dictionary.org/definition/dilemma (accessed January 3, 2007).

4. *Wikipedia, the Free Encyclopedia*, s.v., "Dilemma," http://en.wikipedia.org/w/index.php?title=Dilemma&oldid=92850225 (accessed May 2006).

5. *MSN Encarta Dictionary*, s.v. "problem," www.dictionary.msn.com.

6. Alan W. Watts, *The Wisdom of Insecurity* (New York: Pantheon Books, 1951)14–16.

7. Institute for the Future, *Toward a New Literacy of Cooperation in Business: Managing Dilemmas in the 21st Century*, SR-851 (Palo Alto, CA: IFTF, June 2004), 1.

Chapter 5

1. Joe Lambert and Nina Mullin are master storytellers for the Center for Digital Storytelling at UC Berkeley: www.storycenter.org.

2. AnnaLee Saxenian has compared the cultures of Silicon Valley and Route 28, near Boston-Cambridge. She has pointed out that Silicon Valley is distinctly more open, more willing to share ideas and to trust that all will benefit in the long run. AnnaLee Saxenian, *Regional Advantage: Culture and Competition in Silicon Valley and Route 128* (Cambridge, MA: Harvard University Press, 1996).

3. Karen Miller-Kovach, *Weight Watchers Family Power: 5 Simple Rules for a Healthy-Weight Home* (Hoboken, NJ: John Wiley, 2005).

4. Jim Loehr and Tony Schwartz, "The Making of a Corporate Athlete," *Harvard Business Review* (January 2001), 120–128.

The program is managed by the Human Performance Institute: www.energyforperformance.com

5. Cait Murphy, "Secrets of Greatness: How I Work," *Fortune*, March 16, 2006.

Chapter 6

1. John Raser, *Simulation and Society: An Exploration of Scientific Gaming* (Boston: Allyn and Bacon, 1969), ix.

2. David Ignatius, "Lessons for Iraq from Gettysburg," *Washington Post*, May 4, 2005, 19.

3. Peter Drucker, interview by author, Claremont, CA, July 26, 2001.

4. Serious Games Initiative, "Serious Games Initiative: About Us," Serious Games Initiative, http://www.seriousgames.org/about2.html.

5. Ibid.

6. Henry Jenkins, quoted in Clive Thompson, "Saving the World, One Video Game at a Time," *New York Times*, July 23, 2006. Also see Henry Jenkins, *Convergence Culture: Where Old and New Media Collide* (New York, New York University Press, 2006).

7. See www.peacemakergame.com. Many of these games are either in development or are likely to change online locations, so I recommend the the reader simply Google any games listed in this chapter to find appropriate information.

8. See www.darfurisdying.com/.

9. Massachusetts Institute of Technology, "Charles River City (CRC)," MIT Teacher Education Program and the Education Arcade, http://education.mit.edu/ar/crc.html (accessed January 3, 2007).

10. Jane McGonigal and Ian Bogost, "Cruel 2 B Kind: About the Game," Cruel 2 B Kind, http://www.cruelgame.com/about/ (accessed January 3, 2007).

11. Reena Jana, "Taking the Pulse!!! of Medical Training," *BusinessWeek Online*, April 6, 2006, http://www.businessweek.com/innovate/content/apr2006/id20060410_051875.htm (accessed January 3, 2007).

12. Rob Swigart, "Satisfying Ambiguity," *Tamara: Journal of Critical Postmodern Organization Science* 1, no. 4 (2001).

13. James Paul Gee, quoted in Thompson, "Saving the World, One Video Game at a Time."

14. Robert Johansen, Jacques Vallee, and Kathleen Spangler, *Electronic Meetings: Technical Alternatives and Social Choices* (Reading, MA: Addison-Wesley, 1979), Appendix.

15. Garry Shirts, "Ten Secrets of Successful Simulations," *Training Magazine,* October 2002, accessible online at http://www.stsintl.com/articles/tensecrets.html.

16. Will Wright, quoted in Steven Johnson, "The Long Zoom," *New York Times Magazine*, October 2006, 55.

Chapter 7

1. The father of modern group graphics and mentor to many of today's practitioners is David Sibbet. Sibbet is also the founder of Grove Consultants International, which does content facilitation and offers graphic templates for use in workshops. For information, see the Grove website at www.grove.com. These templates allow some of the advantages of a live graphic artist, but normal people can fill in the templates to create the group memory graphic.

Chapter 8

1. The wonderful title of Peter Schwartz's book *The Art of the Long View* (New York: Currency Doubleday, 1991) picks up this same theme. This important book brought the perspective of scenario planning into wide use in the world of business.

2. Willie Pietersen, *Reinventing Strategy: Using Strategic Learning to Create and Sustain Breakthrough Performance* (New York: John Wiley, 2002).

3. Ibid., 145.

4. Roger Martin, "Why Decisions Need Design," *BusinessWeek Online,* August 30, 2004. http://www.businessweek.com/innovate/content/aug2005/id20050830_416439.htm (Accessed January 3, 2007)

5. Devin Leonard, "The Only Lifeline Was Wal-Mart," *Fortune*, October 3, 2005, 80.

6. Ibid.

7. Jimmy Wales, "Vision: Wikipedia and the Future of Free Culture" (lecture, The Long Now Foundation, San Francisco, April 14, 2006).

8. Ibid.

9. Ibid.

10. *Wikipedia, the Free Encyclopedia*, s.v. "C. K. Prahalad," http://en.wikipedia.org/wiki/C. K. Prahalad.

11. See Kenan Institute, "Case Studies," Kenan Institute, http://www.kenan-flagler.unc.edu/ki/cse/newcasestudies.cfm.

12. See http://www.ashoka.org

13. Pierre Omidyar, quoted in Connie Bruck, "Millions for Millions," *New Yorker* (October 2006).

Chapter 9

1. Robert Johansen and Rob Swigart, *Upsizing the Individual in the Downsized Organization: Managing in the Wake of Reengineering, Globalization,*

and Overwhelming Technological Change (Reading: Addison-Wesley Publishing, 1994), 8.

2. Ibid., 15.

3. Institute for the Future, *Toward a New Literacy of Cooperation in Business: Managing Dilemmas in the 21st Century*, SR-851 (Palo Alto, CA: IFTF, 2004). The primary researchers leading this work are Andrea Saveri, Howard Rheingold, and Kathi Vian.

4. Dexter Filkins, "Profusion of Rebels Helps Them Survive in Iraq," *New York Times,* December 2, 2005, A1.

5. Dee Hock is the founder and former CEO of Visa International, which he argues was the first "chaordic" organization. Dee Hock, *Birth of the Chaordic Age* (San Francisco: Berrett-Koehler, 1999).

6. Ellen Galinsky, *Ask the Children: The Breakthrough Study That Reveals How to Succeed at Work and Parenting* (New York: William Morrow, 1999).

7. Malcolm Gladwell, "The Cellular Church: How Rick Warren's Congregation Grew," *New Yorker*, September 2005, 62.

8. I first heard the term *officing* from Duncan Sutherland in the early days of office automation. It was a term that was ahead of its time. Now, officing is actually possible.

9. Carol Hymowitz, "Have Advice, Will Travel: Running a Virtual Company on the Fly." *Wall Street Journal Online*, (June 5, 2006) http://www.career journal.com/myc/officelife/20060607-hymowitz.html.

10. Mary O'Hara-Devereaux and Robert Johansen, *GlobalWork: Bridging Distance, Culture, and Time* (San Francisco: Jossey-Bass, 1994).

11. William Mitchell, phone interview by Alex Pang and Anthony Townsend, November 10, 2005.

12. See Hof, "The Power of Us." See also David Kirkpatrick, "Money Makes the World Go Round—Or Does It?" *Fortune* (June 2005) on the "contribution economy."

13. See Robert Grossman, "The Truth about the Coming Labor Shortage," *HR Magazine* 50, no. 3 (March 2005).

14. Ibid.

Chapter 10

1. Larry Huston and Nabil Sakkab, "Connect and Develop: Inside Procter & Gamble's New Model for Innovation," *Harvard Business Review* (March 2006).

2. The Social Venture Network, "Social Venture Network: About SVN," http://www.svn.org/organization.html (accessed October 25, 2006).

3. Hock, *Birth of the Chaordic Age*.

Chapter 11

1. Department of the Army, *A Leader's Guide to After Action Review,* U.S. Army Training Circular 25–20 (September 1993), 4.

2. "After Action Reviews" (lecture, Army War College and Columbia Business School Strategic Leadership Forum, July 19, 2006).

3. Bill Drayton, quoted in "What Is a Social Entrepreneur?" Ashoka: Innovators for the Public, http://www.ashoka.org/social_entrepreneur (accessed November 4, 2006).

Conclusion

1. Rick the peanut vendor is a great example of what Joe Pine and Jim Gilmore call the "experience economy," where we see an evolution from products to services, to experiences to transformations. Joe Pine and James Gilmore, *The Experience Economy.*

2. Peter Drucker, interview by author, Claremont, CA, July 26, 2001.

3. Frank Stockton, "The Lady or the Tiger?" *east of the web,* http://www .eastoftheweb.com/short-stories/UBooks/LadyTige.shtml (accessed January 3, 2007).

4. This hint originated with Rebecca Henderson's observations based on her studies of high-conflict cultures in successful companies.

5. For a convincing case regarding the need to constrain extreme negative behavior, see Bob Sutton, *The No Asshole Rule* (New York: Warner Business Books, 2007).

6. I first heard the term "urgent patience" from Bill Walsh, the former San Francisco '49ers football coach, in a late 1980's conversation.

Bibliography

Barnett, Thomas P. M. *The Pentagon's New Map: War and Peace in the Twenty-first Century.* New York: G. P. Putnam's Sons, 2004.

Becker, Franklin, and Fritz Steele. *Workplace by Design: Mapping the High-Performance Workscape.* San Francisco: Jossey-Bass, 1995.

Belitz, Charlene, and Meg Lundstrom. *The Power of Flow: Practical Ways to Transform Your Life with Meaningful Coincidence.* New York: Three Rivers Press, 1998.

Bennis, Warren, and Patricia Ward Biederman. *Organizing Genius: The Secrets of Creative Collaboration.* Reading: Addison-Wesley Publishing, 1997.

Brown, John Seely, Stephen Denning, Katalina Groh, and Laurence Prusak. *Storytelling in Organizations: Storytelling Is Transforming 21st Century Organizations and Management.* Burlington: Elsevier Butterworth-Heinemann, 2005.

Brown, Juanita. *The World Café: Living Knowledge through Conversations That Matter.* Mill Valley: Whole Systems Associates, 2001.

Burud, Sandra, and Marie Tumolo. *Leveraging the New Human Capital: Adaptive Strategies, Results Achieved, and Stories of Transformation.* Mountain View: Davies-Black Publishing, 2004.

Christensen, Clayton M. *The Innovators Dilemma: When New Technologies Cause Great Firms to Fail.* Boston: Harvard Business School Press, 1997.

Collins, Jim. *Good to Great.* New York: HarperCollins Publishers, 2001.

Csikszentmihalyi, Mihaly. "If We Are so Rich, Why Aren't We Happy?" *American Psychologist* 54 (October 1999): 821–827.

Davis, Stan. *Future Perfect.* New York: Addison-Wesley Publishing, 1996.

Davis, Stan, and Bill Davidson. *2020 Vision: Turbocharge Your Business Today to Thrive in Tomorrow's Economy.* New York: Simon & Schuster, 1991.

de Chardin, Teilhard. *The Phenomenon of Man.* New York: Harper Torch-
books, 1959.

Dee, Jonathan. "Playing Mogul." *New York Times Magazine*, December 21,
2003, 36–68.

Drucker, Peter. "The Coming of the New Organization." *Harvard Business
Review*, January-February 1988, 45–53.

———. *The New Realities: In Government and Politics, in Economics and
Business, in Society and World View.* New York: Harper & Row, 1989.

Edmunson, Mark. "Freud and the Fundamentalist Urge." *New York Times
Magazine*, April 30, 2006, 15–18.

Eliade, Mircea. *Myths, Dreams, and Mysteries: The Encounter between
Contemporary Faiths and Archaic Realities. New York*: Harper Torch-
books, 1957.

Freedman, Marc. *Prime Time: How Baby Boomers Will Revolutionize
Retirement and Transform America.* New York: Public Affairs, 1999.

Fuller, R. Buckminster. *Operating Manual for Spaceship Earth.* New York:
Simon & Schuster, 1969.

Garvin, David A., and Lynne C. Levesque. "Strategic Planning at United
Parcel Service." *Harvard Business School Cases* N9-306-002, November
16, 2005.

Gladwell, Malcolm. "The Cellular Church: How Rick Warren's Congregation Grew." *New Yorker*, September 12, 2005, 60–67.

Gottschang, Suzanne Z., Lyn Jeffery, Nancy N. Chen, and Constance D
Clark, eds. *China Urban: Ethnographies of Contemporary Culture.*
Durham: Duke University Press, 2001.

Hayes-Bautista, David E. *La Nueva California: Latinos in the Golden State.*
Berkeley: University of California Press, 2004.

Heider, John. *The Tao of Leadership: Lao Tzu's Tao Te Ching Adapted for a
New Age.* Atlanta: Humanics New Age, 1985.

Hock, Dee. *Birth of the Chaordic Age.* San Francisco: Berrett-KoehlerPub-
lishers, 1999.

Hoffer, Eric, *The True Believer.* New York: Harper & Brothers, 1951.

Huston, Larry, and Nabil Sakkab. "Connect and Develop: Inside Proctor
and Gamble's New Model for Innovation." *Harvard Business Review* 84
(March 2006), 58–66.

James, William. *The Varieties of Religious Experience.* New York: Crowell-
Collier, 1961.

Jantsch, Erich. *Design for Evolution: Self-Organization and Planning in the
Life of Human Systems.* New York: George Braziller, 1975.

Johansen, Robert. *Groupware: Computer Support for Business Teams.* New York: Free Press, 1988.

Johansen, Robert, Jacque Vallee, and Kathleen Spangler, *Electronic Meetings.* Reading: Addison-Wesley Publishing, 1979.

———. *Teleconferencing and Beyond: Communications in the Office of the Future.* New York: McGraw-Hill Publications, 1984.

Johansen, Robert, and Rob Swigart. *Upsizing the Individual in the Down-sized Organization.* New York: Addison-WesleyPublishing , 1994.

Johansen, Robert et al. *Leading Business Teams: How Teams Can Use Technology and Group Process Tools to Enhance Performance.* Reading: Addison-Wesley Publishing, 1991.

Johnson, Steven. *Emergence: The Connected Lives of Ants, Brains, Cities, and Software.* New York: Scribner, 2001.

———. *Everything Bad Is Good for You.* New York: Penguin, 2005.

Keen, Peter G. W. *The Process Edge: Creating Value Where It Counts.* Boston: Harvard Business School Press, 1997.

———. *Shaping the Future Business: Design through Information Technology.* Boston: Harvard Business School Press, 1991.

Kelley, Tom, and Jonathan Littman, eds. *The Ten Faces of Innovation: IDEO's Strategies for Beating the Devil's Advocate and Driving Creativity throughout Your Organization.* New York: Doubleday, 2005.

Kollock, Peter. "Social Dilemmas: The Anatomy of Cooperation." *Annual Review of Sociology* 24 (1998), 183–214.

Kuhn, Thomas S. *The Structure of Scientific Revolutions.* Chicago: The University of Chicago Press, 1962.

Le Guin, Ursula K. *Lao Tzu: Tao Te Ching: A Book about the Way and the Power of the Way.* Boston: Shambhala, 1997.

Linstone, Harold A., and W. H. Clive Simmonds, *Futures Research: New Directions.* New York: Addison-Wesley Publishing, 1977.

Mahler, Jonathan. "The Soul of the New Exurb." *New York Times Magazine*, March 27, 2005, 30–57.

Maslow, Abraham H. *Toward a Psychology of Being.* Princeton: D. Van Nostrand, 1962.

Matsumoto, Michihiro. *The Unspoken Way Haragei: Silence in Japanese Business and Society.* New York: Kodansha International, 1988.

Michael, Donald N. *On Learning to Plan and Planning to Learn.* San Francisco: Jossey-Bass, 1973.

Mills, C. Wright. *The Sociologic Imagination.* New York: Oxford University Press, 1959.

Mindell, Arnold. *The Leader as Martial Artist: Techniques and Strategies for Resolving Conflict and Creating Community.* San Francisco: HarperSan Francisco, 1993.

Morrison, Ian, and Greg Schmid. *Future Tense: The Business Realities of the Next Ten Years.* New York: William Morrow, 1994.

O'Hara-Devereaux, Mary, and Robert Johansen. *Global Work: Bridging Distance, Culture, and Time.* San Francisco: Jossey-Bass, 1994.

Orbel, John, Robyn Dawes. "Social Dillemas." *Progress in Applied Social Psychology* 1 (1981), 31–65.

Pfeffer, Jeffrey, and Robert Sutton. *The Knowing-Doing Gap: How Smart Companies Turn Knowledge into Action.* Boston: Harvard Business School Press, 2000.

Pietersen, Willie. *Reinventing Strategy: Using Strategic Learning to Create and Sustain Breakthrough Performance.* New York: John Wiley, 2002.

Porter, Michael E. "What Is Strategy?" *Harvard Business Review* (November–December 2000), 61–80.

Rogers, Everett M. *Diffusion of Innovations.* New York: Free Press, 1995.

Saxenian, Annalee. *Regional Advantage: Culture and Competition in Silicon Valley and Route 128.* Cambridge: Harvard University Press, 1994.

Schwartz, Peter. *Inevitable Surprises: Thinking Ahead in a Time of Turbulence.* New York: Penguin, 2003.

Sutton, Robert I. *The No Asshole Rule: Building a Civilized Workplace and Surviving One That Isn't.* New York: Warner Business Books, 2007.

Thompson, Clive. "Meet the Life Hackers." *New York Times Magazine*, October 16, 2005 .

Toffler, Alvin, ed. *Learning for Tomorrow: The Role of the Future in Education.* New York: Vintage Books, 1974.

Turkle, Sherry. *The Second Self: Computers and the Human Spirit.* New York: Simon & Schuster, 1984.

Updike, John. "The Future of Faith." *New Yorker*, November 29, 1999, 84–91.

Watts, Alan. *The Wisdom of Insecurity: A Message for an Age of Anxiety.* New York: Vintage Books, 1968.

Wheatley, Margaret J. *Leadership and the New Science: Discovering Order in a Chaotic World.* San Francisco: Berrett-Koehler Publishers, 2006.

Zuboff, Shoshana. *In the Age of the Smart Machine: The Future of Work and Power.* New York: Basic Books, 1988.

Acknowledgments

This book was more than twelve years in the thinking. During that period, I was president of Institute for the Future for eight intense years. I've been writing in a focused way on this book for more than two years now, since I asked our board to allow me to go back to research—working on IFTF projects with our clients and writing.

The early work on this book was supported by Deloitte & Touche USA LLP, which published some of these ideas internally as part of its Talent Market Series. Our sponsor Stan Smith from Deloitte was so much more than a sponsor. Stan provoked our thought and modeled how to live a creative life in the midst of incredible health challenges.

Sponsors for IFTF's forecasting efforts are critical, because we have no endowment. People in the following organizations, in particular, have contributed profoundly to the experience base of this book—either directly or indirectly:

Alegent Health
BP
Campbell's Soup
Centers for Disease Control and Prevention (CDC)
DARPA (Defense Advanced Research Projects Agency)
National Horizon Scanning Centre, Office of Science and
     Technology (U.K. government)
KnowledgeWorks Foundation

Procter & Gamble
Reuters
McKinsey & Company
State Farm Insurance
Target
Time Warner
United Cerebral Palsy
United Parcel Service (UPS)
Walt Disney World

Originally, I imagined this as a co-authored book, based as it is on Institute for the Future's research and experience. As the book took shape, however, we all realized that this had become a very personal book—the most personal I've ever written. I've included many personal stories from my life, while also drawing from ongoing research programs at IFTF: the Ten-Year Forecast, Technology Horizons, and Health Horizons. Having been with Institute for the Future since 1973, I've now lived through three generations of ten-year forecasts. My personal stories and the Institute for the Future are thoroughly mixed.

I had an inner core of colleagues who contributed greatly as the book was getting going, especially Kathi Vian, Lyn Jeffery, Jean Hagan, and Rob Swigart. Marina Gorbis, the IFTF executive director, has added greatly to my thoughts about this project and has been very supportive all the way through. Susannah Kirsch has been a close colleague on many projects for the past few years, and her influences are reflected often in the book. Stephanie Schachter contributed greatly to most of the custom forecasting efforts that provided deep learning experiences that are reported in this book. Matt Chwierut joined me for the home stretch of the book and added a wonderful burst of energy and thoughtful creativity. My assistant, Kathy Seddiqui, helped me keep up with all the other challenges I had while still needing to make time for writing.

My dedication for this book is to the Institute for the Future community, which is now evolving into a "future commons" of fellow travelers. Gregory Schmid was the founder of the Ten-Year Forest Program. Andrea Saveri and Howard Rheingold have been instrumental in bringing this larger community to life—beyond the core of full-time IFTF researchers. I feel so fortunate to be part of this community.

Roy Amara was president of IFTF when I joined, and he has been a faithful mentor to me all these years. We are all grateful for what Roy has done to create a sustainable culture of futures research. Generations of board members, including recent chairs Willie Pietersen, Wolfgang Berndt, Bill Fuller, and Lawrence Wilkinson, have brought outside strategic wisdom to IFTF. Our board members over the years have added incredibly to our work.

Ruann Ernst and Cora Tellez were remarkable in offering their strength and insight during the challenges I faced as president of IFTF. During that same period Steve David, Mark Ciccone, and Mark Schar were there for me in ways for which I will be forever grateful.

Publishing with Berrett-Koehler has been a unique and thrilling experience for me—unlike anything I have ever experienced with other publishers. BK is truly a team, but I must mention Steve Piersanti, who has been an enthusiastic critic from the time he first saw our book proposal. Steve has an amazing ability to be both critical and constructive simultaneously—which I found very motivational. I was exhausted after every editorial meeting with him, but it was always a good tired. Steve has added enormously to the ideas and clarity of the book. Berrett-Koehler also has a very unusual book draft review process that was created by Jeevan Sivasubramanian. The reactions and suggestions from this process were all very helpful, but the review of this book by Valerie Andrews was the most detailed and constructive review that I have ever received.

My literary agent, Jim Levine, helped me think through the initial ideas that led to this book, as well as to find the right publisher and the right process to make it work. Jim is a remarkable agent who understands both content and process.

Visualization is a critical part of foresight for me, as will be clear in this book. My own visual education began with David Sibbet, who has contributed so much to me and to IFTF. Kathi Vian, Jean Hagan, and Anthony Weeks—all gifted artists and information designers, each in their own way—have taught me the value of visual thinking.

My family has always been a great source of energy for me. Remembering how stressed out I got writing earlier books, I doubt that they looked forward to me reentering the world of book writing. My wife and I have been married even longer than I have been at IFTF (thirty-eight years), and she is so much a part of my thoughts. Our children are now adults, and it has been amazing to be able to talk through the ideas in this book with them as I was writing. My mom, still going strong at ninety-four, will remember many of the personal stories in this book, and she is a constant inspiration for me.

To all of my colleagues and friends in the IFTF community, I offer my deepest thanks for the experiences that grounded this book.

Over the years, Paul Saffo's ideas have contributed greatly to IFTF forecasts and to my own thinking.

Our current board is a wonderful mix that includes Wolfgang Berndt, Aron Cramer, Steve David, Karen Edwards, Debra Engel, Marina Gorbis, Ellen Marram, Bob Sutton, Kathi Vian, and Lawrence Wilkinson.

Current full-time staff members of Institute for the Future are Alex Pang, Andrea Saveri, Anthony Townsend, Chris Sumner, Crystal Lynn Keeler, Dale Eldredge, Jason Tester, Jean Hagan, Jeannie Swanson, Jody Ranck, Kathi Vian, Kathy Seddiqui, Kim Lawrence, Lea Gamble, Lyn Jeffery, Mani Pande, Marina Gorbis, Matt Chwierut, Maureen Davis, Mike Liebhold, Mike Love, Rachel Maguire, Robin Bogott, Rod Falcon, Sean Ness, and Susannah Kirsch.

About the Author

Bob Johansen has worked for more than thirty years as a forecaster. Focusing on the human side of new technologies, Bob was one of the first social scientists to study the human and organizational impacts of the Internet when it was called the ARPANET. He also has a deep interest in the future of religion and values.

Bob served as Institute for the Future's president from 1996 to 2004. Still on IFTF's board, he now spends most of his time with IFTF sponsors, engaged in writing, public speaking, and facilitating top-executive workshops across a wide range of industries.

He is the author or co-author of six previous books, including *Upsizing the Individual in the Downsized Organization*, a guide for organizations undergoing technological change and reengineering, and *GlobalWork*, a guide to managing global cross-cultural teams.

A social scientist with an interdisciplinary background, Bob holds a BS degree from the University of Illinois, which he attended on a basketball scholarship, and a PhD from Northwestern University. Bob also has a divinity school degree from what is now called Colgate Rochester Crozer Divinity School, where he studied comparative religions.

About IFTF

The Institute for the Future (IFTF) is an independent nonprofit research group in Silicon Valley. We work with organizations of all kinds to help them make better, more informed decisions about the future. We provide the foresight to create insights that lead to action. The Institute is based in Palo Alto, a community at the crossroads of technological innovation, social experimentation, and global interchange. IFTF was founded in 1968 by a group of former RAND Corporation researchers with grants from the Arthur Vining Davis Foundation and the Ford Foundation to take leading-edge futures research methodologies beyond the world of classified defense work.

For more information, please visit www.iftf.org.

Index

Note: Page numbers in *italics* refer to figures.

AAR. *See* After Action Reviews (AARs)

Absolute answers, search for, 75

Absolutely, use of word, 2

Action, 141
  defined, 146
  introduction to, 143–145
  learning from, 9
  operational problem solvers and, 147–148
  readiness and, 220
  stories about
    Campbell's Soup, 160–162
    cell phones in Caracas, 154–158
    Omidyar network, 158
    TerraPass, 162–163
    Wal-Mart, 148–152
    Wikipedia, 152–154

Ad hoc immersive experiences, 105, 111–112

Administrative waste, 42

Adversaries, learning from, 206–207

After Action Reviews (AARs), 169–170, 200–204

Agility, ambiguity and, 53, 227

Alegent Health, 122–123, 207, 224–225

Amara, Roy, 15, 19

Ambiguity
  agility and, 53, 227
  for creativity, 119
  learning from, 218–219
  learning to be comfortable with, 118–121
  as satisfying/productive experience, 101–102

Anderson, Chris, 34

Answers
  psychological benefits of having, 78–81
  search for absolute, 75

Anthony, Susan B., 213

Apple Computer, 3, 137

Apprenticeships, 112, 113

Army War College, U.S., 1–2, 46–47, 55, 109

Army War College *(continued)*
    AAR guidelines of, 203
Arquilla, John, 55
Artifacts from the future, 21
Ashoka, 212–214

Baby boomers
    dilemmas and, 71–73, 82
    health economy and, 40–41
    personal empowerment and, 29
    as problem solvers, 71
    retirement and, 29
Baran, Paul, 168
Beane, Billy, 5
Biehl, Amy, 63
Biotech Reverse Mentoring
        Program (P&G), 10
Blair, Tony, 94
Blogs, defined, 174
Bogost, Ian, 117
Bottom-up participation patterns,
        gaming and, 32
Buying cards, 205

California Coastal Commission, 3
Campbell, Doug, 101
Campbell's Soup, 160–162
Caracas, cell phones in, action
        story about, 154–158
Case studies, 106
Cell phones in Caracas, action
        story about, 154–158
Cellular churches, 170
Centers for Disease Control and
        Prevention (CDC), 55–56
    strategic imperatives of, 56–57
Change, directions of, 25–26
Charles River City, 116–117
Ciccone, Mark, 110

Citizen journalists, 209–211
Clarity, complexity and, 52–53, 55,
        226
Clean Air Act (1990), 212
Climate change, 41–42, 43, 94–100
Closed mind-sets, 80
Cloyd, Gil, 186–187
Comfort zones, 182
Commander's intent, 54–55
Community schools, VUCA, 58–59
Complexity, clarity and, 52–53,
        226
Computer connectivity, 37
Connections, 9
Consumers, engaged, behaviors
        of, 27–29
Content facilitators, 126–127, 129,
        132
Content synthesis, 20
Corporate Athlete, 91
Corporations, *get there early* and,
        3
Crest toothpaste, 4
Cruel 2 B Kind Self-Organizing
        Game, 117–118
Cruise lines, VUCA world and, 62–
        63
Cyberspace, 33

Dalkey, Norman, 21
Darfur Is Dying, 116
Dark innovation, 39
Dark mobs, 35, 38
Data books, 22
Davis, Chip, 224, 226
Deloitte & Touche, 112, 172–173
    use of simulation at, 114–116
Delphi Technique, 21
Digital youth, flexing and, 179–183

Dilemmas. *See also* Problem
    solving
    baby boomers and, 71–73
    characteristics of, 74
    defined, 73–74
    leadership shifts required for,
        75–77
    modern strategic, leadership
        and, 147
    vs. problems, 73–77, 147–148
    problem solving and, 69–73
    as source of inspiration, 81–84
    stories about, 87, 88
        fitness, 90–93
        of future collaboration for
            global warming, 94–100
        parenting, 93–94
        Silicon Valley, 89–90
    tuning levers for, 83–84
    words and, 71
Direct simulations, 102
Dobson, Terry, 220
Drayton, Bill, 211–214
Drucker, Peter, 29, 113, 218

Economies of scale, 31
Education, in VUCA world, 57–60
Employees, engaged, 28
Empowerment, personal, 27–31
Engaged employees, 28
Environment, health concerns
    and, 43–44
Environmental Protection Agency
    (EPA), 211–214
Ethnography, 21, 23, 105
Expert opinion aggregation, 20
Expert workshops, 20, 22
Extended selves, creating, 40–41
Extreme networks, 38

Extremes, polarization of, 37–40,
    205–206

Face-to-face communication, 175,
    176
Feedback, flexibility and, 169
Fishnet organizations, 165–166,
    166
Fitness dilemma story, 90–93
Fixed-mind sets, 79
Flexible firms
    stories about
        external R&D, 186–187
        IBM, 184–186
        for near future, 190–194
        Walt Disney World, 187–190
Flexible media, 173–178
Flexing/flexibility, 7–11, 164–165
    developing ability for, 167
    digital youth and, 179–183
    places for, 170–173
    principles for, 196–199
    tuning levers for, 167–170
        feedback, 169
        identity, 170
        memory, 169–170
        resources, 168–169
        rules, 168
        structure, 168
        thresholds, 169
Forecast Map, 26–44
    hot zones in, 127
    storylines of
        grassroots economics, 31–35
        health insecurity, 40–44
        personal empowerment, 27–
            31
        polarizing extremes, 37–40
        smart networking, 35–37

Forecasts/forecasting, 16–17
  approaches to, 19–23
    artifacts from the future, 21
    content synthesis, 20
    ethnography, 21
    expert opinion aggregation, 20
    expert workshops, 20
    historical analogy, 20
    scenarios, 20
    survey research, 20
    visualization, 21
  directions of change and, 25–26
Foresight
  developing, 8
  listening and, 13
Foresight to Insight to Action
    Cycle, xiii, 9–11, *10*
  foresight to insight, *86*
  immersion experiences for
      adding value to stages of,
      121
  Insight to Action, *142*
  preparing groups for, 17
  putting it together and, 223–227
  VUCA dangers and, 50
Foresight to Insight to Action
    Workshops, 123–136
  chunks of provocative insights
      for, 127
  content facilitators for, 126–127,
      129, 132
  diverse groups for, 126
  graphic artists for, 129–131, *130,*
      131
  ingredients for successful, 124–
      127
  introductions, allowing time for,
      127–129
  meeting owners for, 124–125
  planning, 124

PowerPoint for provocation in,
    136–139
  preparing minds for successful,
      132–133
  prioritizing in, 131–132
  target outcomes for, 125–126
  tips/techniques for successful,
      134–135
  venue/mood of room and, 129
Fox, Joe, 148
Framing, 226
Fundamentalism, 38, 78–79

Galinsky, Ellen, 169
Gaming, bottom-up participation
    patterns and, 36
Gandhi, Mahatma, 32, 213, 214
Gee, James Paul, 118
General Motors, 205
Geoweb, 33, 36, 187–190
  insuring against loss and, 66
Get there early, 3–7
  for corporations, 3
  defined, 3–4
  flexibility principle of, 196–197
  for nonprofits, 3
Gettysburg Battlefield, "staff ride"
    at, 107–109
Gibson, William, 33
Gilmore, Jim, 62
Global warming, 41–42, 43, 139
  story about future collaboration
      to address dilemma of, 94–
      100
Gore, Al, 139
Grameen Bank, 50–51, 52, 154
Graphic artists, 129–131, *130, 131*
Graphic game plan, *131*
Graphic recording, group, *130,* 131
Grassroots economics, 31–35

Group graphic recording, 131
Group participation, 36

Hacking, 39–40
Hagan, Jean, xviii, 15
Health economy, 40–44
  baby booms and, 40–41
  effect of climate change on, 41–
    42
  environmental concerns and,
    43–44
  impediments to, 42
  language changes and, 41
  nutrition and, 42–43
  in VUCA world, 55–57
Health status, determinants of,
    42–43, *43*
Helmer, Olaf, 21
Historical analogy, 20
Hock, Dee, 168, 196
Holmes, Oliver Wendell, 70
Home monitoring systems, 66–67
Hope, 223–224

IBM, 83, 184–186
IDEO, 146
Ignatius, David, 109
Immersion experiences, 101, 122.
    See also Simulations.
  for adding value to stages of
    Foresight to Insight to
    Action Cycle, 121
  ad hoc immersive experiences,
    105, 111–112
  alternate-reality games, 104
  case studies, 106
  improvisational acting experi-
    ence, 110–111
  learning to be comfortable with
    ambiguity and, 118–121

mentoring, 105
  scenarios, 104
  simulation gaming, 102–104
  theatrical improvisations, 105–
    106
  3-D immersive environments,
    104
Immersive learning, xiv
Improvisational acting experi-
    ences, 110–111
Improvisations, theatrical, 105–
    106
Insight
  to action (*see* Action)
  developing, 8
  leaders and, 8
Inspiration, dilemmas as source
    of, 81–84
Instant messaging (IM), defined,
    174
Institute for the Future (IFTF), logo
    of, 15–16
  operational principles of, 196–
    199
  organization chart, *198*
Insurance, in VUCA world, 66–68
Iraq Study Group, 125–126

Jardine, Ed, 155
Jeffery, Lyn, 181
Jenkins, Henry, 114
Jung, Carl, 19

Kahn, Herman, 16–17
Kay, Alan, 202
King, David, 94
King, Martin Luther, Jr., 72–73
Kirsch, Susannah, 128
Knowledge Works Foundation
    (KWF), 58

Kyoto Protocol, 212

Labor shortages, 30, 42
Lafley, A. G., 10, 91–93, 186, 218
Lambert, Joe, 88
Lao Tzu, 15, 143, 200
Leaders
  insight and, 8
  prepared minds and, 18
  sensing and, 8
Leadership
  hints and hows for, 221–223
  modern strategic dilemmas and,
    147
  sensing and, 122, 224
  shifts in, for problems/dilem-
    mas, 75–77
  simulation gaming for develop-
    ing, 119–121
Learning
  from After Action Reviews, 200–
    204
  from ambiguity, 218–219
  in the field
    from adversaries, 206–207
    from citizen journalists, 209–
      211
    from employee experiences,
      208–209
    from field locations, 207–208
    from what people buy, 204–
      206
Learning ecologies, pervasive, 59
Learning economy, 59
Learning professions, realignment
  of, 59
Lee, Harry, 151
Lee, Robert E., 108
Le Guin, Ursula, 70
Leisure, in VUCA world, 62–64

Lightweight infrastructures, 33
Listening, 226
  for stories, 88
  understanding and, 52
Locative activity, 37
Long-tail economics, 34
Loyalty cards, 204–205

Martin, Roger, 147
McGonigal, Jane, 117
Media
  flexible, 173–178
  networked, 34
  personal, 32–33
Medical error, 42
Meeting owners, 124–125
Meetup, 208
Megacities, 39
Memory, flexibility and, 169–170
Mentoring, 105, 112–113
Microfinance, 50–51
Military simulations, 106–110
Military strategy, 145–146
Mind-sets
  closed, 80
  fixed, 79
Mitchell, William, 177–178
"Moneyball" approach, 5
Morrison, Ian, 146
Muir, John, 213
Mullen, Nina, 88
Myers-Briggs Type Indicator
  (MBTI), 19

National Training Center, U.S.
  Army, 106–107
Net warfare, 55
Network communication skills,
  175–176
Networked media, 34

Networked organizations, 183
  memory in, 169–170
  options for communicating in,
    173, *174*
Networking, smart, 35
Networking IQ, factors for, 36–37
Networking knowledge, 36
Networks, extreme, 38
Network structures, flexibility and,
  168
Nonprofits, *get there early* and, 3
Nutrition, health and, 42–43

Oakland A's, 5
Offices, corporate, 182
Officing, 171–172
Omidyar, Pierre, 158–159
Online lifestyle, 36
Online personnas, 190–194
OnStar service (General Motors),
  205
Open-source technology, 29
Operational problem solvers, 147–
  148
Opinion aggregation techniques,
  21–22
Organizational memory, 169–170
Outrage industry, 64–66
Oxfam, 206–207

Pandemics, 41, 56
Pang, Alex, 33
Parenting dilemma story, 93–94
Parks, Rosa, 72
Pasteur, Louis, 45
PeaceMaker, 116
Peoplecentric offices, 30, 176
Personal empowerment, 27–31
Personal media, 32–33
Personal mobile computing, 37

Pietersen, Willie, 144
Pike Place Market, fish throwers
  from, 217
Pine, Joe, 62
Pottery Barn rule, 109
Powell, Colin, 109
PowerPoint, for provocation in
  workshops, 136–139
Prahalad, C. K., 154
Prediction, 16
Preparedness, disciplines of, 220
Preparing one's mind
  for attending workshops, 132–
    133
  for sensing, 18–19
Problems
  defined, 75
  vs. dilemmas, 73–77
  leadership shifts required for,
    75–77
Problem solvers, operational, 147–
  148
Problem solving. *See also*
  Dilemmas
  cooperative models for, 83
  dilemmas and, 69–73
  language and, 71
Procter & Gamble, 4, 9–10, 186–
  187, 206–207
Public education, in VUCA world,
  57–60
Public policy strategy, 145–146
Pulse!!!, 118

Questionnaire results, 22–23

Radio Frequency Identification
  (RFID) tags, 34
Raser, John, 102
Rauschenbusch, Walter, 72

Readiness, disciplines of, 220
Referral behavior, 36
Resources, flexibility and, 168–169
Retirement, baby boomers and, 29
Reuters, 209–211
Reverse mentoring, 105
Rheingold, Howard, 32, 83
Rick, the peanut vendor, 215–218
Role-play simulation games, 104
Rules, flexibility and, 168

SARS outbreak, 33
Satyagraha, 72
Sauers, Len, 10
Saveri, Andrea, 83
Scale thresholds, flexibility and, 169
Scenario planning, 23
Scenarios, 20, 22, 104
Schar, Mark, 128
Science, in VUCA world, 60–62
Scott, Lee, 149, 151
Seamless mobility, 177
  defined, 174
Self-agency, 27
Self-customization, 28
Self-organization, 28
Sensing, 7–11
  deep, 18
  leaders and, 8
  leadership and, 122
  open mind and, 18
  preparing one's mind for, 18–19
  requirements for, 19
  true, 18
Sensor, Wayne, 122–123
Serious Games Initiative (SGI), 113–114
"Serious games" movement, 102–103

Shadowing, 105, 112–113
Sharing economy, 32, 178
Shirts, R. Garry, 120–121
Sibbet, David, 131
Silicon Valley story, 89–90
Simulation and Society (Raser), 102
Simulation gaming, 102–104, 109, 119, 121
  for business, 102
  for developing leadership, 119–121
  role-play, 104
Simulations, xiv. *See also* Immersion.
  at Deloitte & Touche, 114–116
  examples of, 113–118
    Charles River City, 116–117
    Cruel 2 B Kind Self-Organizing Game, 117–118
    Darfur Is Dying, 116
    PeaceMaker, 116
    Pulse!!!, 119
    Serious Games Initiative, 113–114
    Virtual Team Challenge, 114–116
  military, 106–110
Simulation Training Systems, 120
Smart mobs (swarms), 35
Smart networking, 35–37
Smith, Kenneth W., 72
Social software, 35
Social Venture Network (SVN), 195–196
Sony, 3
Southwest Airlines, 145
Spore, 121
Sport-utility vehicles (SUVs), 43
"Staff rides," 107–109
Starbucks, 182

Stata Center, 177–178
State Farm Insurance, 67
Stategic intent, 54–55
Stockton, Frank, 218–219
Stories, 121
  about dilemmas, 87, 88
    about Silicon Valley, 89–90
    fitness dilemma, 90–93
    of future collaboration to
        address global warming,
        94–100
    parenting dilemma, 93–94
  about flexible firms
    about near future job inter-
        views and, 190–194
    external R & D, 186–187
    IBM, 184–186
    Walt Disney World, 187–190
  about learning in the field
    Alegent Health, 207–208
    Environmental Protection
        Agency, 211–214
    Procter & Gamble, 206–207
    Reuters, 209–211
    Tesco, 204–206
    UPS, 208–209
  about strategic foresight/in-
        sight/action, 148–163
    Campbell's Soup, 160–162
    cell phones in Caracas, 154–
        158
    Omidyar Network, 158–159
    TerraPass, 162–163
    Wal-Mart, 148–152
    Wikipedia, 152–154
  listening for, 88
Storytelling, 87
Strategic intent, in VUCA world,
    54–55
Strategy, 145

military, 145–146
sustainability, Wal-Mart story of,
    148–152
Structures, network, flexibility
    and, 168
Stuart, James Ewell Brown (Jeb),
    108
Survey research, 20, 22 23
Sutton, Bob, 146
Swarms (smart mobs), 35
Swigart, Rob, 118, 164
Synthesis workshops, 203

Target, 64–65
Teilhard de Chardin, Pierre, 72
Ten-year forecasting, 13, 15
TerraPass, 162–163
Tesco, 204–206
Theatrical improvisations, 105–
    106
"The Lady or the Tiger" (Stock-
    ton), 218–219
Theme parks, VUCA world and,
    63–64
3-D immersive environments, 104
Thresholds, scale, flexibility and,
    169
Tolkien, J.R.R., 45–46
Toyota Corporation, 3

Uncertainty, understanding and,
    52, 226
Understanding, uncertainty and,
    52, 226
Uninsurance, 42
UPS, 4, 208–209

Vian, Kathi, 24, 83, 164
Video chat, defined, 174
Video gaming, xiv

Virtual Team Challenge, 114–115

Vision, volatility and, 51–52, 225–226

Visualization, 21

Voice over Internet Protocol (VoIP), defined, 174

Volatility, vision and, 51–52, 225–226

VUCA (Vision, Understand, Clarity, and Agility)
  dealing with, 224–227
  health in, 55–57
  insurance in, 66–68
  leisure in, 62–64
  opportunity in, 49–54
  outrage industry and, 64–66
  public education in, 57–60
  science in, 60–62
  strategic intent in, 54–55

VUCA (Volatility, Uncertainty, Complexity, and Ambiguity)
  world, xiii, 45–46
  dealing with, 224–227
  health in, 55–57
  insuring against loss in, 66–68
  leisure in, 62–64
  opportunity in, 49–54
  origin of term, 1–2
  outrage industry in, 64–66
  public education in, 57–60
  roots of, 46–49
  science in, 60–62
  story about, 47–49
  strategic intent in, 54–65

Wales, Jimmy, 152–154

Wal-Mart, 148–152

Walsh, Bill, 5

Walt Disney World, 63–64, 187–190

Warfare
  asymmetrical, 55
  net, 55

War games, 107

Warren, Rick, 170

Watts, Alan, 79–80

Weeks, Anthony, 131

Weight Watchers International, 90

Wikipedia, 152–154, 169, 208

Wikis, 169
  defined, 174

Win-win strategies, 83

Wisdom of Insecurity: A Message for an Age of Anxiety, The (Watts), 79–80

Words
  dilemmas and, 71
  limitations of, 70–71

Workforce, future backgrounds and styles of, 175–176

Workforce diversity, 30, 175

Workforce shortages, 31, 42

Workshops. See Foresight to Insight to Action Workshops

World of WarCraft, 208

Wright, Will, 121

Yunus, Muhammad, 50–51, 52, 53, 158

Zero-sum games, 83

About Berrett-Koehler Publishers

Berrett-Koehler is an independent publisher dedicated to an ambitious mission: Creating a World that Works for All.

We believe that to truly create a better world, action is needed at all levels—individual, organizational, and societal. At the individual level, our publications help people align their lives with their values and with their aspirations for a better world. At the organizational level, our publications promote progressive leadership and management practices, socially responsible approaches to business, and humane and effective organizations. At the societal level, our publications advance social and economic justice, shared prosperity, sustainability, and new solutions to national and global issues.

A major theme of our publications is "Opening Up New Space." They challenge conventional thinking, introduce new ideas, and foster positive change. Their common quest is changing the underlying beliefs, mindsets, institutions, and structures that keep generating the same cycles of problems, no matter who our leaders are or what improvement programs we adopt.

We strive to practice what we preach—to operate our publishing company in line with the ideas in our books. At the core of our approach is stewardship, which we define as a deep sense of responsibility to administer the company for the benefit of all of our "stakeholder" groups: authors, customers, employees, investors, service providers, and the communities and environment around us.

We are grateful to the thousands of readers, authors, and other friends of the company who consider themselves to be part of the "BK Community." We hope that you, too, will join us in our mission.

Be Connected

Visit Our Website

Go to www.bkconnection.com to read exclusive previews and excerpts of new books, find detailed information on all Berrett-Koehler titles and authors, browse subject-area libraries of books, and get special discounts.

Subscribe to Our Free E-Newsletter

Be the first to hear about new publications, special discount offers, exclusive articles, news about bestsellers, and more! Get on the list for our free e-newsletter by going to www.bkconnection.com.

Get Quantity Discounts

Berrett-Koehler books are available at quantity discounts for orders of ten or more copies. Please call us toll-free at (800) 929-2929 or email us at bkp.orders@aidcvt.com.

Host a Reading Group

For tips on how to form and carry on a book reading group in your workplace or community, see our website at www.bkconnection.com.

Join the BK Community

Thousands of readers of our books have become part of the "BK Community" by participating in events featuring our authors, reviewing draft manuscripts of forthcoming books, spreading the word about their favorite books, and supporting our publishing program in other ways. If you would like to join the BK Community, please contact us at bkcommunity@bkpub.com.